THE WESTERN LIVING COOKBOOK

Recipes by Eileen Dwillies. Photography by Derik Murray

COMAC

MURRAY/LOVE

WHITECAP

Vancouver, British Columbia, Canada 1987

A COMAC
MURRAY/LOVE
BOOK

Produced by Murray/Love Productions Inc.,
1128 Homer Street, Vancouver, B.C.

This edition published by Whitecap Books,
1086 West 3rd Street,
North Vancouver, B.C.

Designed by Chris Dahl

Typeset by The Typeworks

CANADIAN CATALOGUING IN PUBLICATION DATA

Dwillies, Eileen.
The Western living cookbook
ISBN 0-921061-12-9

1. Cookery   I. Western living.   II. Title TX715.D85 1987   641.5   C87-091419-7

Printed and bound in Canada by D. W. Friesen & Sons Ltd., Altona, Manitoba

ISBN 0-921061-12-9

CONTENTS

Foreword 5
Introduction 6

AUTUMN

The Fine Art of Giving Thanks 10
Hungarian Rhapsody 14
Out of the West 18
Favor Curry 22
A Taste of the Past 26
Hunter's Feast 30
A Most Astonishing Vegetable 33
Creole Time 38
Rise & Dine 42
Dynamite Dinner 46
A Tuscan Bias 50
Mad About Mushrooms 55
In a French Mood 60

WINTER

A Classic Christmas Feast 66
A Festal Affair 72
Festive Pheasant 78
Five Courses to Midnight 86
Mid-Winter Nibblies 92
The Salad in Winter 96
Breakfast for Lovers 100
One for the Heart 104
Minestrone! 107
Thali 110

SPRING

From Sorrel to Strawberries 118
Earl Grey & All That 121
Meal from Morocco 126
A Delicate Meal for May 130
Fancy Fish 134
Chinese Sweets and Savories 138
Uptown Grill 142
A Chinese Family Meal 145
California Bistro Meal 148
Food in the Fast Lane 152

SUMMER

Summer Coolers 158
Brunchtime 160
Sea Fare 164
Breaking Bannock 167
Garden Harvest 172
Perfect Picnicking 176
Newest New Mex 180
Buen Apetito! 186
Paella by the Pool 189
Meals On Ice 192

Index 196

ACKNOWLEDGEMENTS

....

We would like to extend our sincerest thanks and gratitude to the following people.
Without the contributions, assistance and hard work of these individuals,
this book would not have been possible.

For their generous contributions to the introductions and recipes in our food features:

Scott Mowbray—*Meal from Morrocco, Dynamite Dinner, In a French Mood*
Edwin Lee—*A Chinese Family Dinner*
Julia Garcia—*Buen Apetito!*
Claude Teton & Olivier Chalier—*Summer Coolers*
David Eaton—*Favor Curry*
Janice Silver—*Breaking Bannock*
Raymond Port—*Chinese Sweets and Savories*
Kerry Sear—*The Fine Art of Giving Thanks*
Shirin Sondhi—*Thali*

For their help in providing props to enliven our photography:

Mikasa, Presents of Mind, W.H. Puddifoot, Basic Stock, Market Kitchen,
Scandinavian Antiques, Kelly's Collections, Hollingdales, Old Country Antiques,
Echo's China and Silver, The Bay, Eatons, Birks, Ming Wo, Kaya Kaya,
Inform, Chachkas, Marilyn's Kitchen Shop, Salt Box, Design Furniture Gallery,
George Jensen, Room Service, Terra Cotta, Murchies and Wise Owl.

For their creative contributions to the cuisine section of *Western Living* over the years:

Ron Starr and Paula Brook, who wrote many of the introductions.
Peter Manning, who art directed many of these photographs.
Judy Bates, Rob Scott and Murdine Hirsch, who provided prop co-ordination.
Liz and Jack Bryan, who founded *Western Living*.

For their hard work and long hours, which contributed to the success of this book:
Patricia Thorvaldson, who copy-edited and proofread the manuscript.
David Counsell, who co-ordinated the production of the book.

FOREWORD

Welcome to the *Western Living Cookbook*. We are fortunate in western Canada that the enjoyment of fine food and good cooking can play such an important part in our lives. For 17 years now, *Western Living* magazine has reported on all that's best about living in the West, and we've offered readers regular, lively editorial coverage on many different aspects of cuisine. We've published thousands of innovative recipes, and our staff and contributors have become experts in presenting stimulating ideas about food. It seems only natural that we pull this exciting material into one high-powered package and share it with our readers and with food lovers everywhere.

Not surprisingly, both *Western Living* and its cuisine section have changed over the years. In order to present our recipes in an up-to-date and easy-to-use fashion, we have chosen only the best and most recent material—from 1984 onwards. Each group of recipes is arranged as a feature. Many features offer recipes that form a complete menu and these are indicated; others explore tempting themes or cooking styles. All features, in turn, are organized by season to help focus your cooking and entertainment needs.

Many people have contributed to *Western Living*'s cuisine section since our beginnings in 1971, but it is primarily the work of Eileen Dwillies and Derik Murray that we celebrate here. Without Eileen's comprehensive co-ordination, recipe development and food-styling skills, this cookbook could not exist. And Derik's photography has brought vivid color and life to Eileen's talents; I believe he is the best food photographer working in Canada.

Andrew Scott, Editor, *Western Living* magazine.

INTRODUCTION

Cooking is my passion. I like the whole process: planning menus, shopping for wonderful fresh produce, meats and seafood, devising delicious dishes that can be prepared with a minimum of effort and, finally, presenting food that is a visual delight.

Planning a meal takes time and imagination. First, I consult my guests-to-be (it's amazing how many people react to onions, garlic and shellfish). Then my menu plan starts with an idea that intrigues me—maybe a fabulous dessert or an unusual entrée that uses some ingredient I've just discovered. Working around that special dish, I choose recipes compatible in color and taste. For instance, with spicy golden chicken, I'd pick a cool green soup, crunchy yellow and green vegetables, a crisp red and green salad and a smooth, creamy dessert. As I consider various dishes, I ask myself if the flavors seem to meld, remembering what Julia Child once said about running her mental taste-buds over the menu. If one dish is complex and time-consuming, I make sure that the others are simple. I don't mean plain or boring—just easy to prepare.

Shopping comes next. I spend a great deal of time engaged in this activity, both professionally and personally, and what I see in western Canadian supermarkets convinces me that future generations of cooks will know no seasons. Asparagus, once a spring treat, now comes to us in the summer from Mexico and in the fall from New Zealand. Stores everywhere sell ingredients from all over the world: we can buy hearts of palm from Brazil, lemon grass from Indonesia and soon, kiwifruit grown by our own farmers.

Canadian cooks are especially fortunate. Even now we can take our good local produce and combine it with the culinary knowledge of the entire world to create our own kitchen masterpieces. We are no longer afraid to devise combinations of foods and food styles. We might, for instance, serve our native saskatoon berries with Italian mascarpone or begin a meal with a New Mexican appetizer and end it with a dessert from France.

If I have a culinary motto, it is "Simple yet Elegant." And my forte is developing ideas into recipes that exemplify this motto. As my lifestyle has changed over the past few years, I have learned to rely more on prepared stocks and sauces that are sold in specialty shops. I find that I put more emphasis on grilled and sautéed dishes in my daily cooking, while creative cooking has become a luxury to look forward to on weekends. I like great flavors and enjoy the challenge of using herbs and spices with a deft touch, or with gusto when it's appropriate. My favorite herbs are oregano, thyme, savory, tarragon, basil and, always, parsley. And among the spices, I like my own Creole mixture (see page 41), as well as cayenne, nutmeg, pepper, pepper and more pepper.

In the years I have been preparing food to be photographed, I've learned that presentation is the final touch that makes a meal rise above the ordinary. Now, at home, rather than passing food around the table, I prefer to prepare each guest's plate in the kitchen. My husband, Paul, and I make a great team, placing vegetables, spooning on sauce and zipping beautiful plates out onto the table. Six or eight people for dinner seems a manageable number to me. Often, I will already have the salad at each place when I call the guests to dinner. Then I will serve the main dish from the kitchen, putting any extra food on the sideboard for those who wish to help themselves. Often, I set the dessert on the sideboard, too.

Enthusiasm for eating and good food is the beginning for anyone starting in the kitchen. A few good tools will also make life there much easier. My favorites are a 25-centimetre (10-inch) Castoflon pan by Le Creuset, a two-litre (two-quart) copper (nickel-lined) saucepan, a 22-centimetre (9-inch) Henckels chef's knife and a 20-centimetre (8-inch) Henckels bread knife.

All the recipes in this book have been tested many times, in both metric and imperial measures. Except for the desserts, all measurements are "ballpark"—guidelines to how a dish tastes when I cook it. You should feel free to taste and adjust according to your preference. Desserts and baked goods are another matter; if you do not follow these recipes closely, the chemistry may be altered and the results disappointing. Although I haven't specified it, I use unsalted butter at all times.

Because we at *Western Living* believe that most people want complete menus, we have presented many of our recipes in this format. Occasionally, we have chosen to explore themes that have interested us. In these features, we focus on fish or delve into pumpkin, soups, salads or mushrooms. Feel free to create your own menus from any of our recipes, minding, of course, your mental taste-buds.

Wonderful food. Simple preparation. Careful choice of ingredients and good presentation. All these sum up my philosophy. Bon appetit!

Eileen Dwillies, *Western Living* magazine.

AUTUMN

California cornucopia: terrine of ham and sweet potatoes for the first course; escalopes of turkey with cranberry coulis and a cornet of vegetables; a dessert as light as falling leaves.

The Fine Art of Giving Thanks

When we decided to ask a professional chef to devise an innovative menu based on traditional Thanksgiving ingredients, we turned to Kerry Sear, now executive chef at the Four Seasons hotel in Vancouver. And when we saw his proposed menu, we knew our choice had been the right one: his four-course dinner for 10 is stunning to look at and equally impressive to taste.

Young, enthusiastic and creative, Sear applies food to the plate with an artist's touch. To devise our Thanksgiving menu, he first drew up a list of foods common to the Thanksgiving table: turkey, cranberries, pumpkin, sweet potatoes, corn and ham. Wanting to suggest bounty in the entrée, he devised a cornucopia theme, with colorful vegetables pouring out of a pastry cornet onto a plate whose focal point is sautéed escalopes of turkey breast on a brilliant cranberry sauce.

The meal begins exquisitely with one of the finest and most unusual terrines we've tasted, a combination of Black Forest ham slices, sweet potatoes blended with cream, and a centre of ham mousse; a smooth horseradish mayonnaise is served alongside.

Simplicity governs the next course, a corn consommé (not pictured) whose presentation is made dramatic by a dome of hot pastry over each diner's bowl.

Dessert, which follows the turkey entrée, is a light pumpkin-hazelnut mousse on a silky nougat sauce.

Kerry Sear is English, and he apprenticed in a hotel in Stratford-Upon-Avon in the mid-'seventies. In 1978, he came to Canada and worked for a summer in Jasper. The following year, he began working at the Chateau Laurier in Ottawa. By 1980, he had joined Delta Hotels as executive sous chef at the chain's Ottawa hotel. After being promoted to executive chef, he moved in 1983 to the Delta River Inn in Richmond, and from there to the Four Seasons.

Sear says he has no mentor or hero in the culinary world, but looks south to California for inspiration. "The nouvelle cuisine style is too sparse. I like the California style, which puts a bit more food on the plate — but food that is artistically arranged, maybe into a picture or theme."

Preparation and Planning

The key to preparing a complex, multi-course dinner without anxiety is planning and preparation. Most of the components in this meal can be made or readied for cooking in advance, so that final preparation largely entails assembly and sautéeing rather than chopping and cooking. In the case of the entrée, for example, Sear says, "a lot of people don't realize that you can blanche your vegetables in advance and reheat them in butter." Indeed, the carving and blanching of the vegetables can be done the day before; they keep well if undercooked, immersed in water and chilled.

There should be no rush between courses; this is, after all, a meal of thanksgiving. Let the guests enjoy their wine while you reheat the vegetables, sauté the turkey slices, and assemble all the elements of the entrée on the plates. Ideally, the cook should have someone in the kitchen helping assemble the food on the plates — which is good fun. Warm dinner plates will ensure that the food remains hot.

The terrine, soup and dessert mousse should be made a day or two in advance, while garnishes and sauces will keep for hours if properly handled (details for doing so are in the recipes).

Keep in mind that the garnishes can be replaced with simpler garnishes of your own.

This is obviously not a meal for an inexperienced cook to attempt without assistance, but for anyone who knows his or her way around the kitchen, the challenge is exciting and the rewards are not only delicious but beautiful.

Here is a suggested schedule for preparation of this meal.

One or two days before: make terrine; make corn consommé; make and roll out pastry for consommé, then freeze; make pastry cornets from leftover pastry and store.

The day before, or morning of meal: make hazelnut mousse and refrigerate in moulds; carve and lightly blanche vegetables for entrée, place in water in fridge.

Morning of meal: make autumn leaves; make cranberry coulis; put soup in individual bowls, cover with pastry and refrigerate.

Afternoon of meal: make julienned vegetables for terrine garnish; make apple pots or slices for terrine garnish; make horseradish mayonnaise; make garlic-sage sauce for entrée; slice terrine and place slices on platter (under airtight plastic) in the refrigerator.

Final preparation and assembly: the soup, which is the second course, will take 25 to 30 minutes to cook, so place soup in oven five to 10 minutes before serving the terrine; when soup is ready, serve immediately; sauté turkey; reheat vegetables and sauces; assemble entrée and serve; assemble dessert and serve.

MENU *(Serves Ten)*

- Terrine of Ham and Sweet Potatoes
- Consommé of Corn Topped with Fresh Herb Pastry
- Escalopes of Turkey with Cranberry Coulis and Garlic-Sage Sauce
- Cornet of Vegetables
- Pumpkin-Hazelnut Mousse with Autumn Leaves

TERRINE OF HAM AND SWEET POTATOES

This terrine consists of pieces of

ham wrapped around a sweet-potato mixture. In the centre is a circle of ham mousse. A look at the photograph will indicate the way the terrine is constructed (though you may use a rectangular mould).

1 kg (2 lbs.) sweet potatoes, peeled and boiled
30 mL (2 tbsp.) butter
1 medium onion, chopped
30 mL (2 tbsp.) parsley, chopped
30 mL (2 tbsp.) chives, chopped
175 mL (¾ cup) whipping cream
4 45-g pkgs. gelatin, soaked in cold water just to cover
Salt and pepper to taste

Purée the cooked and peeled sweet potatoes in a food processor or mash with a potato masher until smooth. Set aside in a large bowl.

In a medium frying pan, melt the butter. Add the onions and sauté gently until tender. Add the parsley, chives and cream. Bring to a boil. Add the softened gelatin. Stir until dissolved. Remove from heat and blend into the puréed sweet potatoes. Season with salt and pepper. Set aside.

Ham Mousse
30 mL (2 tbsp.) butter
½ medium onion, chopped
250 g (½ lb.) Black Forest ham, diced
60 mL (4 tbsp.) brandy
125 mL (½ cup) whipping cream
1 28-g pkg. gelatine, soaked in cold water just to cover
Salt and pepper to taste

In a medium saucepan, melt the butter and sauté the onion until soft. Add the ham and cook briefly; do not let it color. Add the brandy and, wearing an oven mitt or with a long match, flame the mixture. Stand well back. When the flames die down, add the cream and bring to a boil. Remove the ham with a slotted spoon. Add the softened gelatine to the cream mixture and stir until dissolved. Remove from heat.

Purée the ham in a food processor or blender. Add the cream mixture and purée until very smooth. Season with salt and pepper.

Assembly
125 g (4 oz.) ham, thinly sliced
125 mL (½ cup) savory jelly such as aspic, melted

To make aspic, add one package (½ oz.) softened gelatine to 500 millilitres (2 cups) of beef broth and stir until completely dissolved. Let aspic cool slightly, but don't let it gel. An alternative to aspic is any commercial savory jelly, such as blackcurrant, which isn't too sweet. The purpose of the jelly is to thinly coat the ham slices that envelope the terrine, allowing them to stick together.

Dip each slice of ham into the savory jelly and line a small (25-cm/10-in.) terrine mould or loaf pan until the lining is several slices deep. The ham should cover the sides and bottom of the pan.

Spread half the sweet-potato mixture into the ham-lined mould. With a piping bag or large spoon, place the ham mousse down the centre. Cover with the remaining potato mixture. Fold over the ham slices and chill for at least three hours.

A few hours before serving time, make the horseradish mayonnaise and garnishes.

Horseradish Mayonnaise
2 egg yolks
60 mL (4 tbsp.) apple cider
30 mL (2 tbsp.) mustard
250 mL (1 cup) olive oil
60 mL (4 tbsp.) horseradish, or to taste
Salt and pepper

Place the egg yolks, cider and mustard into a bowl and whisk well. Gradually (very slowly, drop by drop) pour in the oil, whisking continuously. Fold in the horseradish. This is a fairly thin, creamy mixture. Season to taste with salt and pepper. Note that a good commercial mayonnaise mixed with a few drops of cider, mustard and horseradish can be used.

Garnishes
There are two garnishes with this dish. The mayonnaise is placed inside a small pot made from a cored apple. For contrasting color, a nest of julienned vegetables with

a few pearl onions sits on the plate. The apple pot can be replaced with a few sliced apples if necessary; either way, the apple will keep if thoroughly coated with lemon juice and water and refrigerated. The julienned vegetables will keep in cold water.

10 apple pots
250 mL (1 cup) or more of julienned carrots, leeks, tomatoes and cucumbers
20 raw pearl onions

Apple Pots
10 Granny Smith apples
1 L (1 qt.) cold water
2 lemons

Cut lemons in half and squeeze out the juice into the water. Add the leftover lemon skins.

If you possess a cookie cutter with a long, tubular blade, it is ideal for cutting the apples in one downward motion; you can then core them to yield an apple "pot." Alternatively, cut away the skin and flesh of the apple to make a small, pot-shaped container, then core it. Remember to keep the tops of the apples for lids. Place pots and lids in lemon water. Before serving, dry with a cloth and fill with mayonnaise. Replace lids.

Assembly and service: dip the mould into warm water (not letting water touch the terrine itself) and turn terrine out onto a plate. Cut two slices per person and place on serving plates, which should be chilled. Arrange the julienned vegetables into a nest and top with the pearl onions. Add filled apple pots.

CONSOMME OF CORN TOPPED WITH FRESH HERB PASTRY

Each bowl of consommé arrives at the table covered with a lid of pastry which has been puffed into a dome by the steam of the soup. A simple trick but spectacular. A pastry recipe involving beef lard or shortening is given below, but any favorite pastry recipe will work (though some puff better than others). This recipe will leave enough dough to make the pastry cornets for the entrée, and preparation details are given. Commercial puff pastry works well for both purposes; you can roll herbs into it.

Consommé

250 g (½ lb.) minced lean beef
250 mL (1 cup) corn kernels, fresh or canned
3 egg-whites
3 L (3 qts.) chicken stock or canned broth
250 mL (1 cup) celery, leek, onion and carrot, peeled and finely chopped
30 mL (2 tbsp.) peppercorns
Salt and pepper

Mix together the beef, corn, egg, salt and 250 millilitres (1 cup) of stock. Place in a large saucepan. Add vegetables and peppercorns along with the remaining stock. Bring slowly to a boil and boil for 20 seconds. Turn down heat and simmer 90 minutes.

Strain mixture through damp cheesecloth or a clean, damp J-cloth. Discard meat mixture. Taste consommé for seasonings. Cool thoroughly or freeze.

Pastry

2.5 L (10 cups or 2½ lbs.) all-purpose white flour
Salt and pepper
5 mL (1 tsp.) each of thyme, dill, sage and oregano
625 mL (2½ cups or 1¼ lbs.) beef lard (or pork lard, or shortening)
Cold water

Sift flour and salt. Add herbs and pepper. With your hands, quickly rub in the fat until mixture is of a sandy texture. Add enough water to make a dough that will form a ball and pull away from the bowl.

Roll pastry out on a floured board until about ⅓-centimetre (⅛-in.) thick, and cut out 10 rounds large enough to cover tops of soup bowls. If you wish to freeze the pastry rounds, stack them with wax paper between each layer or place side by side on a cookie sheet, then freeze.

Note: there should be enough dough left over to make pastry cornets for the entrée. You'll need

a set of cream horn moulds to make these (they're available at cooking departments and stores, and look like small metal cones). Simply roll dough out until thin, then cut into long strips about 1.25 centimetres (½ in.) wide. Wind strips around cream horn moulds, overlapping the dough slightly. Place on a baking sheet and bake at 190°C (375°F) until golden. Cool and remove pastries from moulds. Store in an airtight tin at room temperature.

Up to six hours before serving time, assemble some corn kernels, diced carrots and celery in a pile for garnishing the soup.

Fill small ovenproof soup bowls (individual soufflé dishes are ideal) half full with consommé. Add a little of each garnish. Dampen outside of bowl with a little water and cover with a pastry round, pressing gently around the sides to ensure that the pastry will remain fixed to the bowl. Brush the pastry with a little egg and water mixture (one egg, whisked with a little water) to glaze. Place pastry-covered soup bowls in the fridge until a half hour before serving time.

To Serve: preheat oven to 200°C (400°F). Thirty minutes before serving, place cold soup bowls on a large baking sheet and place in oven. Bake until top is puffy and golden, about 25 to 30 minutes. Serve immediately.

ESCALOPES OF TURKEY WITH CRANBERRY COULIS AND GARLIC SAGE SAUCE

The carving and cooking of the vegetables for this entrée do take a little time but are easily done the day before. The sauces can also be made ahead and gently reheated. The cornets are also made ahead (from the leftover consommé pastry), as indicated in the meal plan, above. The turkey slices will cook in two to three minutes.

This recipe calls for three escalopes of turkey per person. An escalope (also known as a scallop or a cutlet) is simply a thin, usually fairly narrow slice of meat taken from the breast of the

turkey. A knowledgeable butcher should be able to supply you with pre-cut escalopes. The alternative is to buy a nine-kilogram (18 to 20-lb.) turkey and cut your own. To do so, remove the raw, skinned breast meat from the turkey and lay it on a counter. Place your hand on the meat and, with a sharp knife, cut thin cutlets from the breast against the grain of the meat (parallel to your hand). If these cutlets are wider than those shown in the meal photograph, cut them in half. If the breast does not yield enough escalopes, take some from the thighs (or do so anyway, if dark meat is preferred). Leftover turkey can be roasted.

425 mL (1¾ cups) all-purpose white flour
30 mL (2 tbsp.) fresh sage, chopped
Salt and pepper
30 escalopes of turkey, 50 to 75 g (2 to 3 oz.) each
60 to 75 mL (¼ to ⅓ cup) butter

Mix together flour, sage, salt and pepper. Melt butter in a sauté pan. Dip escalopes in the flour and sauté quickly – do not brown! This takes only a few minutes. Keep turkey warm while you assemble the dish.

Garlic-Sage Sauce

75 to 125 mL (⅓ to ½ cup) butter
3 or 4 cloves garlic, chopped
3 medium red shallots, chopped
30 mL (2 tbsp.) fresh sage, chopped, or a couple of pinches of dried
250 mL (1 cup) white wine
250 mL (1 cup) whipping cream
Salt and pepper

Add garlic and shallots to the butter, and sauté until tender over medium heat. Add sage, white wine and cream. Bring to a boil and cook until reduced by half and slightly thickened and smooth; this takes 10 to 15 minutes. Strain through a sieve. Season to taste with salt and pepper. If not serving immediately, strain into a bowl and cover with plastic wrap. Reheat gently in a saucepan. Sauce will thicken on standing but will become thin again over heat.

Cranberry Coulis

1 kg. (2 lbs.) fresh cranberries
125 mL (½ cup) white wine

Bring wine to a boil and add cranberries. Simmer until tender. Reserve a few berries for garnish, then purée the remainder in a food processor or blender. Strain through a fine sieve. Set aside until serving time. Reheat gently.

CORNET OF VEGETABLES

10 pastry cornets
1 medium yellow turnip
2 small white turnips
4 large carrots
1 small pumpkin
250 mL (1 cup) peas
1 medium acorn squash
250 mL (1 cup) cooked corn

To make cornets, see pastry recipe for consommé, above.

Peel all the vegetables, and with a small melon baller (we used one that was about the diameter of a dime) scoop out each vegetable, leaving a little skin on if desired for added color. Keeping them separate, blanche each vegetable in boiling water (vegetables should be undercooked). Set aside. Make ahead and keep in small bowls of water to keep from drying out. At serving time, combine all vegetables plus corn in a pan and sauté in butter, just until hot.

Assembly: at serving time, the vegetables should have been reheated, the turkey sautéed, the sauces warmed and the cornets laid out.

Spoon a little of the garlic and sage sauce onto each warmed dinner plate. Spoon cranberry coulis around the edges. Place turkey slices on the sauces and garnish with sprigs of fresh sage and reserved cranberries.

Place the pastry cornet to one side and fill remaining space with the tiny vegetable balls.

PUMPKIN-HAZELNUT MOUSSE WITH AUTUMN LEAVES

This is a creamy smooth pumpkin mousse made occasionally crunchy with chopped hazelnuts. It sits on a hazelnut sauce. The nougat paste called for in the recipe is available in specialty shops and delicatessens. The mousse can be made a day ahead; the leaves should be made the day of the dinner, as they are soft and don't keep well. If you don't have 10 individual moulds, set the mousse in a large, decorative bowl and carefully turn out individual servings with a spoon.

2 28-g pkgs. gelatine
3 egg yolks
150 mL (⅔ cup) fine berry sugar
250 mL (1 cup) milk
250 mL (1 cup) pumpkin purée
500 mL (2 cups) whipping cream
125 mL (½ cup) hazelnuts, chopped

Soak the gelatine in cold water, just to cover.

Cream egg yolks with sugar until white. Bring milk to a boil and add to eggs and sugar. Stir in pumpkin and mix well. Add gelatine and return mixture to the heat, stirring continuously until mixture coats the back of a spoon. Strain and cool.

When the pumpkin is nearly set, whip the cream and fold into gelatine mixture, along with the hazelnuts. Pour into moulds or large bowl. Chill for three hours, at least.

Hazelnut Sauce
4 egg yolks
75 mL (⅓ cup) sugar
125 mL (½ cup) white wine
125 g (4 oz.) hazelnut nougat paste
250 mL (1 cup) whipping cream

Whisk eggs, sugar and white wine together in a medium bowl.

In a medium saucepan, melt the nougat paste, then add the egg mixture. Whisk over a double boiler until mixture is similar to thick cream. Cool.

Stir in cream and chill.

Autumn Leaves
These are basically soft, thin cookies shaped like leaves. Kerry Sear garnished the dessert plates with four leaves; if you wish to reduce the work involved, two leaves or even one leaf will do.

125 mL plus 15 mL (½ cup plus 1 tbsp.) soft butter, creamed
500 mL (2 cups) icing sugar
5 egg-whites
300 mL (1¼ cups) all-purpose white flour
Drop each of green, red and yellow food colorings

Cream the butter until white. Add the sugar and egg-whites. Fold in flour. Separate mixture into four parts and mix one with yellow food color, one with red and one with green, leaving one plain.

Draw several leaves on a sheet of cardboard and cut them out with a sharp blade. This sheet is your stencil. Place the stencil on a greased cookie sheet. Using a spatula (preferably metal), "paint" bits of colored dough through the stencil cutouts, much as you would fill in shallow holes in a wall with a putty knife. To obtain a multicolored leaf, use one color of dough after the other to fill different sections of the same leaf. Keep adding dough until each stencilled pattern is filled from edge to edge with dough (this actually takes only two or three quick strokes with the putty knife). Then remove stencil. You should have several flat, thin, leaf-shaped cookies on the sheet.

Bake leaves in a hot oven, 190°C (375°F), for five minutes. Remove from baking sheet and place each leaf over the bottom of an upturned glass, small enough to allow the cookie to sag and curl. Cool.

To Serve: when ready to serve dessert, run a knife around the moulds of mousse and dip moulds briefly in hot water. Turn out onto a chilled dessert plate. Spoon hazelnut sauce around mousse and garnish with autumn leaves. □

Hungarian Rhapsody

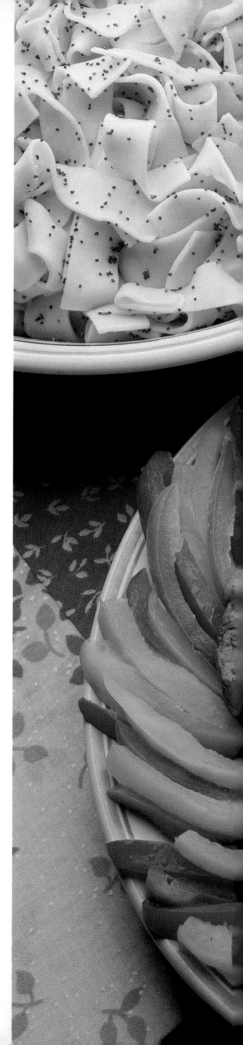

Paprika is mostly used in Canada to tart up cocktail and picnic food. It is not thought to have much flavor of its own, beyond a vague musty taste and a little sharpness on the tongue – not an unfair judgment, considering the quality of many long-bottled varieties.

To read, then, in George Lang's *The Cuisine of Hungary,* that some Hungarians can identify by taste at least six kinds of paprika (exquisite delicate, delicate, noble sweet, semi-sweet, rose and hot) is like hearing that certain northern Canadians can identify 20 kinds of snow. The *origin* of much paprika sold in Canada is often not even mentioned, let alone its flavor classification.

A brief history: The paprika pepper was brought to Europe shortly after the discovery of the Americas, where it originated. The Turks acquired the peppers and brought them to Hungary. In Hungary the *émigré* pepper had found a home where it could flourish as it never had in the wild. It entered the fabric of Hungarian society, rising from peasant usage (peasants could not afford the more exotic imported spices like black pepper) to aristocratic pretensions. In modern times it has passed into the hands of agricultural scientists, who have genetically manipulated the peppers to yield many shades of sweetness from once-spicy plants.

This spice is the soul of Hungarian cooking, the foundation on which a multitude of soups, stews and meat dishes depend for their character. A dish cannot be better than its paprika.

So shop for paprika in a specialty spice store, one run by a knowledgeable importer who specifies the origin and characteristics of the merchandise. For starters, buy a medium paprika, which will lend both sweetness and spice to your cooking. It will improve many dishes – even devilled eggs.

Hungarians eat paprika peppers not only dried and ground, but fresh. Our recipe for pork medallions with peppers calls for both varieties. The pork is pounded with paprika, sautéed and served on a multi-colored fresh pepper bed. Alongside are sautéed onions, another typical Hungarian ingredient. If at all possible, buy at least one yellow pepper for this dish. Yellow peppers are alarmingly expensive but incomparably sweet and mild.

Sour cream is also typically Hungarian; it's found in the recipe for Liptauer cheese, a blend of cream cheese, butter, sour cream, mustard, onions and paprika, which goes well with the unusual homemade crackers detailed below.

MENU *(Serves Six)*

- Liptauer Cheese
- Homemade Crackers
- Kohlrabi with Remoulade Sauce
- Pork Medallions with Julienne of Sweet Peppers
- Poppy Seed Noodles
- Walnut Soufflé Torte

LIPTAUER CHEESE

This dish will keep for about one week, refrigerated. Makes about 500 millilitres (2 cups).

1 250-mL pkg. cream cheese, at room
   temperature
125 mL (½ cup) soft butter
125 mL (½ cup) sour cream
5 mL (1 tsp.) Dijon mustard
10 mL (2 tsp.) Hungarian paprika
Dash of salt and pepper
30 mL (2 tbsp.) chives or chopped
   green onions
1 clove garlic, crushed
Caraway seeds to taste (optional)

Paprika power: pork medallions served on a bed of sweet mixed peppers with cold kohlrabi relish and poppy seed noodles on the side; for dessert, a delicate walnut torte.

Cream the cheese and butter together until smooth (do not use the food processor as it will overprocess the cream cheese). Stir in all remaining ingredients and pack into a serving dish. Serve with homemade crackers or assorted fruit such as apples, pears or oranges.

HOMEMADE CRACKERS

This is a two-in-one recipe. Use half of the dough for the Crackers and the other half for small rolls, which can be served with the kohlrabi course. The crackers will stay crisp for several days, but the rolls will dry out quickly, so freeze any leftovers.

375 mL (1½ cups) warm water
5 mL (1 tsp.) sugar
15 mL (1 tbsp.) yeast
1.25 to 1.5 L (5 to 6 cups) all-
*   purpose white flour*
5 mL (1 tsp.) salt

Mix the water and salt together in a small bowl and sprinkle on the yeast. Let stand until the yeast is dissolved and bubbles.

Place 1.25 litres (5 cups) of flour in a large bowl and make a well in the centre. Stir in the salt. Pour in the dissolved yeast and mix until dough pulls away from the sides of the bowl, adding more flour if needed.

Turn out onto a floured board and knead until dough is smooth and silky, adding flour to make a firm dough. Place in a greased bowl and let rise in a warm place until doubled in bulk.

Punch dough down and divide in half. Cut one half into 16 equal pieces and form into small balls. Place on a greased cookie sheet, slash the tops with a sharp knife or razor blade and let rise until double, about 30 minutes. Brush with a little milk or egg glaze and bake at 180°C (350°F) until golden brown and slightly crisp, about 20 to 25 minutes.

In the meantime, cut the remaining half of the dough in 16 equal pieces and also form into small balls. Mix together 50 millilitres (¼ cup) each of flour and cornmeal. On a board that has been liberally sprinkled with the flour/cornmeal mixture, roll the balls into very flat circles, about 15 centimetres (6 in.) in diameter, turning to coat both sides with cornmeal. Prick the flat discs all over with a fork or the dough will puff as it bakes (just like pita bread).

Preheat your oven to very hot, 240°C (475°F), and place a large cookie sheet in it to preheat.

Place two or three of the dough discs on the heated sheet and bake for about two to three minutes on each side, watching carefully (they burn quickly), or until the crackers are lightly browned in spots and have dried out. Cool on racks. These crackers are meant to be served broken in halves or quarters.

KOHLRABI WITH REMOULADE SAUCE

Hungarians like to serve cold root vegetables in a light oil and vinegar dressing. Kohlrabi is a crunchy, tart example.

3 or 4 bulbs of kohlrabi, peeled and
*   cut into julienne strips*
60 mL (4 tbsp.) vegetable oil
22 mL (1½ tbsp.) vinegar or fresh
*   lemon juice*
Dash of salt and pepper
Remoulade sauce (recipe follows)
Bright green leaves of lettuce or
*   spinach*
Tomato wedges for garnish

Prepare the kohlrabi and place in a bowl. Mix together the vegetable oil, vinegar and salt and pepper and pour over the vegetable strips. Toss to coat. Cover and refrigerate for a few hours. The kohlrabi will keep for several days at this point.

Meanwhile, make the remoulade sauce.

Remoulade Sauce
15 mL (1 tbsp.) Dijon mustard
250 mL (1 cup) good mayonnaise
30 mL (2 tbsp.) capers
15 mL (1 tbsp.) fresh chervil,
*   tarragon, watercress or parsley,*
*   chopped*

Mix together the mustard and the mayonnaise. Squeeze the juice out of the capers in a paper towel. Fold the capers and the herbs into the mayonnaise. Place in a small bowl and refrigerate until serving time.

Just before serving, drain the kohlrabi, reserving the marinade for another salad. Place the julienne strips over the pieces of bright green lettuce leaves, spoon on some of the remoulade sauce and garnish with the tomato wedges.

Serve with the small rolls. Pass extra remoulade sauce around the table.

PORK MEDALLIONS AND JULIENNE OF SWEET PEPPERS

This dish can be partially prepared earlier in the day, covered and kept at room temperature until 40 minutes before serving time.

12 60-g (2-oz.) slices pork tenderloin
10 to 15 mL (2 to 3 tsp.) Hungarian
*   paprika (or more if desired)*
30 mL (2 tbsp.) butter
30 mL (2 tbsp.) oil
1 whole clove of garlic, peeled
1 medium sweet red pepper, cut into
*   thin strips*
1 medium sweet yellow pepper, cut
*   into thin strips*
1 medium sweet green pepper, cut into
*   thin strips*
1 small onion, peeled, cut into thin
*   strips*
30 mL (2 tbsp.) dry white wine
Extra paprika

Sprinkle the paprika evenly over the pork slices, then gently pound the slices until they are slightly larger. Melt the butter with the oil and garlic in a large frypan until sizzling. Remove garlic. Brown the pork slices on both sides. Remove from pan and set aside. In the same pan, lowering the heat to medium, cook the peppers and the onion for about five minutes.

Transfer the peppers and onions to an ovenproof serving dish. Arrange the pork tenderloin in one layer over top. Cool. Cover with foil. This dish can be made ahead to this point.

About 40 minutes before serving time, preheat the oven to 180°C (350°F). Place the foil-covered dish in the oven and bake for 30 minutes.

Remove from the oven and uncover. Place the meat on a warm platter and keep warm. Add the wine to the peppers and return to the oven, uncovered, for another five minutes.

Remove the peppers from the oven, return the meat to the serving dish or place the peppers on the individual serving plates with the meat arranged on top, allowing two slices per person. Spoon some of the sauce over top and sprinkle with paprika.

POPPY SEED NOODLES

Traditionally, Hungarians would add a little sugar to the poppy seeds, which they use in both sweet and savory recipes. Sour cream should be served on the side.

4 L (4 qts.) water
10 mL (2 tsp.) salt
15 mL (1 tbsp.) oil
500 g (1 lb.) wide egg noodles
45 mL (3 tbsp.) butter, melted
60 mL (4 tbsp.) poppy seeds (or more, if desired)
Sour cream

In a large saucepan, bring the water to a rolling boil. Add the salt and oil. Add the noodles and cook, uncovered, until just tender to the bite, about eight or 10 minutes.

Drain in a colander and then rinse under cold running water. The dish may be made ahead to this point. Toss with a little oil to prevent sticking and store at room temperature.

Just before serving time, melt the butter in a large sauté pan or saucepan and add the noodles, cooking over low heat until heated through. Add the poppy seeds and toss to coat. Serve with sour cream on the side.

WALNUT SOUFFLE TORTE

A light and delicate cake. The white torte is actually a fallen soufflé. Don't be discouraged if your layers are less than perfect. The filling and the whipped cream will cover all, and the result will be beautiful.

White Torte
4 egg yolks
60 mL (4 tbsp.) white sugar
45 mL (3 tbsp.) all-purpose white flour
6 egg-whites
Pinch of salt

Mocha Torte
60 mL (4 tbsp.) unsalted butter, room temperature
15 mL (1 tbsp.) instant coffee granules
2 egg yolks
30 mL (2 tbsp.) white sugar
15 mL (1 tbsp.) all-purpose white flour
15 mL (1 tbsp.) cocoa powder
2 egg-whites
Rum

Butter three 20-centimetre (8-in.) cake tins. Line the bottom of each with a circle of parchment or wax paper. Butter again and dust with flour. Set aside. Preheat oven to 190°C (375°F).

To make the white torte, beat the egg yolks with the sugar until light. Beat in the flour. Whip the egg-whites with the pinch of salt until soft peaks form. Beat one-quarter of the egg-whites into the egg yolk mixture to lighten, then gently fold in the remaining whites. Divide between two of the prepared pans. Bake for 15 to 20 minutes or until puffy and golden and a cake tester comes out clean.

To make the mocha torte, beat the butter, coffee, egg yolks and sugar until light. Sift the flour and cocoa together and blend thoroughly into the yolk mixture. Whip the egg-whites until soft peaks form. Beat a few tablespoons into the yolk mixture to lighten, then gently fold in the remaining whites. Pour into the prepared pan and bake for 10 to 12 minutes or until a cake tester comes out clean.

Cool the cakes in their pans. Turn out onto cake racks as carefully as possible. Moisten each layer with about 15 millilitres (1 tbsp.) of rum. Make sure the cakes are quite cold before continuing.

Meanwhile, make the walnut filling.

Walnut Filling
125 mL (½ cup) light cream
250 mL (1 cup) ground walnuts
125 mL (½ cup) unsalted butter, at room temperature
125 mL (½ cup) icing sugar
2 egg yolks
15 mL (1 tbsp.) rum
125 mL (½ cup) thick jam (apricot, peach or a sieved marmalade)
250 mL (1 cup) whipping cream
Icing sugar (optional)

Bring the light cream to a boil with the ground walnuts. Remove from the heat and cool thoroughly. Beat the butter, sugar and egg yolks together until light. Stir in the rum. When the walnuts and cream are very cold, stir into the butter mixture. Chill, if necessary, to get to a spreading consistency.

Place one of the white torte layers on a cake platter. Cover with one-half of the jam. Spread one-third of the walnut filling over the jam.

Place the mocha torte on top and cover with the remaining jam. Spread with one-third of the walnut filling.

Place the remaining white torte on top of the cake layers and spread with the remaining walnut filling. Allow the torte to mellow for one day. No need to refrigerate.

When ready to serve (or earlier in the day), whip the cream, adding icing sugar to taste if desired. Pipe or spread decoratively around the sides of the cake. Pipe rosettes around the rim where the walnut filling meets the whipped cream. Refrigerate until serving time. □

Out of the West

The trend throughout North America – and it's a good one – is the growth of a network of farmers and food producers serving the specialty market. Increasingly one finds unusual – or simply unusually fresh and good – local foods in farmers' markets, specialty stores, health food stores and, yes, supermarkets. The continuation of this trend (and it will continue if Canadian tastes continue to evolve, and if Canadians remain willing to pay for specialty foods) will be essential in the development of a truly regional cuisine in the West.

For this menu, we hunted out some of the West's fine specialty foods and combined them in a gently adventurous menu centred around a meat-and-potatoes (with a twist) main course. The buffalo steak under wild mushroom gravy, served with thick ranch-cut potatoes and fresh herbed vegetables, yields a hearty *and* interesting entrée. The warm squab salad that precedes it perfectly emphasizes the delicate flavor and texture of this delicious bird. And, as usual, dessert – hazelnut crêpes with a silky chocolate sauce – is outstanding.

MENU *(Serves Six)*

- Warm Squab Salad
- Wild Rice Bread
- Buffalo Tenderloin with Wild Mushroom Gravy
- Ranch-Cut Potatoes
- Squash with Herbed Vegetables
- Hazelnut-Filled Crêpes with Chocolate Sauce

Hurray for homegrown: warm squab salad; hearty bread made with whole and ground wild rice; fillet of buffalo tenderloin in an exotic mushroom sauce with ranch-cut potatoes; hazelnut crêpes to complete the meal.

WARM SQUAB SALAD

Squab, an important part of California's booming food scene, are bred in the West by Vancouver Island Mountain Squab, Canada's largest producer. Ask your local butcher if he has or can get any. Much of the squab eaten in Canada is imported from Europe, where around 100 million of the birds are eaten annually by the French and Italians alone. Squab has a unique flavor, but breast of pheasant or duck could be substituted for an equally delicious salad.

2 squabs, cleaned, lightly salted and
  peppered
2 bunches of watercress or arugula
  (also known as rocket, a peppery
  salad herb)
250 mL (1 cup) chicken stock or
  canned broth
15 mL (1 tbsp.) brandy
75 mL (⅓ cup) sherry vinegar or
  balsamic vinegar
5 mL (1 tsp.) lemon juice
Pinch of dry mustard
1 small shallot, minced
Finely minced thyme to taste
Salt and freshly ground pepper to taste
250 mL (1 cup) olive oil

Roast the whole squab (or duck or pheasant breasts; remove the breasts, reserving the remainder of the bird for another use) at 200° C (400° F) for about 20 minutes; it should be rare. Wash and pat dry the watercress or arugula.

Over high heat, in a small pan, reduce the stock to 45 to 60 millilitres (3 to 4 tbsp.) Cool and add the brandy. Set aside.

In a small bowl, mix together the vinegar, lemon juice, mustard, shallot, thyme, salt and pepper. Slowly whisk in the olive oil to make a vinaigrette. Add the reduced stock and brandy.

Strip the rare meat from the squabs and tear into slivers. Marinate briefly in the vinaigrette and serve on the watercress with additional vinaigrette spooned over top.

This salad can be made ahead. Reheat the squab in the reduced stock before adding to the vinaigrette. The meat should be served slightly warm.

WILD RICE BREAD

DuBois Wild Rice Ltd. (Box 1762, Winnipeg, Man. R3C 2Z9) makes a wonderful ground wild rice pancake mixture that makes excellent pancakes and bakes into delicious bread. (The pancake mix gives this fairly heavy bread an extra boost, making it rise higher than it would with plain flour.) You can also do a rough grind of wild rice in your food processor. Use it to replace up to one-half the flour in a bread recipe. Add some cooked wild rice to give the bread an interesting texture.

175 mL (¾ cup) cooked wild rice
  (see below)
375 mL (1½ cups) warm milk
10 mL (2 tsp.) sugar
15 mL (1 tbsp.) yeast
1 egg
5 mL (1 tsp.) lemon juice or vinegar
250 mL (1 cup) all-purpose white
  flour
250 mL (1 cup) DuBois Wild Rice
  Pancake Mix or wild rice flour
2 mL (½ tsp.) salt
500 to 750 mL (2 to 3 cups)
  additional flour to make a soft
  dough
1 egg yolk mixed with 15 mL (1
  tbsp.) water for glaze

To cook the wild rice, simmer 60 millilitres (4 tbsp.) raw rice in 250 millilitres (1 cup) water until tender, about 30 to 45 minutes. Set aside.

Add the sugar to the milk and stir to dissolve. Sprinkle on the yeast and let it stand until dissolved and bubbly, about 10 minutes.

In a medium bowl or the work bowl of the food processor, place 250 millilitres (1 cup) white flour, 250 millilitres (1 cup) wild rice mix, and salt. Stir to mix.

In a small bowl, beat the egg and lemon juice. Add to the dissolved yeast and stir well. Mix into the flour mixture, beating well.

Add cooked rice and additional flour until the dough pulls away from the sides of the bowl.

Turn out on a floured surface and knead until smooth and silky, adding flour as necessary.

Place in a greased bowl, greasing the dough, and let it rise until it

doubles in size — about one hour. Divide in half and shape into two loaves. Place in greased bread pans and let it rise until the centre of the loaf is about 2.5 centimetres (1 in.) above the sides of the pan. Brush with egg glaze.

Bake at 190° C (375° F) for 35 to 40 minutes or until the bread is golden and sounds hollow when tapped on the bottom. Cool on racks.

BUFFALO TENDERLOIN WITH WILD MUSHROOM GRAVY

Buffalo is very tender and does not need marinating. Buffalo is available from many butchers in the West (ours came from Briscoe's Fine Foods in Vancouver). It is becoming increasingly popular in restaurants and is often promoted for its low-fat, low-cholesterol content (producers claim 25 to 30 per cent more protein and up to half as much cholesterol as some cuts of beef). The low-fat content means that buffalo meat must be cooked with care, lest it dry out and become leathery. The key is slow cooking over moderate heat to a rare consistency. The meat is delicious, noticeably different from beef if cooked properly, and not gamey.

15 mL (1 tbsp.) butter
1 small onion, sliced or chopped
1 clove garlic, crushed
1 small tomato, chopped
1 small carrot, peeled and chopped
A few sprigs of fresh rosemary or 2
  mL (½ tsp.) dried
6 or 8 whole black peppercorns,
  coarsely crushed
16 dried whole juniper berries, coarsely
  crushed
500 mL (2 cups) beef stock or canned
  broth
10 to 12 fresh chanterelle, shiitaké or
  golden oak mushrooms, or 28 g
  (1 oz.) dried shiitaké rejuvenated in
  small amount of water
15 mL (1 tbsp.) butter
6 4-cm (1½-in.) thick buffalo strip
  loin or tenderloin steaks
30 mL (2 tbsp.) butter
30 mL (2 tbsp.) olive oil
10 mL (2 tsp.) red currant jelly
250 mL (1 cup) whipping cream

Over medium heat in a medium saucepan, melt the 15 millilitres (1 tbsp.) butter. Add onion, garlic, tomato, carrot, rosemary, peppercorns and juniper berries. Cook, stirring, until the butter is absorbed. Add the beef broth, bring to a boil, reduce heat to a quick simmer and cook uncovered until reduced by half. Strain and set aside.

Wash and dry fresh mushrooms, removing woody stems, or drain dried mushrooms and remove woody stems. Slice into thick pieces. Melt 15 millilitres (1 tbsp.) butter in a medium frypan and sauté mushrooms briefly. Set aside.

The sauce may be made ahead to this point.

In a large frypan, over medium heat, melt together the butter and olive oil. Add the steaks and cook about four minutes on each side, depending on their thickness. Avoid very high heat or the meat will toughen. Remove to a warm platter while preparing the balance of the sauce.

Drain off any excess fat, pour the strained broth into the steak pan and bring to a boil over high heat, scraping up any bits of meat. This is deglazing. Boil until the sauce is reduced by half and is rich and thick. This will take only a few minutes.

Stir in the red currant jelly and boil until melted, about one to two minutes. Stir in the whipping cream and boil until reduced and thick and smooth. Reduce heat. Stir in the prepared mushrooms and cook for 30 seconds. Taste and adjust seasonings.

Place the steaks on warm plates and spoon some sauce on top with mushrooms along the side. Pass extra sauce. Serve with seasonal vegetables and ranch-cut potatoes.

RANCH CUT POTATOES

Choose oval brown-skinned potatoes.

6 medium-sized potatoes
60 mL (4 tbsp.) unsalted, clarified butter, bacon drippings or cooking oil

Cut the potatoes lengthwise into strips about 1.5 centimetres (½ in.) thick. They can be soaked in cold water until baking time. Dry well. Spread in a single layer in a flat baking sheet. Pour the melted butter over the potatoes and stir until well coated.

Bake at 230° C (450° C) for about 30 to 40 minutes, turning the potato slices several times. Drain on paper towels.

Season with salt and pepper if desired.

SQUASH STUFFED WITH SEASONAL VEGETABLES AND FRESH HERBS

Danish, acorn or pitty pan squash make a nice presentation.

6 slices of squash, centre seeds removed
4 stalks of celery, peeled and thinly sliced
125 mL (½ cup) raisins
125 mL (½ cup) walnuts
1 red apple, diced
Chopped fresh herbs such as parsley, chives, oregano, winter savory and thyme
Nutmeg, salt and freshly ground pepper
Butter

Place the slices of squash on a greased baking sheet.

In a small bowl, mix together the celery, raisins, walnuts, apple and herbs. Taste and add seasonings as desired. Divide this mixture among the squash slices. Top with a dot of butter.

Bake at 180° C (350° F) until the squash is tender. This can be done in the microwave with great success.

HAZELNUT FILLED CREPES WITH CHOCOLATE SAUCE

Local hazelnuts are available in the late fall. The shape seems to vary with the type of tree. The lighter brown oval hazelnuts seem to be more flavorful.

Allow three to four of these small crêpes per person.

90 mL (6 tbsp.) unsalted butter
60 mL (4 tbsp.) berry sugar
175 mL (¾ cup) hazelnuts with skins on, toasted and finely ground
Rum to flavor

Cream butter and sugar until white; the sugar should be almost dissolved. Mix in the nuts and flavor with rum to taste.

Spread the inside of the crêpes with the nut mixture and roll up or fold into triangles. Serve with hot chocolate sauce.

Chocolate Sauce
A wonderful sauce that will keep (if nobody sneaks into the fridge and eats it).

3 28-g (1-oz.) squares semi-sweet chocolate
60 mL (4 tbsp.) unsalted butter
15 mL (1 tbsp.) dark rum
15 mL (1 tbsp.) strong liquid coffee
250 mL (1 cup) unsifted icing sugar
250 mL (1 scant cup) evaporated milk
5 mL (1 tsp.) vanilla

Melt the chocolate and butter in a heavy pan together with the rum and coffee. Remove from heat and stir in sugar alternately with evaporated milk. Cook again on medium heat, stirring constantly until the mixture is thick, smooth and creamy. Remove from heat and stir in vanilla.

Basic Crêpe Batter
Makes 48 15-centimetre (6-in.) crêpes.

425 mL (1¾ cup) all-purpose white flour
5 mL (1 tsp.) salt
90 mL (6 tbsp.) melted butter, cooled
6 eggs
375 mL (1½ cups) milk
375 mL (1½ cups) water

Blend ingredients together and refrigerate at least two hours.

Heat a 15-centimetre (6-in.) crêpe pan. Pour out 25 millilitres (⅛ cup) batter into the pan and roll it around, pouring off excess batter. Cook until the small bubbles burst. Turn and briefly cook the other side.

Crêpes freeze well. Store in packages of 12 for ease in thawing. □

Favor Curry

Curry is a most surprising dish. For one thing, it is surprisingly easy to cook an authentic version. You will no doubt be wondering how easy a recipe that requires you to grind a long list of spices can possibly be. Believe us, *very* easy. Don't make the mistake of equating the use of spices with complexity. It may feel slightly foreign to start a recipe by milling whole peppercorns, mustard seeds, coriander, cumin, fennel, cardamom and cloves, but having done it once you'll find that grinding your own is not much harder than opening a tin of prepared curry, and infinitely more rewarding.

Another surprise: great curry needn't blow the top of your head off. That kind of heat comes from chili or cayenne peppers, neither of which are indigenous to Asia. They were introduced to the region in the sixteenth century by the Portuguese, who had discovered them in the New World. Up to then, the most pungent curries had relied upon cooler spices such as mustard seeds and black peppercorns. So you will not betray tradition by cutting back on the fiery spices, or by leaving them out entirely. In fact, you can call yourself a purist.

And, surprise! No two curries are the same. With a little imagination and the luxury of time to experiment, you will discover amazing ways in which the seductive flavors and tantalizing aromas of curry mingle in your pot as the spices interact with each other and with the meats, fish or vegetables that you've chosen for the meal. If you become hooked, you will want to investigate different cooking techniques, sometimes leaving the spices

Touched with gold: a majestic meal of chicken breasts in a curry sauce richly flavored with fresh ground spices, served with mixed sweet peppers, aromatic basmati rice and crisp poori bread.

with a curry sauce that can be used with slight alteration for chicken, shrimp, pork or lamb dishes. The one we have adapted for home kitchens comes from David Eaton, executive chef of Vancouver's Oriental Mandarin Hotel, where a widely celebrated curry buffet is served for lunch every weekday in the Clipper Lounge. The style here is more Malaysian than strictly Indian, highlighted by the creative use of fruits and condiments. In Eaton's mind, spice must be equalled by sweetness, which "levels people's heads so they don't go through the ceiling."

A meal of curry should be planned as a harmonious whole, the main dish surrounded by fresh and cooked chutneys, chewy or crisp breads, aromatic basmati rice, a palate-cooling cucumber salad and marinated fruit. And because this sensual feast of color, texture, taste and aroma is all fork food, it makes for an extremely practical buffet.

Most large supermarkets carry the basic unground curry spices, but if you can't locate them, or desire something along more exotic lines, you can order by phone from Patel Discount Bulk Foods, a Vancouver store with mail-order services across western Canada. Call (604) 255-8151/6729. Patel also carries a wide range of prepared chutneys.

CURRY SAUCE

This basic recipe can be varied according to your tastes. The powdered spices can be used in any recipe calling for curry powder.

30 mL (2 tbsp.) butter
3 cloves garlic, finely chopped
1 medium onion, finely chopped
15 mL (1 tbsp.) fresh ginger, finely chopped
½ 156-mL can tomato paste
1 recipe curry powder, see below
375 mL (1½ cups) water or chicken stock or canned broth
Juice of 3 lemons
Salt and pepper

Melt the butter in a saucepan. Gently sauté the garlic, onion and

ginger over medium heat for one whole, sometimes roasting and grinding them into a paste which is rubbed onto the food for a dry curry variation.

But we suggest you start simple, minute. Add the tomato paste and cook for another minute. Add the curry powder and mix thoroughly, cooking for 30 seconds to one minute until the spices start to release their aroma. Gradually add the cold water and bring to a boil. Reduce the heat and simmer, covered, for one and a half hours. Add the lemon juice and taste, seasoning with salt and pepper if desired.

CURRY POWDER

A coffee-mill used only to grind spices is a great help in every kitchen.

5 mL (1 tsp.) black peppercorns
5 mL (1 tsp.) mustard seeds
2 mL (½ tsp.) coriander seeds
2 mL (½ tsp.) cumin seeds
2 mL (½ tsp.) fennel seeds
2 mL (½ tsp.) cayenne pepper flakes, optional
1 large bay leaf, broken
8 whole cloves
6 to 12 cardamom seeds (the tiny black ones)

In a spice-mill or blender, grind all the ingredients together until fine. If not using right away, store in an airtight container in the refrigerator.

CHICKEN CURRY

15 mL (1 tbsp.) butter
15 mL (1 tbsp.) oil
4 boneless chicken breast halves, cut into 2.5-cm (1-in.) cubes
½ recipe curry sauce
1 red and 1 green pepper, thinly sliced, or 125 g (4 oz.) seedless red and green grapes and 1 small pineapple, peeled, cored and cut into 1.8-cm (¾-in.) cubes

Melt the butter in the oil and sauté the chicken pieces on all sides, about two to three minutes. Add the curry sauce and bring to a boil. Reduce the heat and simmer gently

for five minutes or until the chicken is cooked through. Add the peppers, or the grapes and pineapple cubes, and simmer another minute. Serve on a bed of basmati rice.

SHRIMP CURRY

250 g (8 oz.) cooked shrimp, hand-peeled if possible
15 mL (1 tbsp.) butter
½ recipe curry sauce
1 red and 1 green pepper, thinly sliced, or 125 g seedless red and green grapes and 1 small pineapple, peeled, cored and cut into 1.8-cm (¾-in.) cubes

Melt the butter in a saucepan and sauté the shrimp for one minute. Add the curry sauce and bring to a boil. Reduce the heat and add the peppers, or the grapes and pineapple. Simmer for one minute. Serve on a bed of basmati rice.

PORK AND BANANA CURRY

Check with your butcher to make sure a pork tenderloin will be available when you want to do this recipe.

2 bananas, sliced
60 mL (4 tbsp.) raisins (optional)
30 mL (2 tbsp.) butter
750 g (1½ lbs.) pork tenderloin, cut into 7.5-cm (3-in.) chunks, then into strips about 7.5 cm by 2.5 cm by 6 mm thick (3 by 1 by ¼ in.)
398-mL can tomatoes, crushed
½ recipe curry sauce

Gently sauté the bananas and raisins in the butter for three or four minutes or until well coated with butter. Remove from the pan and set aside.

In batches, to prevent overcrowding, sauté the pork over medium heat until brown. May be made ahead to this point.

Add the tomatoes and curry sauce and bring to a boil. Turn down heat and simmer until the pork is cooked, about three to five minutes.

Serve on a bed of basmati rice garnished with bananas and raisins.

BASMATI RICE

500 mL (2 cups) basmati rice
10 mL (2 tsp.) turmeric (optional)
8 whole cloves
3 bay leaves

Place the rice in a thick-bottomed saucepan and add enough water to cover the rice by five centimetres (2 in.). Add the bay leaves, cloves and turmeric (if you want a nice yellow color) and bring to a boil, stirring often. When boiling, reduce the heat and cover with a tight-fitting lid. Cook for 15 minutes. Taste for tenderness. Drain off any excess liquid. Serve immediately.

ONION CHUTNEY

The flavor of sweet fruit preserves, combined with the tartness of onion and the sharpness of crushed peppercorns, makes this an exceptional accompaniment for curry dishes; it is also good with meat pâtés. Makes about 375 millilitres (1½ cups).

1 small onion, peeled
1 small orange
30 mL (2 tbsp.) raisins
6 pitted prunes
5 mL (1 tsp.) shallots or green onions,
    minced
45 mL (3 tbsp.) medium dry sherry
    (Madeira will do)
2 mL (½ tsp.) lemon rind, grated
5 mL (1 tsp.) fresh lemon juice
250 mL (1 cup) good quality
    cranberry relish
5 mL (1 tsp.) white peppercorns,
    crushed
45 mL (3 tbsp.) pine nuts, coarsely
    chopped
Dijon mustard, to taste

Slice the onion lengthwise into several pieces and soak in salted water for one hour. Cut half the orange rind into julienne strips. Squeeze the orange and reserve 30 millilitres (2 tbsp.) juice. Combine the raisins, prunes, shallots, sherry, julienned orange rind, orange juice, lemon rind and lemon juice. Bring to a boil and simmer slowly, uncovered, for 20 minutes. Cool and reserve any liquid. Coarsely chop the raisin mixture. Rinse and drain the onion and mince finely.

Key condiments: the crucial side dishes of an Indian feast, offering sharp contrasts of sweet, sour, smooth and spicy. Shown here, a fresh cucumber relish, tomato-onion salad and mango chutney.

Combine the cranberry relish, onion, peppercorns and pine nuts. Stir in the raisin mixture and reserved liquid, if any. Add mustard to taste. Will keep, refrigerated, one month.

FRESH CUCUMBER CHUTNEY

Don't make this more than one hour ahead of serving as it tends to become quite watery.

1 English cucumber
1 medium onion
5 mL (1 tsp.) salt
2 mL (½ tsp.) pepper or chili powder
15 mL (1 tbsp.) fresh lemon juice

Thinly slice the cucumber. Peel and finely chop the onion. Combine in a medium bowl and add seasonings. Cover and refrigerate for up to one hour.

MARINATED FRUIT

A cooling fruit salad is a wonderful way to end a curry buffet. Very little fruit is needed.

Use this opportunity to try new types from other parts of the world.

1 apple
1 pear
1 nectarine
1 banana
1 peach
1 orange
A few grapes
45 mL (3 tbsp.) fresh lemon juice
45 mL (3 tbsp.) liqueur such as
    Grand Marnier, Cointreau,
    Galliano (more is not necessarily
    better!)

Leaving the colorful skin on the apple, peel the other fruits and cut into slices. Place in a large bowl and drizzle on the lemon juice and liqueur. Using your hand, gently lift and stir the fruit until it is coated with the liquids. Cover and refrigerate overnight or for at least five hours, gently lifting and stirring once in a while to mix the flavors. □

A Taste of the Past

....

The dishes for this meal were
adapted from recipes found in the
cookbook collection of the Ladner,
B.C., museum. Ladner, with its
rich soil and proximity to the
Fraser River and the sea, was one
of the first areas in the Lower
Mainland to be settled, but the
objects in the town's small,
pleasant museum describe not the
hardship of early pioneers but the
comfortable surroundings that
residents had created for
themselves by the turn of the
century. Prosperous Ladner homes
were full of elegant tables, delicate
knick-knacks, fine glassware and
china, well-stuffed chairs and
lovely wallpaper. Food, once the
stuff of survival, had become the
stuff of elegant dinner parties.
"From Cape Breton to Vancouver
Island," wrote Pierre and Janet
Berton of the era in their *Canadian
Food Guide*, "*fin de siècle* Canadians
contrived to eat heartily."

In the Vancouver Public
Library's Pacific Northwest
collection are several menus from
gala dinners held in the first
decades of this century. The menu
from the Vancouver Bar
Association's dinner at the Hotel
Vancouver on Wednesday,
December 30, 1908, gives some
idea of what west coast high
society liked to eat: oysters and
cocktails, consommé julienne and
sherry, sole, calf sweetbreads and
Niersteiner, roast lamb, Mumm's
champagne punch, game, cheese,
salad, frozen Napoleon cream,
dessert and coffee.

At home, the housewife in
Ladner (or Saskatoon) had a
number of comprehensive
cookbooks to rely on, the most

*A fabled feast: the classic carrot
consommé for a starter; beer-braised
beef pie in the English tradition;
artful tomato and egg salad with
boiled dressing; a proper rice
pudding for dessert.*

famous being Fannie Farmer's *Boston Cooking School Cookbook*. Also found in many homes, even in Canada, was the *White House Cookbook*. Annie R. Gregory, in 1907, wrote *Canada's Favorite Cookbook*. In addition, the homemaker could rely on flour, baking powder, spice and sugar producers to send her promotional recipe booklets. The style of these, as much as the recipes, illustrated the changing times: drawings from the first 20 years of the century show women at work over huge wrought-iron stoves; suddenly, in the 'twenties, they were wearing flapper outfits and eating dainty tidbits while watching the progress of a tennis game.

In the December 31, 1925, *Vancouver Evening Sun*, Edith Adam's cooking page provided recipes for such delicacies as O'Brien potatoes, Turkish eggs and egg froth (a dessert). The society page was loaded with accounts of fine dinner parties crowded with men and women who wore only the most noteworthy of clothes. Those who suffered dyspepsia on the home and hotel party circuit could resort to the "Health and Diet Advice" column of Dr. Frank McCoy, found on the editorial page. Dr. McCoy identified starch as a major troublemaker, and wrote on December 26, 1925, that "Cakes, Cookies, Ginger Snaps, Macaroons and Lady Fingers are all unwholesome cookies, and should not be considered a suitable food, even by ones whose digestion is strong. They certainly should not be used for your children."

While many cooks were concerned with what they had heard or read about the *haute cuisine* of Europe, they were also blessed by an abundance of local ingredients. Game, wild berries, salmon, trout and the like were emphasized in their season. This produced a distinctively western Canadian table. Imported, easily preserved staples, such as rice and raisins, which had for years helped families through the winter, remained favorites, turning up in puddings even on fancy hotel menus.

These recipes have been taken from several sources and adapted somewhat to modern tastes (generally to make them less heavy). The rice pudding, for example, is made with brown rice, which produces a delicious, chewy texture, and with Australian raisins, which plump up during cooking to a huge size. But dishes like beef braised in beer and stock and served in pastry are timeless examples of good cooking from the past.

MENU *(Serves Six)*

• Sherried Carrot Consommé
• Braised Beef Pie with Beer
• Tomato and Egg Salad with Boiled Dressing
• Brown Rice Pudding with Orange Sauce

SHERRIED CARROT CONSOMME

The ingredients in the consommé have changed little from the days when consommé was a more popular meal opener than it is today. Consommé's decline is unfortunate; it is a light, subtle soup which relies almost entirely on the quality of the homemade stock used. Far from being an easy dish, its clarity and flavor depend on the cook's skilful rendering of chicken bones, vegetables and herbs. There is no substitute for time and care. For details on making clarifying stock, consult any classic cookbook.

4 medium carrots, peeled and shredded or thinly sliced
30 mL (2 tbsp.) butter
750 mL (3 cups) homemade chicken broth
Salt
Freshly ground pepper
Nutmeg
15 mL (1 tbsp.) sherry (or more to taste)
Chervil or parsley, coarsely chopped

Pat the moisture from the shredded carrots. In a medium saucepan, melt the butter and add the carrots. Simmer gently until the butter is absorbed into the vegetable. Add the chicken broth and bring to a boil, turn down the heat and simmer until the carrots are tender. Taste for seasonings.

Add salt and pepper as needed. A dash of nutmeg enhances the soup. May be made ahead to this point and refrigerated or frozen.

When ready to serve, reheat and taste again for seasonings. Add sherry. Serve in preheated soup bowls, garnishing with a sprinkling of coarsely chopped chervil or parsley.

BEEF PIE WITH BEER

Pies of all sorts were popular in the West. In this recipe, lean beef chuck is braised in a blending of beer, beef stock and vegetables, topped with a short-crust pastry and baked until brown. The beef mixture is best if made the day before and allowed to cool in its juices to achieve a wonderful flavor.

1 kg (2 lbs.) lean beef chuck, trimmed of fat and cut into 2.5-cm (1-in.) cubes
10 mL (2 tsp.) salt
Dash of pepper, freshly ground
125 mL (½ cup) all-purpose white flour
125 g (¼ lb.) bacon (about 4 slices)
125 mL (½ cup) onions, finely chopped
15 mL (1 tbsp.) sugar
1 clove garlic, finely chopped
500 mL (2 cups) beer or malt liquor
500 mL (2 cups) beef stock or canned broth
1 medium bay leaf
3 medium potatoes, peeled and cut into cubes (same size as beef)
1 398-mL can Italian tomatoes, chopped
1 medium turnip, peeled and cut into cubes
4 stalks celery, peeled and cut diagonally into slices (or other vegetables of your choice)
60 mL (4 tsp.) finely chopped parsley
Pastry for 1 22-cm (9-in.) pie

Pat the cubes of beef completely dry. In a plastic bag, mix together the salt, pepper and flour. Toss the beef cubes in the bag and shake to coat well.

In a heavy casserole or frypan, fry the bacon until almost crisp. Remove with slotted spoon to drain on towelling. Cut into 2.5-centimetre (1-in.) pieces. Add onions to the bacon fat and fry until soft. Sprinkle on the 15 millilitres (1 tbsp.) sugar and fry until golden. Add garlic and cook for one to two more minutes. Be careful not to burn the garlic. With a slotted spoon remove the onions and garlic to a paper towel to drain.

Brown the floured beef cubes in the remaining bacon fat, adding vegetable oil if needed. Fry only four or five at a time, turning with a spatula until they are nicely brown. As they brown, transfer to an ovenproof casserole.

When all the beef is browned, add 250 millilitres (1 cup) of beef broth to the frypan and bring to a boil, scraping up all the particles on the bottom and sides of the pan. Transfer to the baking dish along with the remaining beef broth and beer. Add the reserved onions and garlic, bacon and bay leaf.

Place in a 180° C (350° F) oven, covered, and bake for one hour. Then add the vegetables and parsley. Cover the casserole and bake for a further 30 to 45 minutes or until the vegetables are tender.

Remove from the oven, uncover, and set aside to cool. Remove bay leaf. This dish may be made ahead to this point. When cool, it freezes well.

About one hour before serving time, place the beef and vegetables in a deep pie dish and cover with pastry dough, crimping the edges tightly. Decorate the pastry with cut-outs from leftover dough. Brush lightly with a mixture of one egg yolk mixed with 15 millilitres (1 tbsp.) water. Cut a few vents in the top.

Bake at 190° C (375° F) for 45 to 50 minutes or until the crust is golden brown and the pie is heated through. Serve at once, directly from the baking dish.

TOMATO AND EGG SALAD WITH BOILED DRESSING

This salad is made with a delicious dressing much like mayonnaise in texture but without the oil.

4 large tomatoes

4 large eggs
Butter lettuce
Boiled dressing (recipe below)
Pimiento, olives or pickles, finely chopped

Plunge the tomatoes into boiling water for 10 seconds, cool under cold running water and peel off the skins. Chill thoroughly. Hard cook the eggs by placing them in cold water in a saucepan and bringing them to a boil. Cover and let stand for 20 minutes. Cool under cold water and refrigerate.

At serving time, arrange the lettuce leaves on a large platter. Cut the tomatoes in half and place on the lettuce, cut side up. Cut the hardboiled eggs in half lengthwise. Sprinkle with a little salt and pepper and place cut side down on the tomato half. Spoon the boiled dressing carefully over the top of the egg and sprinkle on a little of the chopped pimiento.

Boiled Dressing

15 mL (1 tbsp.) all-purpose white flour
7 mL (1½ tsp.) sugar
10 mL (2 tsp.) salt, or to taste
2 egg yolks, beaten
45 mL (3 tbsp.) butter, melted
175 mL (¾ cup) milk
60 mL (4 tbsp.) mild vinegar

Place all the ingredients in a heavy saucepan or top of a double boiler. Stir well and cook slowly on medium heat or over hot water, whisking constantly until mixture coats the back of a wooden spoon. Strain into a small bowl. Cool and adjust seasonings. Add white pepper and chopped or dried tarragon, if desired. Keep refrigerated.

RICE PUDDING WITH ORANGE SAUCE

A delicious brown-rice pudding that can be served directly from the baking dish or cooled slightly and unmoulded onto a serving plate.

15 mL (1 tbsp.) butter
175 mL (¾ cup) raw brown rice
750 mL (3 cups) milk

Pinch of salt
Zest of one orange, finely chopped
125 mL (½ cup) white sugar
60 mL (4 tbsp.) all-purpose white flour
4 egg yolks, beaten
170 g (¾ cup) Australian Lexia raisins soaked in 60 mL (4 tbsp.) rum or brandy
Dash of cinnamon and nutmeg
4 egg-whites

Melt the butter in a medium saucepan and add the raw rice. Stir to coat. Add the milk and salt and bring to a boil. Lower the heat and simmer, uncovered, stirring occasionally, until all the milk is absorbed. This will take 40 to 60 minutes. Cool.

Heat the oven to 200° C (400° F). Stir together the orange zest, sugar and flour. Mix into the cooled rice. Beat in the egg yolks. Add the raisins and their soaking liquid. Stir in cinnamon and nutmeg to taste.

Beat the egg-whites until soft peaks form. Gently fold into the rice mixture. Pour into a buttered 3 litre (3 qt.) soufflé dish or ovenproof casserole. Bake for 35 to 45 minutes or until puffed and a dark golden brown and a skewer inserted in the centre comes out clean. Cool slightly before unmoulding.

Orange Sauce
This sauce is delicious with bread pudding as well.

125 mL (½ cup) sugar
Zest of one orange, finely chopped
15 mL (1 tbsp.) butter
250 mL (1 cup) orange juice, fresh if possible
15 mL (1 tbsp.) cornstarch
60 mL (4 tbsp.) lemon juice
1 egg yolk, beaten
45 mL (3 tbsp.) Grand Marnier

Put the sugar, orange zest, butter and orange juice in a small pan. Bring to a boil. Dissolve the cornstarch in the lemon juice and add. Simmer four to five minutes. Add a little of the hot mixture to the beaten egg yolk, then beat egg mixture back into the sauce. Cook, stirring for two minutes. Remove from heat and stir in Grand Marnier. Best served warm. □

Hunter's Feast

Each fall, a number of western Canadians pull their shotguns out of the closet for another season of game-bird hunting. Our wild duck dinner will easily compensate for stiff joints caused by long, cold hours lying in stubble waiting for quacks.

Wild duck requires special treatment. Before roasting, it should be parboiled for 15 minutes with a small, peeled carrot placed inside the cavity; this should remove any "gamey" flavor (usually evident only in fish-feeding ducks). After this, discard the carrot, lay the duck in fresh water for half an hour, then stuff as desired. When roasting, baste frequently with drippings.

To roast partridge, pheasant, quail or grouse, first wash the bird thoroughly with baking soda and water, and rinse carefully. Stuff with your choice of dressing and sew up; then skewer the legs and wings to the body. Lay thin slices of fatty salt pork or fatty bacon over the entire breast. Add 125 mL (½ cup) of water to the roasting pan, add the bird, and then place in a moderate oven (180°C or 350°F) until tender, allowing 15 to 20 minutes per pound (30 minutes per kilogram). Baste frequently with melted butter, and make a gravy of the drippings.

MENU *(Serves Eight)*

- Carrot Salad in Lettuce Cups
- Warm Red Cabbage
- Wild Duck Calvados Stuffed with Barley Pilaf
- Pear Shortcake

CARROT SALAD IN LETTUCE CUPS

The flavor of this salad improves with time and so it's best made a day or two ahead.

750 g (3 cups) carrots, peeled and cut into thin julienne strips about 5 cm (2 in.) long
60 mL (4 tbsp.) fresh lemon juice
250 mL (1 cup) parsley leaves, loosely packed then finely chopped
2 hard-cooked eggs, peeled and coarsely chopped
½ small onion, peeled and coarsely chopped
1 small dill pickle, coarsely chopped
30 mL (2 tbsp.) capers, drained
30 mL (2 tbsp.) Dijon mustard
5 mL (1 tsp.) chopped fresh tarragon or 2 mL (½ tsp.) dried
250 mL (1 cup) mayonnaise
Lettuce leaves

Place the prepared carrots in a medium bowl. Sprinkle with lemon juice and toss to coat. Add 150 mL (⅔ cup) of the chopped parsley. Set the remainder aside for the mayonnaise.

Mix together the eggs, onion, dill pickle, capers, Dijon mustard and tarragon. Add the reserved parsley. Stir in the homemade mayonnaise. Season to taste. Add the sauce to the carrot mixture. Chill until serving time.

When ready to serve, arrange lettuce leaves on a chilled platter and place carrot mixture in centre of each. Garnish with a whole sprig of parsley.

WARM RED CABBAGE

Red cabbage, lightly cooked, makes a wonderful and tasty garnish. Arrange it around the duck for a colorful presentation.

1 small head red cabbage
60 mL (4 tbsp.) vinegar
60 mL (4 tbsp.) olive oil

Quarter the cabbage, remove the core and shred finely lengthwise to obtain long strips. Place in a medium bowl.

Bring the vinegar to a boil, pour it over the shredded cabbage and

Wild and wonderful: roast duck calvados stuffed with barley pilaf served on warm red cabbage; carrot salad in lettuce cups; and a fluffy pear shortcake for dessert.

mix well. The cabbage will turn bright red. It can be prepared one hour in advance. Keep at room temperature.

Just before serving, heat the olive oil in a large frypan. Add the cabbage and toss until heated through.

WILD DUCK CALVADOS STUFFED WITH BARLEY PILAF

In this recipe, the method used for draining out some of the fat is the Chinese way of preparing the skin for Peking duck. The soy sauce adds a delicious taste to the crispy skin.

2 2.5-kg (5-lb.) ducks
Barley pilaf (recipe follows)
45 mL (3 tbsp.) soy sauce
250 mL (1 cup) sugar
625 mL (2½ cups) water
3 tart apples
30 mL (2 tbsp.) all-purpose white
*   flour*
750 mL (3 cups) chicken stock or
*   canned broth*
30 mL (2 tbsp.) calvados or apple
*   cider*
15 mL (1 tbsp.) apple jelly

Either hang ducks over a pan for 12 to 24 hours or let them sit, uncovered, on a rack over a baking sheet in the refrigerator for two to three days. This will release the fat. If the ducks are frozen, thaw first. Stuff with the barley pilaf, placing any extra in a small casserole to bake alongside the ducks. Tie the legs together so they lie close to the body. Rub the ducks all over with the soy sauce and prick the skin. Place in the oven in a roasting pan, or on a baking sheet with sides, and roast at 200°C (400°F) for 1¼ hours, pricking the skin again after 20 minutes of cooking. During the roasting, drain off the fat as it accumulates, with a bulb baster.

Boil the sugar and water for two minutes. Peel and core the apples, and then slice into eighths. Poach in the sugar syrup until apples are just tender. Set aside.

The ducks are done when the internal temperature reaches 82°C (160° to 180°F) and the juices run clear when a thigh is pierced. Remove from the rack, discard the string and allow to rest while preparing the gravy.

Pour off all but 30 mL (2 tbsp.) of fat from the roasting pan. Over medium heat sprinkle flour over the fat, then cook, stirring, until the flour turns a deep brown color. Pour in the stock and bring to a boil, stirring. Add calvados and apple jelly, and simmer for five minutes. Taste for seasonings. Reheat the apples in the syrup.

Place the ducks in the centre of a large platter, either whole or cut in quarters. Arrange the red cabbage around the edges and garnish with the apple slices. Serve the gravy separately.

Barley Pilaf
This is delicious as a stuffing or as a side dish.

375 mL (1½ cups) pearl barley
1¼ L (5 cups) cold water
5 mL (1 tsp.) salt
75 mL (⅓ cup) butter, melted
1 clove garlic, finely chopped
125 mL (½ cup) chicken stock or
*   canned broth*
125 mL (½ cup) finely chopped
*   parsley*
125 mL (½ cup) chopped walnuts
60 mL (4 tbsp.) chopped green onion
15 mL (1 tbsp.) lemon juice

In a large saucepan, soak barley in the water for one hour. Add salt and bring to a boil, then reduce heat and simmer for 25 minutes or until tender. Drain and rinse under cold water.

Combine the cooked barley with the remaining ingredients.

Stuff the ducks and place remaining pilaf in a small casserole. Baste with the drippings during the roasting. The pilaf should be covered and baked for 20 minutes.

PEAR SHORTCAKE

A surprisingly light dessert that can be assembled hours in advance.

2 23-cm (9-in.) light sponge or genoise cakes (recipe follows), each one sliced in half
75 mL (⅓ cup) apple jelly
15 mL (1 tbsp.) water
500 mL (2 cups) whipping cream
45 mL (3 tbsp.) icing sugar
30 to 45 mL (2 to 3 tbsp.) pear brandy
12 canned pear halves, sliced thinly

Prepare the cakes and set aside.

Melt the apple jelly in the water. Brush the tops of the sliced cakes with the apple jelly glaze. Set aside.

Whip the cream until it begins to thicken. Add the sugar and brandy and continue beating until very stiff.

Place one layer of the cake on a serving platter, glazed side up. Spread with a layer of the whipped cream, about ½-cm (¼-in.) thick. Reserving the best pear slices for the top of the cake, place a quarter of the slices over the cream, spreading evenly. Repeat with two more layers of the cake, cream and pears. Top with the last layer of cake, glazed side up. Frost the entire cake with the remaining cream. Overlap the reserved pear slices in a neat circle around the outer edge.

Chill until serving time.

Basic Genoise Sponge Cake
This recipe makes two 23-cm (9-in.) cakes or one 25×40-cm (10×15-in.) jelly roll or one 25-cm (10-in.) square cake. It freezes well.

6 large eggs at room temperature
175 mL (¾ cup) sugar
2 mL (½ tsp.) vanilla
250 mL (1 cup) all-purpose white
*   flour*
90 mL (6 tbsp.) butter, melted and
*   cooled*

Preheat oven to 180°C (350°F). Butter and flour baking pans. In a medium bowl, beat eggs and sugar until thick and light in color. The mixture should form a thick ribbon when the beater is raised. Whisk in vanilla.

Place flour in a sieve and sift on to the egg mixture. Fold in quickly. Pour in cooled butter and fold gently but thoroughly.

Pour into prepared pans and bake 20 to 30 minutes, depending upon the type of pan used. Turn out onto a wire rack to cool. The bottom of the cake is to be used as the top.

If baking a jelly roll, remove from the oven and sprinkle the top with icing sugar. Turn out onto a sheet of parchment and sprinkle the bottom with icing sugar. Cover the cake with a tea towel and roll up from the long side. Let sit until cool. Unroll, trim crisp edges and fill as desired. □

A Most Astonishing Vegetable

Of course, most of us don't think of it as a vegetable. We see a pumpkin and we think Jack-o'-lantern – or pie. And there it stops. But this American contribution to gastronomy is a versatile vegetable.

Pumpkin makes fine pickles and fruitcake and pretty ice cream. It also turns up in soups, stews and soufflés. Using our recipes, you could make a meal of it: deep-fried blossoms as an appetizer, savory pie as a main course and ice cream for dessert. Pumpkin keeps well too—up to four or five months when stored in a cool spot.

The potential pumpkin eater, however, may be easily dissuaded because opening this culinary treasure is such a daunting chore. If you have a choice, buy a pumpkin of a manageable size – one that will fit into your microwave: a whole pumpkin assaulted with microwaves for one to two minutes (on High) will be easier to cut. Then you can choose one of three methods to produce the purée called for in many recipes.

To steam: cut the top off, ditto the bottom (so that it will sit solidly on your cutting board). Now, slip a sharp knife under the skin and pare it off, as though you were peeling a very large orange. Cut the flesh into five-centimetre (2 in.) cubes, discarding the stringy interior, but saving the seeds for toasting, and steam the chunks over hot water for 20 to 30 minutes until they are tender. Purée them in a blender or mash them like potatoes, then cool and store in ziploc bags.

To bake: cut the pumpkin into halves or quarters and clean out the seeds and strings. Place the pieces cut side down on a greased baking sheet and bake in a 180°C (350°F) oven for about an hour, until a knife pierces the skin easily. After the pumpkin has cooled slightly, scrape out the flesh and purée it.

To microwave: cover quarters or halves (scraped clean of seeds and strings) with plastic wrap and arrange them in the microwave with space between each. Cook for about eight minutes on High until tender, rotating and rearranging at half time. Let stand, covered, for five to 10 minutes before scraping out the flesh and mashing it.

Don't be fooled by a pumpkin's size and seeming impenetrability; this astonishing vegetable is easily bruised, and once bruised, falls quickly into ruination. When you are buying one, check the bottom because that's where decay begins, and pass up any that have soft spots or cracks. If you have one in cool storage, check it frequently and cook it up immediately if you see signs of deterioration.

TOASTED PUMPKIN SEEDS

Rinse the seeds to remove strings and pulp, and pat dry. Spread the seeds out on a baking sheet and allow several hours to dry thoroughly.

Toss the dried seeds with about 25 millilitres (1½ tbsp.) vegetable oil. Season with salt, seasoning salt or pepper. Toast at 180°C (350°F), stirring every five minutes or so until golden brown, about 20 minutes. Cool completely. Add more salt if needed, and serve as a snack or garnish.

FRIED PUMPKIN BLOSSOMS

These fragile fritters are similar to fried zucchini blossoms. Try them as a dessert as well as a vegetable dish.

8 pumpkin blossoms
1 egg, well beaten
250 mL (1 cup) fine cracker crumbs
Salt and pepper, as desired
Oil for frying, to depth of 2.5 cm (1 in.)
Gather the blossoms just before they are ready to open. Wash very

gently and drain on a cloth. Gently press flat with your hands.

Dip the blossoms into the well-beaten egg, then into cracker crumbs seasoned with salt and pepper. Fry in hot oil until golden brown, turning once.

Serve immediately, with chicken or veal. Sprinkle with icing sugar if serving as a dessert. Serves four.

COUNTRY PUMPKIN SOUP

Pumpkin is used extensively in European countries for the flavoring of soups, and a piece of pumpkin is always included with soup greens. This soup is a hearty meal in itself. It can be made ahead; it also freezes well.

250 mL (1 cup) dried white beans
1 bay leaf
Bunch of fresh sage, or 15 mL (1 tbsp.) dried
2 cloves garlic, peeled
15 mL (1 tbsp.) vegetable or olive oil
250 g (8 oz.) slab bacon, or 125 g (4 oz.) of the stronger Italian pancetta, thickly sliced and coarsely chopped
2 large onions, thinly sliced
2 large leeks (white part only), cleaned and sliced
2 cloves garlic, minced
2 medium carrots, peeled and finely sliced
2 stalks celery, peeled and finely sliced
1 large sprig fresh parsley
1 sprig fresh thyme
Freshly ground pepper
398-mL can Italian tomatoes
1.5 L (6 cups) chicken stock or canned broth
375 g (1½ lbs. or 3½ cups) pumpkin, peeled and cut into 1.2-cm (½-in.) cubes
2 spicy wieners or garlic sausage, thinly sliced

Cover the beans with five centimetres (2 in.) cold water and bring to a boil. Cook one minute. Remove from heat, cover and let stand one hour. Add more water, to cover beans by at least five centimetres (2 in.). Add the bay

For pumpkin eaters: the venerable squash takes on new shape in sweet and savory soup, a colorful chutney combining pumpkin with Australian ginger and raisins, and savory pumpkin pie flavored with onions and bacon.

leaf, sage, garlic and oil. Bake at 160°F (325°F) for one and a half to two hours or until very tender. Remove the herbs. Mash or purée half the beans with their liquid. Reserve the purée and the remaining beans.

Sauté the bacon in a large saucepan or stock pot. When lightly browned, remove to a bowl using a slotted spoon, and reserve. Add more oil if necessary. Add the onions and leeks and cook at medium-low setting until soft. Add the garlic and cook another minute. Add the carrots, celery, parsley, thyme and pepper. Cook another minute. Add the tomatoes and stock and bring to a boil. Add the pumpkin and reserved bacon and simmer, covered, for one hour.

Add the reserved beans and the purée. Cook for another 20 to 30 minutes. Discard the sprigs of parsley and thyme. Taste, and add additional seasonings if needed. Add spicy wiener and reheat gently. Serves eight.

PUMPKIN CRANBERRY SAUCE

This tasty sauce is made in the pan juices of roast pork, duck or turkey. The pumpkin adds an interesting texture.

500 mL (2 cups) pumpkin, peeled and cut into 2-cm (¾-in.) cubes
125 mL (½ cup) chicken stock or canned broth
30 mL (2 heaping tbsp.) brown sugar
30 mL (2 tbsp.) cranberry relish
Juice of ½ lemon
15 mL (1 tbsp.) cornstarch, mixed with a little water to make a smooth paste

Cook the pumpkin in boiling, salted water until barely tender, about three minutes. Drain and reserve.

Transfer the roast or poultry to a serving dish and keep warm. Drain off excess fat.

Place the roasting pan over medium heat and add chicken stock to the pan juices. Stir in the brown sugar and cook two to three minutes, scraping the bottom of the pan to loosen roasting

scraps. Bring to a boil. Lower heat.

Add the pumpkin and reheat for two minutes. Add the cranberries and lemon juice. Cook another two minutes. Taste, adding more lemon juice if necessary. This sauce should have a sweet yet tart flavor.

If too thin, whisk in a little cornstarch/water mixture until the sauce just coats a spoon. Transfer to a gravy boat and serve alongside the roast. Serves four.

SAVORY PUMPKIN PIE

Savory pumpkin pie makes a nice appetizer when served in tiny wedges, or a light lunch when served in larger portions with a salad. The chopped green Buderim Australian ginger adds a special touch.

Pastry for 1 25-cm (10-in.) pie shell, made with a combination of cinnamon, nutmeg and pepper (or a pinch of Chinese five-spice mix)
60 mL (4 tbsp.) soft butter
1 large onion, finely chopped
3 leeks (white part only), finely chopped
5 mL (1 tsp.) finely chopped fresh ginger, or green Australian ginger in the jar
Salt and pepper
125 g (4 oz.) bacon
250 mL (1 cup) whipping cream
3 eggs
375 mL (1½ cups) pumpkin purée
Fresh nutmeg
Spoonful sour cream mixed with green onions or chives, for garnish

Prepare pastry and chill. Roll out into a 25-centimetre (10-in.) quiche pan and chill again.

Melt the butter in a medium frypan and add onions and leeks. Sauté until tender. Stir in the ginger. Season with salt and pepper and place on a plate to cool.

In the same frypan, cook the bacon until golden and crisp. Drain on paper towels. Crumble the bacon into the chilled pastry. Layer on the cooled onion mixture.

In a medium bowl, mix together the cream, eggs and pumpkin.

Season with nutmeg. Gently pour mixture over the onions and bacon.

Bake at 190°C (375°F) for 40 to 50 minutes until puffed and set. A knife inserted slightly off centre should come out clean.

Cool to lukewarm and serve immediately for best results. Serves eight to 10.

SPICY PUMPKIN SEED SAUCE

This is a very spicy, rich brown sauce that is wonderful over chicken with extra sauce served separately. It's also good over a vegetable such as cauliflower, topped with a little grated Monterey Jack cheese and briefly set under the broiler to melt the cheese. You can make this sauce ahead.

125 mL (½ cup) unsalted green pumpkin seeds
20 whole almonds, skins on
30 mL (2 tbsp.) sesame seeds
5 mL (1 tsp.) cumin
5 mL (1 tsp.) cinnamon
1 to 2 mL (¼ to ½ tsp.) cayenne
2 to 10 mL (½ to 2 tsp.) chili powder, depending on taste
5 mL (1 tsp.) salt
2 mL (½ tsp.) pepper
30 g (1 oz.) unsweetened chocolate
250 mL (1 cup) chicken stock or canned broth

Toast the almonds, pumpkin seeds and sesame seeds in a dry frypan over low heat. Place in a blender with the cumin, cinnamon, cayenne, chili, salt and pepper. Blend briefly.

Melt the chocolate in a small saucepan. Scrape into the blender and add 60 millilitres (4 tbsp.) stock. Blend to make a smooth paste. Add balance of chicken stock. Blend briefly, then pour out into a small saucepan. Bring to a boil, then reduce heat to very low. Stir until slightly thickened. The sauce should have a gravy-like consistency. Serves four.

Variation: add sautéed onion, garlic and two finely diced tomatoes, either right into the blender or into the pot for a coarser texture.

PUMPKIN CONSERVE
(Chutney)

Delicious with meat and vegetables or on toast, this pumpkin chutney will have your guests wondering what the bright orange chunks are. The finely diced Australian ginger in syrup adds a piquant taste. It can be made ahead and freezes well. The recipe makes five 250-gram (8-oz.) jars.

750 g (1.5 to 1.75 mL, or 6 to 7
    cups) pumpkin
3 lemons
1 orange
500 mL (2 cups) raisins
45 mL (3 tbsp.) ginger, finely
    chopped
1 L (4 cups) white sugar

Peel the pumpkin and dice into 1.2-centimetre (½-in.) chunks. Place in a large bowl.

Slice the citrus fruit paper thin. Remove any seeds. Add the fruit, raisins and ginger. Stir. Add the sugar and stir well.

Leave covered for 10 to 12 hours or overnight at room temperature, stirring occasionally.

Transfer to a large saucepan. Place over medium heat. Simmer two and a half hours or until well reduced and thickened. The mixture will thicken more upon standing. Spoon into hot sterilized jars. Cool. This conserve will keep in the refrigerator for up to three months.

PUMPKIN BARS WITH CREAM CHEESE FROSTING

If you like carrot cake, you'll love this bar. It's a winner.

4 eggs
500 mL (2 cups) white sugar
250 mL (1 cup) vegetable oil
1 398-mL can pumpkin, or two cups
    fresh pumpkin, cooked and mashed
500 mL (2 cups) all-purpose white
    flour
5 mL (1 tsp.) salt
10 mL (2 tsp.) baking soda
5 mL (1 tsp.) cinnamon
125 g (4 oz.) cream cheese
60 mL (4 tbsp.) butter
5 mL (1 tsp.) vanilla
375 mL (1½ cups) icing sugar

Combine the eggs, white sugar and oil in a large bowl. Beat until lemon-colored and thick. Blend in the pumpkin.

In another bowl, mix together the flour, salt, soda and cinnamon. Add this to the pumpkin mixture a half cup at a time, mixing well after each addition.

Pour into a greased and floured pan 22 by 33 centimetres (9 by 13 in.).

Bake at 180°C (350°F) for 35 to 40 minutes, or until a cake-tester comes out clean. Cool.

In a small bowl, mix together the cream cheese, butter and vanilla. Add enough icing sugar to make a thick icing. Spread over the cooled cake. Cut into squares. This recipe can be made ahead and freezes well. Serves 10.

STICKY PUMPKIN BUNS

This fine-textured bread makes 12 delicious, moist buns or two regular loaves. To make the loaves, just leave out the variation for the buns.

2 mL (½ tsp.) white sugar
60 mL (4 tbsp.) warm water
25 mL (1½ tbsp.) yeast
375 mL (1½ cups) warmed milk
30 mL (2 tbsp.) brown sugar
10 mL (2 tsp.) salt
175 mL (¾ cup) mashed cooked
    pumpkin, well drained
45 mL (3 tbsp.) soft butter, melted
1 egg, well beaten
2 mL (½ tsp.) cinnamon
1.25 to 1.375 L (5 to 5½ cups) all-
    purpose white flour
125 mL (½ cup) butter
175 mL (¾ cup) brown sugar
125 mL (½ cup) pecans or walnuts,
    coarsely chopped
250 mL (1 cup) raisins
5 mL (1 tsp.) cinnamon

Stir the white sugar into the warm water and sprinkle on the yeast. Let stand until dissolved and bubbly.

In a large bowl, mix together the milk, brown sugar, salt, pumpkin, butter, egg and cinnamon. Mix well. Stir in dissolved yeast.

Beat in the flour one cup at a time, until the dough forms a ball and pulls away from the sides of the bowl. Knead, adding flour as necessary until smooth. Form into a ball and place in a greased bowl. Let rise until double in size.

For bread: punch the dough down, form it into two loaves and place in well-greased loaf pans. Let rise until the centre of the dough is even with the edges of the pan. Bake at 190°C (375°F) for 30 to 40 minutes, until the bread is a golden color and sounds hollow when tapped on the bottom.

For buns: in a small bowl, cream together 75 millilitres (⅓ cup) of the butter with 60 millilitres (4 tbsp.) of the sugar. Spread a thin layer on the bottom of a pan 22 by 33 centimetres (9 by 13 in.). Scatter the nuts on top.

On a lightly floured surface, roll the dough into a rectangle 30 by 40 centimetres (12 by 16 in.). Brush with remaining 45 millilitres (3 tbsp.) butter. Mix cinnamon with the remaining brown sugar and sprinkle over the surface. Scatter on the raisins.

Roll up from the long side. Cut into 16 pieces. Place in pan. Let the dough rise about a half hour.

Bake at 200°C (400°F) for five minutes. Turn oven to 190°C (375°F) and bake a further 20 to 25 minutes, or until done.

Invert onto a platter. Let stand one minute. Remove pan.

PUMPKIN ICE CREAM

This unusual treat is just like frozen pumpkin pie. For variation, you can spoon it into a gingersnap crust or garnish with crumbled gingersnaps. Makes one litre.

1 398-mL can pumpkin, or 2 cups
    fresh pumpkin, cooked and mashed
250 mL (1 cup) packed brown sugar
Pinch of cinnamon, nutmeg and
    ginger, or to taste
250 mL (1 cup) Creamo
Pinch of grated orange peel
60 mL (4 tbsp.) fresh orange juice
500 mL (2 cups) whipping cream

Mix all the ingredients together in a large bowl and freeze according to instructions for your ice-cream maker. This dessert doesn't keep, so enjoy it as soon as it's made. Serves six. □

Creole Time

The last several years have seen a revival of American regional cookery, or more accurately, an increased *acceptance* of American regional cookery among those who pontificate about food. This is a pleasant side-effect of the renewal of flag-waving and chest-thumping as American pastimes. Down home is where Americans proudly want to be, and they want the cooking that goes with it. And those who live in cities like New York and Los Angeles – not exactly down-home places – want authentic southern lard biscuits and genuine Texas Barbecue in their fashionable restaurants, as they wanted the regional specialties of France and China before.

Not surprisingly, then, the food of New Orleans is being much crowed about these days. New Orleans boasts a style of cooking that has remained famous even when most eyes were focused on foreign shores: Creole. And, with the rise to international prominence of New Orleans chef Paul Prudhomme, it has probably become the foremost regional cuisine of the United States.

Creole itself is a mixture of French, Caribbean, Spanish, Black and other influences, locally combined and interpreted. Its country cousin is Cajun cookery, which features hearty, spicy dishes originally brought to the area by Acadians from Nova Scotia, and the two styles have been combined to yield the confusing but delicious mix of influences that comprises the cooking of New Orleans today.

There is concern with being *au courant* in New Orleans as well. The blending of Cajun and Creole with modern preferences can be seen in many of the gumbos

The new New Orleans: lightly battered trout fillets with roasted pecans and a creole-style meunière sauce; a dish of fresh vegetables; and "green" wild rice on the side.

served in New Orleans restaurants. A gumbo, traditionally, is a one-pot meal flavored and thickened with okra or filé (ground sassafras leaves). Many restaurants now lighten the dish so that it can be incorporated as a soup into a multi-course meal.

Characteristic of New Orleans cooking is the use of a roux (a mixture of flour, butter and sometimes other fat) to thicken; for flavor variations, the roux is cooked golden, brown or even black before being added to a dish. The roux is, of course, a French device, but in New Orleans it is often cooked darker than a French chef would be accustomed to, and the flavorings added to a roux-based Creole dish are decidedly more vigorous than a French chef would dream of: cayenne pepper, black pepper, paprika and a complex mixture of herbs. The exact combination of spices and herbs remains every New Orleans chef's great secret.

The abundance of local ingredients also influenced New Orleans cooking. Rice became a staple and soft-shelled crabs a world-famous delicacy. Even the end of the meal is distinctive: New Orleans coffee (available in some Canadian coffee shops) contains a touch of chicory. Bread puddings, so common in New Orleans, were developed for the simple reason that there was always so much leftover French bread about; local imagination dictated the addition of nuts, coconut and fruit to these puddings. Paul Prudhomme may be correct when he claims that the cooking of Louisiana is the most vital regional cuisine still evolving in North America.

CREAM OF OYSTER AND ARTICHOKE SOUP

This soup will bring raves. It is at its best when served immediately, but it will reheat – be careful not to boil – and it can be frozen. It makes 20 generous half-cup servings.

2 255-g pkgs. of frozen artichoke hearts, quartered
1 dozen large fresh oysters or 2 227-g containers of fresh oysters, cut into bite-sized pieces

1 L (4 cups) strong chicken stock or canned broth
10 mL (2 tsp.) thyme
125 mL (½ cup) chopped green onions
15 mL (1 tbsp.) parsley, chopped
Cayenne to taste
125 mL (½ cup) melted butter
175 mL (¾ cup) all-purpose white flour
250 mL (1 cup) whipping cream

Combine artichokes, oysters and any of their liquids. Add stock, thyme, onions and parsley. Heat to almost boiling.

In a small saucepan, melt the butter and combine with the flour. Cook a few minutes, stirring, until the roux is light golden. Slowly whisk or stir into the soup. Bring up to a boil and cook until thickened. Add the cream. Taste for seasonings and add some cayenne, starting with a very small pinch. Serve immediately with a good French bread.

TROUT WITH ROASTED PECANS AND CREOLE MEUNIERE SAUCE

This is our adaptation of a beautiful recipe created by Lawson of The Olde N'Awlins Cookery restaurant in The French Quarter (he a former football player who once tried out for the B.C. Lions football team). It may seem long, but it can be done in stages, as described below, and it comes together quickly at serving time.

First, make the pecan butter:

125 mL (½ cup) roasted pecans (see note below)
60 mL (4 tbsp.) butter, softened
Juice of half a lemon
5 mL (1 tsp.) Worcestershire sauce
Dash of Cajun seasoning mix (see recipe below)

Purée the roasted pecans in the food processor or blender. Add the butter, lemon juice, Worcestershire and seasonings. Blend well. Taste and adjust seasonings. Set aside. This can be refrigerated.

Note: to roast pecan halves, place on a cookie sheet in a 180°C (305°F) oven for 10 minutes, until slightly brown. Be careful not to burn the nuts.

Second, make the Creole meunière sauce:

125 mL (½ cup) fish brown sauce or rich chicken stock thickened with a little flour (see below)
125 mL (½ cup) butter, softened and cut into chunks
15 mL (1 tbsp.) Worcestershire sauce
15 mL (1 tbsp.) water
Dash of Tabasco
Juice of half a lemon
30 mL (2 tbsp.) parsley, chopped

To thicken chicken stock, melt 15 millilitres (1 tbsp.) butter in a small pot, whisk in about 15 millilitres (1 tbsp.) flour and cook until very golden brown, about 15 minutes. Slowly whisk in the stock and cook until slightly thickened.

Bring the 125 millilitres (½ cup) of sauce to a boil, turn down the heat, and, using a whisk, add the butter piece by piece until completely absorbed. Whisk in the remaining ingredients. Check for seasonings. Keep warm or reheat gently at serving time.

Third, make the trout batter:

1 egg, beaten with a little milk
250 mL (1 cup) all-purpose white flour mixed with 15 mL (1 tbsp.) Cajun seasoning mix (recipe below)

Place the egg mixture in one shallow pan and the flour mixture in another.

Fourth, prepare the trout:

8 trout fillets, approximately 125 g (4 oz.) each, skin on
60 mL (4 tbsp.) butter
60 mL (4 tbsp.) oil
A few lemon slices and toasted pecan halves, for garnish

Dip the trout fillets in the seasoned flour, then in the egg mixture and back again into the flour. Set on a cake rack to dry slightly.

A few minutes prior to serving time, heat the butter and oil in a large skillet. Add the trout to the pan and sauté quickly. Turn the trout fillets only once (approximately three minutes on each side). The fish should be crisp and golden brown when done. It does not take long. Keep warm.

Place one fillet on each individual plate, skin-side up. Spread with a heaping teaspoon of the pecan butter, covering the entire fillet. Sprinkle with a few toasted pecans. Cover trout and topping with a few spoonfuls of Creole meunière sauce. Garnish with lemon slices. Serve immediately with more sauce on the side.

Cajun Seasoning Mix

Most Creole and Cajun recipes use a seasoning mixture that varies only slightly according to the whim of the chef. The mixture is made up ahead of time and added as needed instead of salt, pepper, etc. This is one variation – change it according to your tastes.

15 mL (1 tbsp.) salt
15 mL (1 tbsp.) paprika
3 mL (¾ tsp.) cayenne pepper
2 mL (½ tsp.) white pepper
2 mL (½ tsp.) black pepper
2 mL (½ tsp.) dry mustard
1 mL (¼ tsp.) oregano
1 mL (¼ tsp.) thyme
Pinch of crushed bay leaf

Mix all ingredients together.

GREEN RICE

Of the many kinds of rice grown in Louisiana, some have a very nutty flavor. Canadian wild rice is as close as we can get to this taste.

75 mL (⅓ cup) butter
250 mL (1 cup) long grain rice
250 mL (1 cup) wild rice, rinsed under cold water and well drained
1L (4 cups) chicken stock or canned broth
30 mL (2 tbsp.) butter
1 small green pepper, finely chopped
125 mL (½ cup) parsley, finely chopped
3 green onions, finely chopped
1 clove garlic, minced

Melt the 75 mL (⅓ cup) butter in a heavy casserole. Add the rice and cook over medium heat, stirring frequently, until butter is absorbed into the rice, about five minutes. Stir in the chicken stock and bake, covered, at 180°C (350°F) for 45 minutes, or until the liquid is absorbed and the rice is tender. Add more liquid if necessary.

Meanwhile, in the remaining butter, sauté the green pepper until

slightly soft, add the parsley, onions and garlic and sauté for one minute. Set aside.

When the rice is cooked, remove from the oven and stir in the vegetables, mixing well.

This dish may be made ahead and reheated.

BREAD PUDDING WITH MERINGUE AND LEMON SAUCE

Serve this pudding directly from the baking dish and present the sauce on the side.

1 L (4 cups) whole milk or light cream
3 large eggs
3 large egg yolks
500 mL (2 cups) white sugar
Dash of salt
5 mL (1 tsp.) vanilla
250 mL (1 cup) raisins (optional)
125 to 250 mL (½ to 1 cup) coarsely chopped pecans (optional)
250 mL (1 cup) coconut (optional)
1 loaf day-old French bread, approximately 300 g (10 oz.)
45 mL (3 tbsp.) butter
3 large egg-whites
30 mL (2 tbsp.) white sugar

In a large bowl, mix together well the milk, eggs, egg yolks, sugar, salt, vanilla, raisins, pecans and coconut. Beat to mix well. Break or cube the bread into bite-sized pieces and add to the milk mixture. Let the bread soak in the mixture for at least 30 minutes.

Melt the butter in a 22-centimetre (9-in.) square baking pan and tilt to coat all sides. Pour the melted butter into the pudding and stir. Pour the pudding into the pan, place in the oven and bake at 180°C (350°F) for one hour or until puffy and golden brown.

Beat the egg-whites until soft peaks form. Gradually add the remaining sugar, beating until stiff peaks form and the sugar is dissolved.

Remove the pudding from the oven. Spread the meringue over the top and return it to the oven. Bake for a further 10 minutes or until the meringue is golden brown. The pudding will remain hot for quite a while after it is removed from the oven.

Lemon Sauce

125 mL (½ cup) butter
250 mL (1 cup) white or brown sugar
1 egg, beaten
125 mL (½ cup) bourbon or lemon juice

Melt the butter and sugar together in a small saucepan. Add the beaten egg gradually, stirring with a whisk. Do not boil. Cool slightly. Whisk in lemon.

CREAMY PRALINES

There are many variations of this famous New Orleans praline. This is the one from the New Orleans School of Cookery. The recipe, which makes about 20, does not double. It is a very sugary confection.

375 mL (1½ cups) white sugar
175 mL (¾ cup) brown sugar
125 mL (½ cup) milk or cream
90 mL (6 tbsp.) butter
375 mL (1½ cups) pecans, whole or coarsely chopped

Combine all the ingredients in a large, heavy saucepan and bring to a boil, stirring constantly.

Boil until it reaches the soft ball stage (115°C/238 to 240°F). Test by dropping a little into a glass of very cold water. Roll the cooled test drop in your fingers. If it forms a ball easily, it is ready.

Immediately remove from the heat and stir until mixture cools slightly and thickens. This happens almost instantly. It will become cloudy and creamy-looking and there will be a coating on the nuts.

Spoon on to buttered wax paper, aluminum foil or parchment. Let cool and firm. Best eaten on the day it is made.

For a praline sauce, take the boiling mixture off the heat just before it reaches the soft ball stage. It is a wonderful syrup for ice cream. Do not refrigerate. □

Rise & Dine

A lot of nutritional advice has been dished out in recent years on the subject of breakfast, probably the best being that one should eat it. Apparently this idea has finally sunk in: surveys show that breakfasts at home and in restaurants are on the rise. According to the *New York Times*, 96 per cent of us start our day with a meal, which is a marked improvement over the old get-up-and-go attitude that led to major mid-morning mood swings followed by oversized lunches and the mandatory afternoon snooze. Starting your day with a full stomach leads to a much healthier nutritional balance, particularly if you fill it with wholesome foods that are low in sugar and high in protein.

That's easier said than done on those harried weekday mornings, with three kids vying for two pairs of socks, the wrong lunch kit leaving with the right carpool and Aunt Ida on the phone, collect. Your instinct is to reach for the Shreddies and be done with it, ignoring your culinary conscience until Saturday when you can unfurl a more ambitious breakfast menu in your own sweet time. We sympathize (having been there ourselves) but cannot condone the standard mad-rush excuse for an unsatisfying breakfast. If you take a moment to collect yourself, you will realize how many wholesome, tasty dishes you can cook up in virtually the same time it takes to toast bread. The key ingredient is organization. In fact, once you get rolling, you'll find yourself planning tomorrow's breakfast each night, whipping up some muffin dough or layering a cheese puff, ready to be popped into the oven next morning as you stumble from bedroom to shower.

Berry good: a nouveau version of the Monte Cristo sandwich combines creamy Brie or Camembert with fresh strawberries.

This month we offer a classic breakfast selection, with a few easy-to swallow variations for gourmets and health buffs. Morning tastebuds are a tender lot. No matter what the latest diet and fitness gurus say about the *right* way to start the day, most of us are inclined towards good old-fashioned, North American fare. Somehow, waking up to the sound of brewers' yeast foaming in the blender or to the smell of sweetbreads poaching in goat's milk will never offer the same kind of comfort as the sizzle of eggs and the hiccup of coffee perking on low.

GRANOLA

Once you have made your own granola, you will never use store-bought again. You can add or subtract nuts, seeds and spices, keeping roughly to these same proportions. Serve with cream or milk and top with fresh, sliced fruit. Makes 1.5 litres (6 cups).

625 mL (2½ cups) quick-cooking oatmeal
250 mL (1 cup) coconut, sweetened or unsweetened, long or medium thread
125 mL (½ cup) sunflower seeds (unsalted)
60 mL (4 tbsp.) sesame seeds
1 100-g pkg. flaked almonds
125 mL (½ cup) wheat germ
60 mL (4 tbsp.) unsalted butter
60 mL (4 tbsp.) brown sugar (heaping spoonfuls)
60 mL (4 tbsp.) liquid honey
Pinch of salt, optional
7 mL (1½ tsp.) vanilla
250 mL (1 cup) raisins

Preheat the oven to 150°C (300°F). Toss the oatmeal, coconut, seeds, almonds and wheat germ in a large roasting pan. Bake for about 20 minutes, stirring occasionally.

Combine the butter, brown sugar, honey and salt in a small saucepan and bring to a boil. Reduce the heat and cook, stirring, until the sugar is dissolved, about three to five minutes. Remove from the heat and stir in the vanilla. Turn up the oven to 180°C (350°F) and stir in the butter mixture until all the dry ingredients are evenly coated. Return to the oven and bake for a further five minutes. Add raisins. Cool.

OATMEAL IN A TRICE

Stove-top porridge takes too long and leaves you with a sticky pot. This microwave method avoids the pot and takes half the time. Serves one.

250 mL (1 cup) hot tap water
75 mL (⅓ cup) large-flake oats
5 mL (1 tsp.) brown sugar
Dash of cinnamon
Pinch of salt (optional)
Scattering of raisins

Put the water in a serving bowl and microwave on high for three minutes. Stir in the oats, sugar, cinnamon, salt and raisins. Microwave on high uncovered for seven minutes. Stir, cover and let sit for two minutes. Serve with milk and fresh fruit.

MAKE AHEAD MUFFINS

This recipe can be varied by adding raisins, nuts or fruit. The dough will change color in the refrigerator; just stir it up. Makes six dozen.

320 mL (10 oz.) bran cereal
500 mL (2 cups) boiling water
250 mL (1 cup) butter
1 L (1 qt.) buttermilk
8 eggs, beaten
1.25 L (5 cups) all-purpose white flour
500 mL (2 cups) sugar
20 mL (4 tsp.) baking powder
20 mL (4 tsp.) baking soda
10 mL (2 tsp.) salt

Place the bran in a large bowl and stir in the boiling water. Add the butter and stir until melted. Add the buttermilk and eggs. Mix well. In another bowl, stir together the flour, sugar, baking powder, baking soda and salt. Add all at once to the cereal mixture, stirring just until the dry ingredients are moistened. Store in the refrigerator up to four weeks.

Bake in greased muffin tins at 200°C (400°F) for 20 minutes.

EASY OMELETTE WITH SALSA

Omelettes are fast. Add any topping that you have handy—sweet or savory. Serve with toast and tea. Makes one.

15 mL (1 tbsp.) butter
2 eggs, lightly beaten
15 mL (1 tbsp.) water
Chopped fresh herbs, for a savory omelette
Salt and pepper, if desired
Salsa for garnish (or jam)

In a 20-centimetre (8-in.) non-stick frypan, melt the butter. Mix the eggs and water and pour into the hot pan. Reduce the heat to medium and cook, lifting the edges slightly with a spatula. Once the mixture starts to look set on top, scatter on the herbs, if you are using them, and salt and pepper. Cook a few seconds more. Slide the omelette out onto a warmed serving plate, folding one half over the other. (This will require a little practice.) Garnish with salsa, sauce, jam or jelly and serve immediately.

DIANE'S PUFF PANCAKE

A baked pancake that is much like a popover. Quick and easy, it will bake while you get dressed. If you don't have a cast-iron frypan, wrap two or three layers of foil around the handle of your regular frypan to protect it in the oven. This recipe makes one pancake. If you want two, double everything but the eggs. For three, triple everything but use only three eggs. Serve with a sprinkling of icing sugar and top with fruit or jam.

125 mL (½ cup) milk, at room temperature
5 mL (1 tsp.) vanilla
Pinch of nutmeg
2 eggs, at room temperature
125 mL (½ cup) all-purpose white flour
Butter
15 mL (1 tbsp.) icing sugar
Fruit or jam

Beat together the milk, vanilla, nutmeg and eggs. Whisk in the flour. The batter will be lumpy.

Heat the oven to 200°C (400°F). Lightly butter a cast-iron frypan and heat in the oven (do not burn the butter). Pour on the batter. If you are baking two or three, use one cup of batter for each. Bake each pancake for 15 minutes or until well puffed and golden. Add sugar, fruit or jam and serve immediately.

SOUR CREAM PANCAKES

The light and fluffy kind. Makes 14 to 16.

250-mL container sour cream
2 eggs (see note)
500 mL (2 cups) pancake mix, any type

Mix together the sour cream and eggs. Stir in the pancake mix. It will be a very thick mixture. Drop by large tablespoons onto a preheated, non-stick frypan. Because sour cream burns easily, fry over low heat. As the pancakes set, spread them out a little. They will puff and expand to almost double. When they are golden brown, turn and cook the other side. Serve with warmed syrup.
Note: for an even lighter result, if you have the time, separate the eggs, beat the yolks with the sour cream and stir in the pancake mix. Beat the whites until soft peaks form, and fold into the pancake mixture.

POTATO LATKES

This version of a popular pancake can be made the night before and refried or heated in the microwave in the morning. Makes 12 to 14.

3 large potatoes
½ medium onion
Juice of 1 lemon
6 eggs
125 mL (½ cup) all-purpose white flour
125 mL (½ cup) oil
Salt, pepper
Chopped garlic, optional
Butter

Peel and grate the potatoes and onion. Place in a bowl of cold

water with the lemon juice.
Beat together the eggs, flour, oil and salt and pepper to taste. Add the drained vegetables and garlic, if you like, and mix well.
Drop by tablespoons onto a lightly buttered frypan, spreading out slightly. Fry over medium heat until golden brown on each side.

FRENCH TOAST SANDWICH

On restaurant menus, this type of sandwich is often called a Monte Cristo. Quick and easy. Take the second one with you for lunch; it tastes great cold. Makes two.

4 slices bread
2 slices cheese
2 slices corned beef
2 eggs
15 mL (1 tbsp.) milk
Freshly ground pepper
Butter

Cover two slices of bread with the cheese and beef. Top with the remaining bread. Lightly beat the eggs, milk and a little pepper. Place the sandwiches into the mixture and let stand for a few minutes. Turn and let the other side soak up the remainder of the egg mixture.
Heat a lightly buttered frypan over medium heat. Add the sandwiches and fry until golden brown on each side.
Serve with warmed syrup and freshly ground pepper.

NOUVELLE FRENCH TOAST

A tasty, light version of the above sandwich, this French toast is a great luncheon dish as well. Serves two.

4 to 6 large ripe strawberries
100 g (3½ oz.) Brie or Camembert
4 thick slices French bread
2 eggs
30 mL (2 tbsp.) milk
Pinch of nutmeg
Butter

Slice two or three of the strawberries, reserving nice whole ones for the garnish. Spread two slices of bread with the soft cheese.

Top with sliced strawberries. Cover with another slice of bread.
Lightly beat the eggs, milk and nutmeg in a large flat container. Place the sandwiches into the mixture and let stand for a few minutes. Turn and let the other side soak up the remainder of the egg mixture.
Heat a lightly buttered frypan over medium heat. Add the sandwiches and fry until golden brown on each side.
Serve with whole strawberries and warmed syrup.
Note: this is even more delicious if the egg/milk mixture has 30 millilitres (2 tbsp.) maple syrup added to it.

CHESHIRE CAT'S CHEESE PUFF

Santa Barbara's Cheshire Cat Inn serves this piping hot from the oven along with freshly squeezed orange juice and the biggest croissants you have ever seen. Serves 10 to 12.

16 slices enriched bread, crusts removed and cubed
250 g (½ lb.) sharp Cheddar, grated
6 eggs
1 L (4 cups) milk
25 mL (1¾ tbsp.) salt
1 mL (¼ tsp.) dry mustard
Freshly ground black pepper
8 mL (1¾ tsp.) Worcestershire sauce

Layer the bread and cheese in a large flat casserole dish. Beat together the remaining ingredients and pour over top. Press the bread down to absorb the liquid. Refrigerate overnight. Bake at 180°C (350°F) for one hour. Serve immediately, while puffed.
Note: vary with bits of ham, sausage and chilies, if desired, or add slivers of tomatoes and red or green pepper halfway through the baking time. □

Dynamite Dinner

From the first bite, the food of Thailand announces itself to be unlike any other Asian cuisine. There are hints of Chinese, Malay and Indian influences, but, like Thailand itself, Thai food has preserved its independence and character. It is unique and delicious.

This surprising, lively cuisine shares with the trendiest of North American cooking an emphasis on freshness and short cooking times and on startling juxtapositions of flavor and texture. Ingredients are usually not disguised to achieve a subtle effect, but presented in their naked, natural glory.

The difference, of course, is that Thai ingredients, in Thai quantities, are not at all what many of us are used to. Consider the naked, natural glory of the tiny red chili pepper, which one Bangkok restaurateur calls the "dynamite chili." In Thai cuisine, chilies are scattered like depth charges throughout curries, soups, sauces and the like. Diners supping on a coconut milk and chicken dish, having carefully fished out these chilies, might then, with quickly mounting vexation, find themselves chewing on equally hot fresh green peppercorns. They may bite into a pungent bit of lemon grass, or a small, bitter ping-pong-ball-sized eggplant. They may detect, in the heady steam of *dom yam gung*, fresh coriander, fresh lemon juice and some fragrance that hints of lime (it comes, in fact, from the leaves of the kaffir lime tree). Tucking into an innocuous-looking coconut

Thai this: a hot and sour prawn soup loaded with spices and fresh herbs; an entrée of mussels accented with green pepper and tomato cooked in a freshly ground curry paste; tender chicken in nam prik sauce; and an unusual salty-sweet pudding made with coconut and rice.

pudding, they may be startled to find the sweetness of the pudding contrasting with a very salty topping. This is, above all, a cuisine of spice and contradiction.

The recipes here were obtained from Thai restaurateurs and cooks (namely, Charlermpol Charnvises of the D'Jit Pochana restaurant and Tong Jeng Loh of the Royal Orchid hotel). I have adapted them to local ingredients where necessary, and reduced the chili content by a large amount. Still, some people may find this food too hot, particularly the mussel dish; an option is to further reduce the number of chilies. Those wanting more fire can spoon on some of the *nam prik* sauce, (see recipe, below).

The easiest way to cook and eat this meal is in courses. Serve the soup first, then the mussels, then the chicken. It is a good idea to have rice with the mussels, however, so serve it Chinese-style in small bowls, which the diners can refill for the chicken course. I served a simple salad of vinegar and thinly sliced cucumber with the chicken; it had a cooling effect and increased vegetable content in the meal.

Many Thai ingredients are used in Vietnamese, Chinese, Indian and Indonesian cuisines, and so your best source of supplies may be a store that caters to an Asian population. We were able to find all the ingredients at two stores in Vancouver's Chinatown.

Fish sauce is a distillation of shrimp or small ocean fish and is used in many Thai dishes; it is pale brown and transparent. Its aroma varies from the slightly fishy to the intensely so. If you can't find any, ask a local Vietnamese restaurant where they buy theirs.

Lemon grass is a fragrant, lemony plant sold in stalks similar to those of green onions, though much tougher. The flavorful part is closest to the root; the upper parts should be discarded. Dried lemon grass has a faint flavor, and so you should substitute 10 pieces of dried for one stalk of fresh. If you can't find fresh or dried, use thinly sliced lemon peel.

Select small, fresh red chilies, and remove the seeds if you don't want the food to be too hot. Wear rubber gloves when you slit and clean the chilies. Dried red chilies can be used, but are not as good.

Palm sugar is made from the sap of palm trees and is sold in dark brown chunks or discs. It goes by names such as Gula Merah and Gula Jawa (Indonesian), Gula Melaka (Malay) and Jaggery (Hindi). The easiest way to use palm sugar, I find, is to boil it into a thick syrup, as you would for any sugar syrup. If you can't find palm sugar, substitute the darkest, least-refined cane sugar available.

Laos powder, a spice used in many Asian cuisines, is sold in small bottles by the Conimex company. If you can't find it, leave it out.

Shrimp paste is often called *trassi*. It is a pungent, brown, clay-like mixture.

Magrut (kaffir lime) leaves impart a unique flavor and fragrance but are not easily found in the West. Try substituting a few leaves from a lime, lemon or orange tree, or add a little lime peel.

Fresh coriander is essential to Thai cooking, and you cannot substitute the dried variety. The best coriander is that sold with the white roots attached. Coriander is also called cilantro and Chinese parsley. Many supermarkets now carry it.

Coconut milk is not the sour-tasting juice of a young coconut, but a liquid derived from the flesh of an old coconut. To make thick coconut milk, purée in the blender 500 millilitres (2 cups) of warm water (or half water, half milk) and 375 millilitres (1½ cups) of dried or fresh unsweetened coconut. Squeeze this mixture through cheesecloth into a bowl and discard the coconut. You can buy canned coconut milk; Selecta brand has the best flavor of several on the market.

Coconut oil will lend an authentic flavor to Thai dishes, but it is expensive and high in saturated fat. Substitute corn or other vegetable oil.

—Scott Mowbray

MENU *(Serves Four)*

- Hot and Sour Prawn Soup
- Mussel Curry
- Chicken in Screwpine Leaves
- Nam Prik
- Coconut and Rice Flour Pudding

DOM YAM GUNG
(Hot and Sour Prawn Soup)

This is one of Thailand's most famous dishes and, I think, one of the world's best soups. It is simple, delicious and fiery. The proper pink color and sea flavor can be obtained only by frying the prawn heads and shells as described below. The shells and heads are strained out, but you often find chili pieces, lemon grass and coriander floating in this soup. In Thailand, this is a very lemony, fragrant soup, so add plenty of lemon juice and several spoonfuls of fish sauce just before serving; it will have a pronounced sour flavor.

1 kg (2 lbs.) fresh prawns, in the shell
45 mL (3 tbsp.) coconut or vegetable oil
2 L (2 qts.) hot water
4 stalks lemon grass, bruised
4 magrut leaves; or lime, lemon or orange leaves
3 or more small red chilies, seeds removed
15 mL (1 tbsp.) bottled chili paste
Fish sauce
Lemon juice
Handful of fresh coriander, chopped
Green onions, chopped

Remove shells and heads of the prawns and set aside. Refrigerate the prawn meat for later use. In a large pot, fry heads and shells in oil for two or three minutes, stirring constantly. Add water, lemon grass, citrus leaves, chilies and chili paste and cook for 20 minutes. Strain the soup and discard shells, lemon grass, etc.

Bring stock to a boil, add prawn meat and cook until barely done (only three or four minutes). Add lemon juice, fish sauce and coriander to taste and serve immediately, garnished with green onions and coriander.

Serve *nam prik* sauce alongside, so that those who want to can bring the soup up to Thai standards of spiciness.

MUSSEL CURRY

The curry sauce in this dish is not soupy, but it is thick and clings to the mussels.

45 mL (3 tbsp.) coconut oil or
*   vegetable oil*
Curry paste (recipe below)
45 mL (3 tbsp.) fish sauce
15 mL (1 tbsp.) sugar
2 green peppers, cut into large chunks
2 ripe, medium-sized tomatoes, cut
*   into pieces*
Fish stock or water
8 to 10 live mussels per person

Heat coconut oil in pan and fry curry paste over low heat for about five minutes, until it is fragrant. Add fish sauce, sugar, peppers and tomatoes and cook for 15 minutes or until peppers are tender (if mixture seems dry, add some water or fish stock). Add mussels, cover pan and cook until mussels open; this takes only a few minutes. Serve with steamed rice and *nam prik*.

Curry Paste
5 small red chilies, seeded and chopped
5 mL (1 tsp.) fresh black pepper
2 shallots
4 cloves garlic
15 mL (1 tbsp.) fresh coriander root,
*   or 30 mL (2 tbsp.) coriander leaves*
2 magrut or citrus leaves, or 2 mL
*   (½ tsp.) lime-skin zest*
15 mL (1 tbsp.) lemon grass, sliced
2 mL (½ tsp.) salt
5 mL (1 tsp.) laos powder
5 mL (1 tsp.) shrimp paste

Grind ingredients to an almost-smooth paste with a mortar and pestle, or use a food processor. Add a small amount of water if paste is too dry.

GAI HOR BAI TOEY
(Chicken in Screwpine Leaves)

This recipe yields chicken that is tender and sweet. It is an adaptation of a Thai recipe in which the chicken is wrapped in the leaves of the pandan tree and deep-fried. In my version, you

simply sautée the chicken and finish cooking it with the sauce. Instead of chicken thighs, you might use a whole chicken, cut into small pieces, Chinese-style.

15 mL (1 tbsp.) dark soy sauce
5 to 10 mL (1 to 2 tsp.) freshly
*   ground pepper, to taste*
10 mL (2 tsp.) brown sugar
A palmful of fresh coriander leaves,
*   chopped*
15 mL (1 tbsp.) sesame oil
45 mL (3 tbsp.) evaporated milk
15 mL (1 tbsp.) nam prik (see below)
2 cloves garlic
30 mL (2 tbsp.) corn oil
6 chicken thighs
Lime juice
Green onions, chopped

Combine the soy sauce, pepper, sugar, coriander leaves, sesame oil, milk and *nam prik*. Crush the garlic and add to soy mixture. In a heavy frypan, heat the corn oil and sautée the chicken until brown on both sides. Pour on soy mixture and continue to cook chicken until it is done. Turn several times to coat the pieces with the soy mixture, which will thicken slightly as it cooks. Sprinkle some lime juice or, for additional spiciness, some *nam prik* over the chicken before serving. Garnish with chopped green onions.

NAM PRIK

This hot sauce is as common in Thailand as ketchup is in America (though far tastier). It can be used during cooking and should be served with every Thai meal. It calls for salted fish, which Chinese people sometimes refer to as Bombay duck.

45 mL (3 tbsp.) dried, salted shrimp
*   or fish*
4 cloves garlic
6 to 8 fresh red chilies
10 mL (2 tsp.) palm sugar or palm
*   sugar syrup*
60 mL (4 tbsp.) fish sauce
45 mL (3 tbsp.) fresh lime juice
Fresh red or green chilies for garnish
*   (optional)*

Remove the seeds from the red chilies if you don't want the sauce to be as hot. In Thailand, the seeds

are left in. In a mortar or food processor, grind the salted fish, garlic, red chilies and palm sugar into a paste. Add fish sauce and lime juice and mix until you have a liquid. Put into a bowl and sprinkle bits of chopped red or green chilies on top. This recipe makes enough to cook with, and to serve with the meal.

KHANOM TALAI
(Coconut and Rice Flour Pudding)

An unusual but delicious sweet pudding with a salty topping, which again demonstrates the Thai love for contrasting flavors. The Thais sometimes garnish this dish with sliced green onions, but we don't go that far.

150 mL (½ cup plus 2 tbsp.) rice
*   flour*
125 mL (½ cup) evaporated milk
500 mL (2 cups) thick coconut milk
75 mL (⅓ cup) palm sugar syrup

Topping
250 mL (1 cup) coconut milk
2 mL (½ tsp.) salt
30 mL (2 tbsp.) rice flour

Garnish
Toasted coconut

Heat oven to 160°C (325°F). Mix evaporated milk and rice flour until smooth, and add to coconut milk and sugar. Pour the mixture into six small oven-proof cups or ramekins. Place ramekins in a pan with water coming about halfway up the sides. Bake 45 minutes to one hour, or until the puddings have set. Mix the remaining coconut milk, salt and rice flour and gently pour into the cups. Bake another 20 to 30 minutes, until the topping has slightly set. Let puddings cool before refrigerating, to set further. Garnish with toasted coconut if desired. □

A Tuscan Bias

If any part of Italy provided the inspiration for this feature, it was Tuscany. That region, north of Rome, is known for its plain, hearty cuisine — a cuisine that celebrates the seasons and incorporates the best ingredients. Our first recipe, for instance, is for *bruschetta*, a dish traditionally served in the fall when the first olive oil comes off the press. The Florentines call the dish *fett'unta*, and they make it by toasting bread over an open fire, rubbing it with garlic and drenching it with olive oil. It becomes *bruschetta* when chopped tomato and fresh basil are added. The Umbrians, who consider their Tuscan neighbors humorless and severe, would add a chopped truffle to their *bruschetta*.

Tuscan bread is traditionally made without salt. There are two good reasons: the Tuscans eat a lot of salty meat, notably prosciutto, and so need a blander bread; and salt attracts moisture and causes bread to go mouldy. Country cooks who normally make bread once a week have devised ways of using up stale bread; ladling soup over thick slices, as we do in our leek soup, is one of the best.

Rabbit is plentiful in Tuscany and is eaten as often as chicken. It is sometimes roasted with a stuffing of aromatic vegetables, but we combine it in a stew with a *mélange* of mushrooms, tomatoes and celery.

Risotto is a dish common to all Italy. A sort-of-savory rice pudding, it must be made with arborio, a short-grain rice that absorbs much more liquid than the usual two-to-one formula. Italians like their rice hard in the centre, and their risotto creamy. And they often flavor the dish with the best parmesan cheese – Parmigiano Reggiano, made in the valley between Parma and Reggio. This superlative, nutty and expensive cheese is a special treat and deserves to be used in dishes where its unique flavor can be appreciated. The tinned imposter will not do.

Nor should you use an inferior quality when we call for olive oil. Our vegetable frittata deserves the compliment of a fine virgin olive oil. Once you have tasted the fruity flavor of Olio Extravergine d'Oliva, you'll understand why the Tuscans drizzle it on everything.

BRUSCHETTA ROMANA

This toasted, garlic-flavored bread is traditionally eaten at the time of the olive harvest. It's good as an appetizer with wine.

Slice of Italian bread, 1.2 cm (½ in.) thick
Peeled garlic clove
Virgin olive oil
Fresh tomatoes, peeled and cut into small dice
Fresh basil, coarsely chopped
Salt and freshly ground pepper, to taste

Toast the slices of bread under the broiler until golden on the outside but still soft inside. Rub one side with the raw garlic. Drizzle on the olive oil. Add tomatoes, herbs, salt and pepper.

CALZONE

Shaped like turnovers and filled with the usual pizza ingredients, our calzone are gently fried in olive oil until golden. Traditionally, they are baked in very hot brick ovens. Serve hot with a salad or as a snack with wine.

Basic Dough
300 mL (1¼ cups) warm water
15 mL (1 tbsp.) sugar
30 mL (2 tbsp.) oil
15 mL (1 tbsp.) yeast
750 mL (3 cups) all-purpose white flour, more or less

Place the warm water in a medium-sized bowl and stir in the sugar and oil. Sprinkle on the yeast and let stand until bubbly.

Stir to mix and whisk in the flour, 250 millilitres (1 cup) at a time until the dough pulls away from the sides of the bowl and forms a ball. Add flour until the dough is no longer sticky.

Turn out onto a board and knead until smooth. Place in a greased bowl and let rise for one hour or until double in bulk.

Punch down and divide into four 22-centimetre (9-in.) circles. Fill with some of the suggested fillings. Fold over, crimping the edges with a fork or a pastry wheel. Fry until golden in oil heated to about 180°C (350°F).

Fillings
Tomato sauce (homemade spaghetti sauce is best)
Fresh or dried oregano, basil or marjoram
Salt, pepper
Mozzarella or Jack cheese, thinly sliced or shredded
Anything else you would like: blanched green peppers, salami, pepperoni, anchovies, olives, sautéed onions or sausage

ZUPPA DI PORRI

A very tasty leek soup that is similar to the classic French onion soup. The Tuscan bread served in the soup is made without milk, eggs or salt and is baked on a terracotta tile. Serves four.

5 medium-sized leeks
60 mL (4 tbsp.) unsalted butter
30 mL (2 tbsp.) all-purpose white flour
1 L (4 cups) hot beef, chicken broth or canned stock
Salt and freshly ground pepper, to taste
4 slices Tuscan (or crusty) bread
125 mL (½ cup) Swiss cheese, freshly grated

Rinse the leeks well and cut into 1.2-centimetre (½-in.) slices. Wash carefully to remove all the grit.

Melt the butter in a medium pot, add the leeks and sauté until golden, about 15 minutes. Sprinkle the flour over the leeks and mix it in well. Pour over the hot broth. Stir. Add salt and pepper as needed. Simmer, covered, for 20 minutes.

Toast the bread slices on each side and place in individual soup bowls. Sprinkle 15 millilitres (1 tbsp.) of the cheese over each slice, add soup and sprinkle on the remaining cheese.

Cover the bowls with foil and let rest for 10 minutes before serving.

RAVIOLI ALLA PIEMONTESE

This is quite an elegant dish, meant to use up leftover roasts. It's not a rigid recipe; any meat can be used, as long as you have 750 millilitres (3 cups). The flavor is simple and earthy and should complement the wine.

3-egg pasta recipe (see below)
250 mL (1 cup) roast beef
250 mL (1 cup) roast chicken
250 mL (1 cup) roast pork
Herb such as rosemary or sage
1 or 2 medium onions, finely chopped and sautéed
2 large cloves garlic
375 mL (1½ cups) parmesan cheese, grated
Salt and pepper, to taste
30 to 45 mL (2 to 3 tbsp.) breadcrumbs
2 whole eggs
½ bottle or more of a good Barolo wine such as Fontanafredda

Make the pasta and set aside. Grind or finely chop the meat and add the herb, onions, garlic, 125 millilitres (½ cup) of the cheese, seasonings, crumbs and eggs. Mix well.

Cut the pasta in half and roll out one half into a large sheet about 1.5 millimetres (⅛ in.) thick. Place dabs of the filling on the sheet about 2.5 to four centimetres (1 to 1½ in.) apart. Roll out the second half of the pasta and place it over the first. Cut into squares with a crimp cutter and place the ravioli

on a lightly floured cloth or cookie sheet. (Instant-blending flour is good for this purpose.)

Bring a large pot of water to the boil and cook the ravioli about two to three minutes, or until tender. Drain well and place in a hot buttered serving dish.

Sprinkle on as much wine as you want and scatter on the remaining cheese. Serve at once.

Pasta

4 servings: 2 eggs and 375 mL (1½ cups) flour
6 servings: 3 eggs and 550 mL (2¼ cups) flour
8 servings: 4 eggs and 750 mL (3 cups) flour
15 mL (1 tbsp.) olive oil (optional in all recipes)

Method 1: in a small bowl beat the eggs and add the oil if you are using it. Place the flour in a pile on the table and make a well in the centre. Add the eggs to the well. With a fork, whisk the eggs and gather in a bit of flour until the mixture begins to form a ball. Using your hands, draw in more flour as needed and knead until the ball is smooth and silky. All the flour may not be needed. Form into a ball and let rest 10 minutes before rolling.

Method 2: place the eggs, and the oil if you are using it, in the work bowl of a food processor. Start the machine and add the flour slowly until the mixture forms a ball. Remove from the work bowl and knead a few more times by hand. The dough should be smooth and silky. Let rest 10 minutes before rolling out.

Note: never exceed 250 millilitres (1 cup) flour per egg.

When rolling out the dough, flour the board with instant-blending flour to avoid getting too much flour into the dough.

INSALATA DI FINOCCHI

Fennel, an aromatic flowering plant of Italian origin, is now widely cultivated. it has a slight flavor of aniseed. The bulbous stem at the base of the leaf stalk is cooked like celery or can be eaten raw. Although the feathery leaves

don't have much flavor, they are often served chopped as a garnish. Serves four to six.

2 large fennel bulbs
30 mL (2 tbsp.) parsley, chopped
1 garlic clove, finely chopped
Salt and papper to taste
45 to 60 mL (3 to 4 tbsp.) olive oil
15 mL (1 tbsp.) red wine vinegar

Cut off the long stalks and bruised leaves of the fennel. Slice the root end off the bulbs. Wash thoroughly. Cut the bulbs into quarters and then into thin slices. Place in a salad bowl. Add parsley and garlic. Season with salt and pepper. Add oil and vinegar and toss gently.

VEGETABLE FRITTATA

An Italian omelette with endless variations. Use a heavy frypan for best results. Serves four.

6 eggs
Salt and fresh pepper, to taste
125 mL (½ cup) parmesan cheese, freshly grated
60 mL (4 tbsp.) butter, divided
15 mL (1 tbsp.) olive oil
1 medium onion, thinly sliced
3 zucchini, finely sliced (or other vegetable such as sliced tomatoes, grated carrot, cabbage, broccoli)
30 mL (2 tbsp.) parsley, chopped
2 cloves garlic, finely chopped

Beat the eggs, salt and pepper in a medium bowl. Add the cheese. Melt 45 millilitres (3 tbsp.) of the butter with the oil in a heavy frypan. When the butter foams, add the onion and sauté until tender, about five minutes. Add vegetables, parsley and garlic. Sauté three to four minutes or until slightly cooked. Remove the vegetable mixture from the pan and add to the egg mixture. Mix well.

Melt the remaining butter in the pan and add the egg and vegetable mixture. Mix well. Cook over medium heat for five to six minutes or until the bottom of the frittata is lightly browned. Place a large plate on top of the frypan and turn the frittata out onto a plate. Slide the inverted frittata back into the pan. Or cover the

Generous ravioli squares doused with a good Barolo;
calzone — a pizza with the works, folded like a turnover.

handle of the frypan with several layers of foil and place the pan under the broiler. Cook four or five minutes longer. Serve from a warm plate.

RISOTTO

A classic Italian dish that is easy to make and doesn't take more than 15 to 20 minutes. But it does need a bit of watching. Serves four.

45 mL (3 tbsp.) unsalted butter
15 mL (1 tbsp.) olive oil
1 small onion
500 mL (2 cups) arborio rice (or short grain)
125 mL (½ cup) dry white wine or vermouth
2 mL (½ tsp.) salt
Dash of freshly ground pepper
1 to 1.25 L (4 to 5 cups) chicken stock or canned broth.
30 mL (2 tbsp.) butter
125 mL (½ cup) parmesan cheese, freshly grated

Melt the butter with the oil and sauté the onion until soft. Add the rice, wine, salt and pepper and stir well.

As soon as the liquid is almost evaporated, add enough chicken stock to just cover the rice. Stir again. Simmer steadily, stirring frequently. As soon as the liquid level goes down below the rice, add more chicken stock. It should be added gradually so that the rice never stops simmering.

The rice should take 18 to 20 minutes to cook from the time the first bit of liquid is added. When finished it probably will have absorbed about 1.25 L (5 cups) of liquid and will look creamy. Stir in the butter and the cheese. Taste for salt and pepper. Serve immediately. To vary the dish, stir in one of the following: tiny peas, tips of asparagus, tiny lima beans, chopped raw spinach or chopped tomato.

CONIGLIO ALLA PADELLA

An earthy rabbit stew with onions, garlic, celery, tomato, white wine and mushrooms is richly satisfying. Supermarkets carry frozen rabbits, and a number of butchers have them fresh. Serves four.

1.5-kg (3-lb.) rabbit, thawed and cut up into serving pieces
Salt, pepper, flour
60 mL (4 tbsp.) butter
1 medium onion, finely chopped
2 cloves garlic, chopped
250 mL (1 cup) celery, chopped
175 mL (¾ cup) good white wine
398-mL can Italian tomatoes and juice
125 mL (½ cup) sliced mushrooms

Salt and pepper the rabbit. Roll the pieces in flour. Brown the meat in the melted butter in an ovenproof frypan. As the pieces are browned, removed to a platter. Add onion, garlic and celery to the pan and cook, scraping the bits from the bottom. Return the rabbit to the pan and add the remaining ingredients.

Cover and bake at 160°C (325°F) for one hour or until the meat is tender. This dish may be simmered gently on top of the stove as well. Do not let it boil. When the meat is tender, remove the pieces and put on a serving platter. Skim excess fat from the pan juices and boil until the sauce is slightly thickened. Correct the seasonings and serve over the rabbit.

TORTA TERREMOTO (Earthquake Cake)

The glossy top of this cake is supposed to crack — like an earthquake. Potato flour gives it a unique, densely moist but light texture.

340 g (12 oz.) semi-sweet chocolate
125 mL (½ cup) unsalted butter
4 eggs
425 mL (1¾ cups) icing sugar
60 mL (4 tbsp.) potato flour

Melt the chocolate and butter together in the top of a double boiler. Remove from heat and set aside to cool.

Beat the eggs with the sugar until thick and yellow and the batter forms a ribbon when the beaters are lifted.

Add the chocolate mixture and the potato flour to the eggs and fold well. Pour into a buttered and floured 22-centimetre (9-in.) cake tin.

Bake at 180°C (350°F) for 35 to 45 minutes. Cool and turn out.

FRITTURA MISTA DI FRUTTA

This is a fruit fondue-type dish. Absolutely delicious!

375 mL (1½ cups) all-purpose white flour
Pinch of salt
2 eggs, separated
175 mL (¾ cup) cold water
30 mL (2 tbsp.) brandy
2 large Delicious apples, ripe but firm
2 large Bosc pears, ripe but firm
Lemon juice
16 large strawberries
1 kg (2 lbs.) solid vegetable shortening
250 mL (1 cup) white sugar

Place the flour in a large bowl, add the salt and mix thoroughly. Make a well in the flour and put in the oil and egg yolks. Stir slowly, adding water little by little. When all the water is added, stir in the brandy. It will help form a crust when the batter is fried. Let the batter rest for at least two hours at room temperature. Do not refrigerate.

Peel and core the apples and pears and cut into bite-sized pieces. Sprinkle with lemon juice to prevent browning. Remove the stems from the strawberries.

When the batter is ready, beat the egg-whites until stiff. Gently fold into the batter and mix carefully. Heat the vegetable shortening in a deep fat fryer. Place paper towels on serving dish for draining.

When the shortening is hot, spear each piece of fruit on a fondue fork and dip in the batter, making sure that the fruit is completely covered. Shake off any excess. Fry about one minute on each side or until golden. Remove from the fat with a slotted spoon and place on the paper towels to drain.

Sprinkle with granulated sugar. Place on serving platter and serve immediately.

Oranges, peaches, apricots and bananas also fry well. □

Mad About Mushrooms

Mushrooms are the magical ingredient here—not just ordinary, buy-them-at-the-store mushrooms, but the strange and exotic varieties you see springing up at markets and specialty shops.

When you first dip into mycology books, you are struck by the wonderfully descriptive names that mushrooms have been given. There's the Inky Cap, a variety that deliquesces into a black, slimy mass; the Devil's Snuffbox, an edible puffball that kids like to squeeze to release its cloud of spores, and the Death Cap, the most delicious of all mushrooms, according to those who did not survive long enough to enjoy them twice.

It seems to me, however, that namewise we've abused the common supermarket mushroom. Those mmmmmarvellous, put-them-in-a-brown bag mushrooms are the mushrooms that stand for all mushrooms, the mushrooms you think of when you say "mushroom." But no one has thought to give them a name.

If you send your kid to the store for some mushrooms, he doesn't come back with shiitakés or chanterelles (and at $20-plus a kilo, he'd better not). He brings the no-name mushroom, or what one mycology text with depressing candor calls "the mushroom of commerce." Is this the best we can do for this most versatile and hardworking of all mushrooms?

It's hardly fair that something that supplies us with Vitamin B, amino acids, iron, selenium and copper should go unnamed. It's an especial insult when you consider that the nutritional value of *Cantharellus tubaeformis* is virtually zip, and yet they have been properly and prettily christened. Chanterelles. You could write a song about them. No wonder people plunge about in coniferous forests in the chilly spring and fall, poking in decaying matter to find their trumpet-shaped caps. No wonder the less observant (you

have to be observant to mess around with wild mushrooms, as we've seen) chase the last parking spot at the market to pay up to $22 a kilo for these meaty delicacies. My other mycology book says chanterelles (or the equally melodius *pfifferling* in German) have a peppery taste and an apricot-like fragrance. But wait, we seem to be talking about a different chanterelle—*Cantharellus cibarius*—the best-known species. Let the mycologists distinguish; at least the genus has been accorded a familiar name.

Maybe we are careless about mushrooms of commerce because they are so easy to acquire. *Morchella angusticeps,* on the other hand, are dearly bought. First you burn down a forest, and then a year later you clamber about in a sooty wasteland, getting as dirty as a chimneysweep while you search for tall, narrow caps that look like brains or sponges. Morels. In the city, you'll pay $14 or $15 a kilo. For the residents of burned-out areas, they provide a chance to earn $600 to $700 a day (a bonus, but hardly a reason to burn down a forest).

Now the Japanese, who are careful to name what they value, have a basic word that means mushroom: také. This they attach to other words to name a trio of respected fungi. There's the highly prized matsutaké, which grows abundantly in the forests of the Pacific northwest, earning pickers $30 a kilo for mushrooms in pristine condition. There's the shiitaké, which has a pungent, smoky, almost meaty flavor for which you will pay from $27 to $34 a kilo. There's the baby—the tiny enokitaké with its spaghetti-thin stems and pearl-button tops. And then there's the inevitable linguistic exception—the shimeji. Oyster mushrooms, we call them; they cluster like a pile of ears on deciduous trees and have a floral aroma and flavor reminiscent of gardenias.

That brings us to the *Boletus edulis,* the mushroom that Marial told his fellow Romans made a better present than silver and gold. In feudal times it was reserved for those of noble birth, and so it was called King Boletus or My Lord's Mushroom. We plebes can now eat it, but most often we get it dried and have to soak it to restore its unique flavor. It has a plethora of names: it's the German *steinpilz,* the French *crèpe,* the Italian *porcino* and the English pennybun. No "mushroom of commerce" for this baby.

Our recipes offer you a chance to try some of these exotic and well-named mushrooms. And they also give you a chance to expand your repertoire of uses for old what's-its-name.

—Audrey Grescoe

DOUBLE MUSHROOM SOUP

A delicious creamed soup that goes well with a beef entrée and is best served soon after it has been made. For a more intense flavor, use the dried mushrooms in the stock.

60 mL (4 tbsp.) butter
1 medium onion, chopped
1 clove garlic, crushed
250 g (8 oz.) fresh mushrooms, chopped, or 60 g (2 oz.) dried
625 mL (2½ cups) chicken stock or canned broth
1 bay leaf
2 mL (½ tsp.) salt
1 mL (¼ tsp.) pepper
75 mL (⅓ cup) cream
8 fresh mushrooms
45 mL (3 tbsp.) Madeira or sherry
A few flat leaves of Italian parsley

If you are using dried mushrooms, soak them first in warm water for about five minutes, rinse to remove any sand, and chop.

Melt the butter in a medium saucepan. Add the onion and sauté until soft. Add the garlic and sauté for one minute longer. Stir in the chopped mushrooms. Add the

chicken stock, bay leaf, salt and pepper, and bring to a boil. Reduce the heat and simmer 15 to 20 minutes. Remove the bay leaf.

Cool the soup slightly and purée in a blender. (Be careful the hot liquid does not pop the lid off.) At this point, the soup can be held—frozen or refrigerated if you don't plan to use it that day, or at room temperature if you are using it soon.

Just before serving, slice the eight fresh mushrooms. Return the soup to the saucepan and stir in the cream. Reheat gently, but do not boil. Taste for seasonings. Add the sliced mushrooms and the Madeira. Garnish with a slice of mushroom and a leaf of flat Italian parsley.

MUSHROOM AND ENDIVE SALAD WITH CREAMY TARRAGON DRESSING

This recipe is a jumping off point for your imagination. Mushrooms of any kind make a wonderful addition to all salads. We've chosen a creamy oil and vinegar dressing, but any dressing will work as well.

Mushrooms
Alfalfa sprouts
Belgian endive

Make the dressing and allow it to stand to blend flavors. Arrange the endive spears on chilled salad plates. Garnish with mushrooms and alfalfa sprouts. Spoon a little dressing over all and pass additional dressing.

Creamy Tarragon Dressing
This recipe makes 500 millilitres (2 cups). Keep the dressing refrigerated, but bring to room temperature before serving.

There's magic in these mushrooms: a tangy pâté; a celebration of vegetables in a wild mushroom and bacon sauté; delicate and delicious mushroom tarts with Béarnaise sauce; hearty double mushroom soup.

1 large egg
15 mL (1 tbsp.) Dijon-style mustard
   (more if desired)
30 mL (2 tbsp.) tarragon wine vinegar
5 mL (1 tsp.) dried tarragon or 15 mL
   (1 tbsp.) fresh tarragon, finely
   chopped
Salt and pepper to taste
45 mL (3 tbsp.) good olive oil
Just under 375 mL (1½ cups) light
   vegetable oil

Put the olive oil in a measuring
cup and add the vegetable oil to
make 375 millilitres (1½ cups).

Blend together the egg,
mustard, vinegar and seasonings.
Very slowly pour in the oil—drop
by drop if you are mixing by hand
or in a slow steady stream if you
are using a food processor—until
the mixture becomes thick and
shiny. Taste for seasonings and
add more mustard if desired.

MUSHROOMS IN PARCHMENT

A delightful beginning to any
meal, this dish can be made for
any number of people, but we
have given quantities for two first-
course servings. Chanterelle,
shiitaké or oyster mushrooms can
be used for a change of pace.

250 g (8 oz.) plump, fresh mushrooms
A heaping 30 mL (2 tbsp.) parsley,
   finely chopped
Freshly ground pepper
1 large clove garlic, finely chopped
30 mL (2 tbsp.) fine bread crumbs
Approximately 30 mL (2 tbsp.) olive
   oil
Juice of ½ a lemon
2 thin lemon slices for garnish
Parchment paper

If using wild mushrooms, check
carefully for sand and dirt. Cut the
mushrooms into fairly thick slices
and place in a bowl. Add all the
remaining ingredients except the
lemon slices and parchment. Toss
well.

Cut the parchment into two
rectangles 30 by 45 centimetres (12
by 18 in.) Brush with oil or butter.
Divide the mushroom mixture
between the two pieces of
parchment. Fold each in half and
seal by tightly folding the edges.
Brush the outside with a little
additional oil or butter.

Bake the packages on a baking
sheet at 180°C (350°F) for about
10 to 15 minutes or until they puff
slightly and are golden.

Place on serving plates and tear
open. Serve as a light first course.

MUSHROOM TARTS WITH BEARNAISE SAUCE

This rich pastry can be prepared
ahead and frozen unbaked, or
baked the day before and kept in a
container at room temperature
until serving time. Although
Béarnaise sauce is often difficult to
prepare, this blender method cuts
some of the work. Any mushroom
suits this tart, but the shiitaké or
the common, cultivated white ones
are best. The recipe makes 12
medium or 24 small tarts.

Pastry
310 mL (1 cup, 4 tbsp.) all-purpose
   white flour
90 mL (6 tbsp.) unsalted butter, very
   cold
30 mL (2 tbsp.) Crisco, very cold
1 egg yolk
Approximately 75 mL (⅓ cup) water

Put the flour in the work bowl of
a food processor. Add the butter
and Crisco cut into chunks.
Process until fine—a little smaller
than peas. Turn out into a medium
bowl and make a well in the
centre. In a measuring cup place 75
millilitres (⅓ cup) water and the
egg yolk. Whisk to blend. Pour
half of the liquid into the well and
stir briskly. Add the remaining
liquid and stir, gradually gathering
the dough into a ball. More water
may be added as needed, one
tablespoon at a time. Gather into a
ball, cut in half and form into two
discs. Wrap in plastic wrap and
chill at least four hours.

To bake the empty tarts, preheat
the oven to 190°C (375°F) or
200°C (400°F). Roll out the pastry
on a floured board and cut into
circles to fit your tart pans. To
keep the pastry from puffing, prick
the bottom of each tart, or bake
blind: from a circle of aluminum
foil form a cup to fit into each tart
and fill it with kidney beans;
remove this weight halfway
through the baking period. Bake
for 20 minutes. When the tarts
have cooled, place three or four

slices of mushroom, cooked as
below, in each tart. Spoon on the
Béarnaise sauce and serve.

Filling
250 g (8 oz.) firm mushrooms
30 mL (2 tbsp.) butter
15 mL (1 tbsp.) flour
30 mL (2 tbsp.) sherry

Slice mushrooms thickly and sauté
quickly in a little butter. Season to
taste. Dust with the flour and stir.
Add the sherry and cook briefly.
Place on a plate to cool.

Béarnaise Sauce
A rich, butter and egg sauce
(related to hollandaise, which is so
popular on vegetables and fish),
Béarnaise is usually served on beef
but goes well with mushrooms
because of its sharpness.

60 mL (4 tbsp.) white wine
60 mL (4 tbsp.) white wine vinegar
A slice of onion
6 peppercorns
Pinch of tarragon
3 egg yolks
15 mL (1 tbsp.) lemon juice
1 mL (¼ tsp.) cayenne pepper
120 to 180 mL (8 to 12 tbsp.) very
   soft unsalted butter
Fresh parsley, chopped

Boil the wine, vinegar, onion,
peppercorns and tarragon in a
small pot until reduced to 30
millilitres (2 tbsp.). Strain. In a
blender place the egg yolks, lemon
juice and cayenne pepper. Blend in
the wine-vinegar liquid.

Heat the butter until it is
bubbling and very hot, but not
browned. Turn on the blender to
high and pour in the hot butter in
a thin continuous stream. Do not
pour too fast or the eggs will not
absorb the butter properly. When
the sauce is thick, turn off the
machine. You may not have
needed all the butter. Stir in the
parsley. Serve at once.

If the sauce starts to curdle, pour
in 15 millilitres (1 tbsp.) hot water
and blend again. If the sauce is too
thin, you have added the butter
too quickly and have no alternative
but to serve thin sauce, or try
again.

WILD MUSHROOM AND BACON SAUTE

Prepare all the ingredients ahead of time and toss together over medium heat just before serving. This is a terrific dish for a brunch with a poached egg nestled on top. For variation in the vegetables, try slivers of celery root (celeriac), fennel (finocchio) or endive and prepare as directed below. This recipe will serve four as a side dish, or two as a main dish.

6 small to medium carrots and 2 stalks
celery or 350 g (¾ lb.) various
vegetables
125 g (4 oz.) shiitaké mushrooms
45 mL (3 tbsp.) unsalted butter
30 mL (2 tbsp.) vegetable oil
1 shallot or green onion, finely minced
1 clove garlic, minced
8 slices bacon
15 mL (1 tbsp.) lemon juice
Salt
Freshly ground pepper
Fresh parsley, chopped

Trim and peel the carrots and celery. Cut into strips about six millimetres (¼ in.) long. Cook in boiling salted water until just barely tender, about five to eight minutes. Drain and reserve.

Remove the mushroom stems and cut the remainder into thick strips. Heat 15 millilitres (1 tbsp.) of the butter and the same quantity of the oil in a medium frypan. Add the shallot and garlic, and cook gently until tender. Add the remaining butter and oil, and stir in the mushrooms. Toss frequently until lightly browned. Drain and reserve.

Fry the bacon and crumble coarsely. Drain and reserve. The dish may be made ahead to this point.

Just before serving, reheat the frypan. Add the vegetables and toss to heat. Add the mushrooms and bacon, and tossing frequently, cook until heated through, about five minutes. Add the lemon juice and salt and pepper to taste. Sprinkle with parsley. Serve immediately.

MUSHROOM PATE IN BRIOCHE CASES

Use shiitaké, chanterelle, oyster or common mushrooms (or a combination of all or some) for this mousse-like mixture, which can be served without the bread casing as a spread for crackers. Make the brioche into a loaf or bundt shape if you don't have the fluted brioche pans. The dough will make two small brioches, or one large loaf or bundt, enough to serve 10 to 12 people as a first course.

Brioche dough, chilled (recipe follows
or use a bread dough)
60 mL (4 tbsp.) unsalted butter
500 g (16 oz.) mushrooms, sliced then
coarsely chopped
45 mL (3 tbsp.) all-purpose white or
instant-blending flour
280 mL (1 cup, 2 tbsp.) chicken stock
or canned broth
1 pkg. gelatine
30 mL (2 tbsp.) water
75 mL (⅓ cup) brandy
Salt
Pepper
125 mL (½ cup) whipping cream

Make the brioche dough and chill overnight. The next day, bake and cool.

Melt the butter in a medium frypan. Add the mushrooms and poach gently on low heat until they have given off most of their liquid, about 10 minutes. Remove the mushrooms to a large bowl.

Sprinkle the flour into the pan of mushroom liquid and whisk. Cook one to two minutes. Whisk in the chicken stock and simmer gently for two to three minutes.

Soften the gelatin in the water and stir in the brandy, which has been warmed. Stir to dissolve. Stir into the chicken-stock mixture. Pour the entire chicken-stock mixture into the mushrooms and stir to blend. Cool. Season to taste.

While the mixture is cooling, prepare the bread casings. Cut 2.5 centimetres (1 in.) off the top of the bread, leaving sides and bottom at least 1.2 centimetres (½ in.) thick. Reserve crumbs and top slice for another use. Paint the insides with melted butter.

When the mushroom mixture is cool, whip the cream until soft peaks form and fold it in. Spoon into the prepared bread cases. Chill until firm.

Garnish with chopped fresh herbs and serve in wedges. Béarnaise sauce is a wonderful addition.

Brioche Dough

There are many recipes for brioche dough, but this one is not as rich as some and makes a wonderful casing for varius fillings. The recipe makes two medium brioches, which freeze well; it can be halved successfully.

750 mL (3 cups) all-purpose white
flour
15 mL (1 tbsp.) dry yeast
125 mL (½ cup) warm water
25 mL (1½ tbsp.) sugar
5 mL (1 tsp.) salt
4 large eggs
180 mL (12 tbsp.) soft, unsalted
butter

Place the flour in the work bowl of a food processor. Set aside. In a small bowl, sprinkle the yeast over the warm water. Stir in the sugar. Let stand until dissolved.

Add the salt to the flour in the processor and process briefly. Break the eggs into the flour. Stir the dissolved yeast. With the machine running, pour in the yeast and add the butter in chunks. Do not process any longer than 30 seconds. The dough will not make a ball; it is a cake-like batter.

Scrape the dough into a greased bowl, cover with plastic wrap and let stand for one hour in a warm place. Punch down and refrigerate, covered, overnight.

Grease the baking pans. Sprinkle flour on the work table. Remove the brioche dough from the bowl. It will be soft but cold enough to handle. Gently form it into a ball or oblong in the shape of your pan and place in the prepared container. Let rise until the dough almost reaches the top of the pan, but no longer than one and a half hours.

Brush a mixture of one egg yolk and 15 millilitres (1 tbsp.) water over the loaf and bake at 200°C (400°F) for 30 minutes, or until golden and the bottom sounds hollow when tapped.

Place on a rack to cool, and then proceed with the mushroom paté. □

In a French Mood

A few months ago I had the good luck to meet one of those southern Americans who embody the grace and hospitality we associate with Dixie. Shirley Corriher of Atlanta, Georgia, gave me a small bag of flour. Specifically: White Lily soft winter-wheat, low-protein flour. Flour like finest talc, finer than the finest pastry flour, essential to the baking of southern biscuits. We talked for only a few minutes, but Corriher's Julia Child-like enthusiasm for cooking (and eating) reminded me again of the exuberance and humor that properly belong in every kitchen and at every table. She explained that southern biscuit dough is unusually liquid. Then she showed me with illustrative hand movements how to handle the dough, and gave me a recipe. But biscuits, though simple, are an art-form, and southern biscuits to a Canadian are an arcane art-form at that. I was nervous.

I took the flour home and baked a batch of Super Balls. The two people I served these rubber items to were polite about it. "Good biscuits," my friends lied. It's hard being humorous or exuberant about a *failure*, for God's sake. "Maybe this is the way they eat them in the South," I speculated, dourly.

The right ingredients alone do not a success bake. Expertise is much harder to hand over than a paper bag of flour. I regret not having time to get into a kitchen with Shirley Corriher and watch her handle that flour, cut shortening into it, work that liquid dough and bake those biscuits, because I later learned that her knowledge of food runs the full gamut, from emotional appreciation to the understanding of molecular activity. While describing Paul Prudhomme's

method of blackening fish on red-hot iron, her face was full of wonder at his artistry. In describing the behavior of eggs in soufflés, she has written, in *Cooks* magazine, a passage like this: "Egg proteins as they occur in nature are huge, complex, coiled molecules which are cross-linked and are somewhat similar in concept to the reinforcing springs in mattresses. Heat or mechanical force, like beating with a whisk, causes these cross-links to come apart and the coils to unwind."

So what? Well, Corriher, who is both a chemist and a cooking teacher, obviously understands what is going on inside a soufflé, and an understanding of the principles of cooking is essential to good performance in the kitchen. Cooking without a confident understanding (whether instinctive or learned) of principles is to place undue trust in recipes, which, as any experienced cook knows, are often distressingly inaccurate. To break beyond a workmanlike ability, you have to begin to experiment with ingredients, and to note the different results when you use different flours, fats, liquids and emulsifiers. Of course, experimentation, especially when it's unguided, yields failures, so the best place for it may be a classroom such as Corriher's. Especially if you're mortified by disasters at home and if the dog is no more fond of rubber biscuits than you are. In 500 grams (1 lb.) of cooking, there is always at least 30 grams (1 oz.) of science.

This meal is French in tone, but is the result of successful experimentation. Three of the recipes illustrate how you can express the inner character of foods while outwardly obliterating their shape and texture. The delight comes, in a sense, from the

A formal affair: velvet-smooth broccoli bisque with a swirl of whipping cream; delicate salmon sole mousse spiked with sherry, garnished with watercress, served on caper mayonnaise; broiled marinated flank steak with Madeira sauce and glazed vegetables.

roundabout journey back to the point of departure. Fish is blended with cream and sherry and made into a mousse which fully expresses the delicacy of salmon and sole. The bisque of broccoli transforms a rugged vegetable into a subtle soup that is nevertheless most broccoliesque. And the two sorbets, like all good sorbets, are exquisitely, intensely, single-mindedly fruity. This approach is not always appropriate, of course, and in the case of beef, justice is well served by simply marinating the meat and serving it rare in all its glory.

—Scott Mowbray

MENU *(Serves Six)*

- Salmon-Sole Mousse
- Broccoli Bisque
- Broiled Flank Steak with Madeira Sauce and Glazed Vegetables
- Raspberry and Blueberry Sorbets

SALMON SOLE MOUSSE

60 mL (4 tbsp.) dry sherry
Water
1 450-g pkg. frozen sole fillets, thawed
1 envelope unflavored gelatine
2 mL (½ tsp.) salt
1 225-g can salmon, drained
½ bunch watercress or parsley
250 mL (1 cup) whipping cream
Homemade caper mayonnaise (recipe below)

In a medium skillet, heat the sherry and about one centimetre (½ in.) of water to boiling. Add frozen sole fillets and cover and simmer for 15 minutes, or until fish flakes easily. Remove sole to a platter and set aside. Reserve 125 millilitres (½ cup) of poaching liquid, discarding remainder.

In a small pot, evenly sprinkle gelatine over 60 millilitres (4 tbsp.) of cold water. Let stand one minute to soften, and stir in reserved poaching liquid. Over medium heat, cook the mixture, stirring constantly until gelatine is dissolved.

In a food processor, blend sole with the gelatine mixture and salt until sole is smooth. Pour mixture into a large bowl. Cover and refrigerate until well chilled and almost set, about 45 minutes.

Meanwhile, in a medium bowl, finely flake the drained salmon.

Mince enough watercress to make 75 millilitres (⅓ cup), set aside in a small bowl. Reserve remaining watercress for garnish.

In a mixing bowl, beat whipping cream until stiff peaks form. Fold the whipped cream into sole mixture until blended, then fold 125 millilitres (½ cup) of sole mixture into flaked salmon. Fold another 125 millilitres (½ cup) into minced watercress.

Evenly spoon half of the remaining sole mixture into a greased 22 by 12-centimetre (9-in. by 5-in.) loaf pan. Add the salmon mixture for the second layer, then the watercress mixture. Top with remaining sole mixture, and cover and refrigerate until mousse is set, at least three hours.

Unmould onto a platter or cutting board. For each serving, spoon caper mayonnaise onto a small plate, place a slice of mousse on top and garnish with watercress.

Caper Mayonnaise
1 egg
5 mL (1 tsp.) Dijon mustard
5 mL (1 tsp.) red or white wine vinegar
5 mL (1 tsp.) fresh lemon juice
50 mL (3 tbsp.) good olive oil
Vegetable oil
Capers

Into a food processor, blender or small mixing bowl, place the egg, mustard, vinegar and lemon juice. Mix briefly. Into a measuring cup, place the olive oil, then add vegetable oil until you have 375 millilitres (1½ cups).

Very slowly, start pouring the oils into the egg mixture while machine is running or hand is whisking. The mixture will become thick and shiny.

Before serving, add capers. Mayonnaise will keep up to 10 days in refrigerator.

BROCCOLI BISQUE

60 mL (4 tbsp.) butter
1 medium onion, sliced, or 2 leeks, cleaned and sliced
2 small potatoes, peeled and sliced
500 mL (2 cups) broccoli, coarsely chopped
750 mL (3 cups) chicken stock or canned broth
Salt, pepper to taste
125 mL (½ cup) whipping cream

Melt butter in a large heavy saucepan; do not let it brown. Add vegetables and cover with parchment paper and lid; allow to simmer gently until vegetables are soft but not brown (this is called "sweating the vegetables").

Remove parchment and add chicken stock. Bring to a boil and simmer until vegetables are well cooked. Allow to cool slightly. Purée the mixture in a blender until smooth. Pour it back into the cleaned saucepan. Season with salt and pepper (a dash of cayenne or Tabasco is nice, too). Add whipping cream and bring to a simmer. Do not let boil or the cream may curdle. Serve hot with a swirl of lightly whipped cream as a garnish.

The soup is also delicious served cold, with a topping of sour cream. It will freeze, but may need to be put through the blender again after defrosting, as the cream may have separated.

BROILED MARINATED FLANK STEAK WITH MADEIRA SAUCE AND GLAZED VEGETABLES

This dish requires a bit of organization in order that the meat be presented rare, the sauce hot and the vegetables crisp. The vegetables can be prepared ahead of time — up to the point where they will be glazed in the sauce skillet. The sauce can be made while the uncooked meat stands at room temperature; keep it warm in a double boiler. Cook the meat while the vegetables are being glazed, then quickly arrange meat, sauce and vegetables on serving plates or a platter.

1 large flank steak
60 mL (4 tbsp.) vegetable oil
60 mL (4 tbsp.) red wine
5 mL (1 tsp.) ginger, fresh chopped
1 clove garlic, minced

Mix the oil, wine, ginger and garlic and spread on both sides of the flank steak. Place in a glass container and let meat marinate for one or more hours in the refrigerator; turn the meat at least once during this time. At this point, you can do the preliminary preparation of the vegetables.

A half hour before cooking, remove meat from refrigerator and let stand at room temperature. While meat stands, make the Madeira sauce (see below).

When ready to cook the meat, heat the broiler or frying pan to very hot and cook meat about five minutes on each side for rare, eight minutes for medium rare. Place the meat on cutting board and let stand for five minutes before slicing.

Madeira Sauce

75 mL (⅓ cup) unsalted butter
3 medium shallots or 1 small onion, chopped
1 medium carrot, chopped
½ stick of celery, chopped
25 mL (1½ tbsp.) tomato paste
250 mL (1 cup) red or white wine
1 284-mL can beefstock or canned broth
3 springs parsley
Pinch of thyme
½ bay leaf
20 mL (4 tsp.) flour
20 mL (4 tsp.) soft butter
75 mL (⅓ cup) Madeira

Melt the unsalted butter in a heavy saucepan. Add the shallots and sauté over low heat until golden. Add the carrots, celery, tomato paste and cover and cook for five minutes.

Stir in the wine, stock, parsley, thyme and bay leaf. Bring to a boil, then simmer, uncovered, until reduced to about 375 millilitres (1½ cups). This takes about one hour. Strain and return sauce to pot.

Mix together the remaining quantities of flour and butter. Gradually whisk the mixture into the boiling sauce and cook until thickened and smooth. Add the Madeira and reduce the heat. Simmer for a few minutes. Pour sauce into a double boiler over low heat to keep warm. Do not wash

the pan, but return to the stove for glazing the vegetables.

Glazed Vegetables

500 g (1 lb.) carrots
8 white turnips
750 g (1½ lb.) new peas, or tiny frozen gourmet peas
75 mL (⅓ cup) chicken stock or canned broth
20 mL (4 tsp.) sugar
Salt and pepper

Rinse the carrots and carve into bite-sized ovals. Put carrots in or steam them over boiling water for about six minutes; remove while still crisp. Refresh under cold water until cold, and set aside.

Peel and quarter the turnips, and carve into bite-sized ovals. Cook in boiling water for 10 minutes. Refresh and set aside.

Simmer the peas until barely tender. Drain, refresh and set aside. The vegetables can be prepared to this point ahead of time.

When ready to glaze vegetables, add a few dollops of butter to the same pan the sauce was made in (traces of the sauce should be in the pan) and toss the carrots and turnips. Add the chicken stock, sugar, salt and pepper. Cook over moderate heat, shaking pan until the liquid has evaporated and the vegetables are well glazed. Return the peas to the pan with chopped parsley. Toss gently and transfer to a serving dish, or arrange vegetables on individual plates. Slice meat and arrange with vegetables. Pour Madeira sauce over the meat or serve alongside.

RASPBERRY AND BLUEBERRY SORBETS

To make both of these sorbets, boil together the sugar and water called for in the recipes until the sugar is melted. Add other ingredients, except the fruit, and chill syrup thoroughly. Then purée the fruit and add it to the chilled syrup. Freeze the mixture according to instructions on your ice cream maker, or freeze it in a flat metal tray in the freezer. In the latter case, to make the mixture smooth, you must remove the

frozen mixture from the freezer, whip it up in a blender or food processor, and freeze again. Do this twice for the best texture.

Raspberry Sorbet

1 300-g pkg. fresh or frozen raspberries (will yield 375 mL or 1½ cups of purée)
125 mL (½ cup) sugar
125 mL (½ cup) water
30 mL (2 tbsp.) lemon juice
15 mL (1 tbsp.) Grand Marnier

Blueberry Sorbet

1 300-g pkg. frozen blueberries, unsweetened and without syrup
250 mL (1 cup) sugar
250 mL (1 cup) water
60 mL (4 tbsp.) orange juice
15 mL (1 tbsp.) lemon juice
15 mL (1 tbsp.) vodka □

The yuletide table: seafood in a tarragon and mustard dressing; roasted goose served with a tangy wild rice stuffing and cumberland sauce; creamed potatoes topped with green onions; broccoli dotted with sweet red peppers.

A Classic Christmas Feast

The elegant first dish in our Christmas feast is meant to be served from a coffee table or buffet in the living room, while family and guests survey the lighted tree, enjoy the fireplace and sip champagne. No other drink would be quite as appropriate with an hors-d'oeuvre that features *three* types of caviar on a savory sour cream mousse.

After their appetizers, the diners proceed to the table for a sweet and luscious seafood salad in a Dijon-tarragon dressing. The choice of seafood is left entirely to the cook, though we suggest prawns, scallops and perhaps crab claws. Whatever the choice, cook the seafood just barely.

The entrée is goose. A goose is a succulent and flavorful change, and the main objection to it, its greasiness, can be minimized through proper cooking.

Our goose, roasted to a turn, loaded with orange and wild-rice stuffing and sauced at table with a tart Cumberland concoction, is superb; the skin crisps in the oven deliciously and should be distributed to all the diners, along with the excellent dark meat. Some of the offending fat can be removed from inside the bird before cooking, and the rest will baste the goose while it cooks – a convenience for the chef. When it is time to carve, remove the wings first and discard; they have virtually no meat on them. The leg joints are harder to get at than on a turkey, but it's not necessary to remove the legs; just slice meat from them.

With the crowning goose entrée come outstanding variations on familiar winter vegetable themes: rich mashed potatoes, broccoli made colorful with red peppers, beets in ginger. For dessert, another dollop of tradition: a fine plum pudding from a recipe somewhat lighter than most. The final touch is homemade chocolates to be eaten with coffee and tea.

MENU *(Serves Twelve)*

- Caviar Crowned Mousse
- Rye Bread
- Sea food Salad with Tarragon Mustard Dressing
- Roast Goose with Orange Stuffing
- Cumberland Sauce
- Creamed Potatoes
- Confetti Broccoli with Red Peppers
- Ginger Beets
- Onion Relish
- Traditional Steamed Christmas Pudding
- Brandy Butter
- Mincemeat, Cranberry and Pumpkin Tartlettes
- Homemade Chocolates

CAVIAR CROWNED MOUSSE

Three colorful caviars decorate the top of this savory herbed mousse. If you have trouble locating caviar in your area, have your grocer contact either Continental Importers or National Importers.

60 mL (4 tbsp.) parsley, chopped
60 mL (4 tbsp.) mixed fresh herbs (chives, savory, tarragon, etc.) or 15 mL (1 tbsp.) dried herbs
5 mL (1 tsp.) lemon rind, grated
15 mL (1 tbsp.) lemon juice
5 mL (1 tsp.) Worcestershire sauce
250 mL (1 cup) sour cream
1 envelope unflavored gelatin
60 mL (4 tbsp.) dry white wine or water
125 mL (½ cup) whipping cream, whipped
Freshly ground pepper
2 50-g jars Canadian whitefish golden caviar
1 100-g jar black lumpfish caviar or sturgeon caviar
1 50-g jar of red salmon caviar
Green onion for garnish, chopped
Rye bread, thinly sliced (recipe below)

In a medium bowl, combine the parsley, herbs, lemon rind, lemon juice, Worcestershire sauce and sour cream.

Sprinkle the gelatin over the wine or water in a small saucepan. Let soften five minutes, then cook over low heat, stirring constantly until gelatine is completely dissolved. Stir gelatin into sour cream mixture. Cool thoroughly, then fold in the whipping cream and freshly ground pepper.

Line a 20-centimetre (8-in.) springform mould with parchment or waxed paper and lightly oil with vegetable oil. Spoon the gelatine mixture into the pan and let set for several hours or overnight.

At serving time, carefully remove the mousse from the springform pan and place on a serving plate. Arrange the caviar in 2.5-centimetre (1-in.) rings around the mould. Do not do this too far ahead of time, as caviar does not keep well, and the black caviar may bleed into the yellow and the red eggs (unless you're using a sturgeon caviar). Cover the remaining surface with chopped green onions.

Serve with thinly sliced rye bread.

RYE BREAD

This is a fine-textured bread with an interesting flavor. It can be shaped in a standard bread pan or into a free-form round. Baguette pans can be used to make bread that can be sliced into small rounds.

15 mL (1 tbsp.) dry yeast
45 mL (3 tbsp.) honey
60 mL (4 tbsp.) warm water
250 mL (1 cup) warm milk
125 mL (½ cup) hot water
30 mL (2 tbsp.) soft butter
15 mL (1 tbsp.) salt
625 mL (2½ cups) dark rye flour
750 mL (3 cups) all-purpose white flour, more or less
Cornmeal
1 egg-white beaten with 30 mL (2 tbsp.) water

Dissolve the yeast and honey in the 60 millilitres (4 tbsp.) warm water and allow the mixture to soften for four to five minutes. Combine the warm milk, hot water and softened butter. Stir to melt the butter. Mix into the yeast mixture along with the salt. Mix the rye flour with half of the white flour and add this mixture to milk/yeast mixture, one cup at a time. Then start adding the balance of the white flour. Scrape out the dough onto a floured board and knead to make the dough velvety and elastic; this takes about 10 minutes.

Shape the dough into a ball and place in a well-greased bowl, turning to coat the dough with the butter. Cover and place in a warm area to double in bulk, one to 1½ hours.

Punch dough down and turn out onto a lightly floured board. Divide into two equal loaves. Grease baking sheet, loaf pans or baguette pans, and sprinkle a little cornmeal in the bottom of the pans or onto the baking sheet. Place dough in pans or on sheet and allow to rise until doubled in bulk, about 30 minutes to one hour. Brush the tops of the loaves with the egg-white/water mixture.

Bake at 190°C (375°F) for 40 to 50 minutes or until the loaves sound hollow when tapped on the bottom. Cool thoroughly on racks before slicing.

SEAFOOD SALAD WITH TARRAGON AND MUSTARD DRESSING

This salad can be made with any combination of seafood you like. Do not serve it too cold as the dressing is best at room temperature.

3 or 4 medium or large raw shrimp per person, shelled
2 or 3 scallops per person (quartered if large)
500 mL (2 cups) uncooked tiny peas, fresh or frozen
5 or 6 green onions, trimmed and cut into 1-cm (½-in.) pieces
Salt and freshly ground pepper to taste
Dressing (recipe below)
Romaine leaves, coarsely shredded

Bring a large pot of water to boil and drop in the raw shrimp. Cook one minute and add the scallops. Cook two minutes or just until the water returns to the boil. Pour through a strainer. Cool seafood to room temperature by running under water. Reserve a few shrimp for garnish and toss the remainder with the peas (you may not want to use the entire two cups) and green onions. Season lightly.

Stir in some of the dressing. Toss lightly. Place the shredded romaine on serving plates and spoon the salad into the centre. Garnish with reserved shrimp.

Serve immediately, with additional dressing on the side.

Dressing
1 large egg
15 mL (1 tbsp.) Dijon-style mustard, more if desired
30 mL (2 tbsp.) tarragon wine vinegar
5 mL (1 tsp.) dried tarragon
Salt and pepper to taste
45 mL (3 tbsp.) good olive oil, plus enough light vegetable oil to make 375 mL (1½ cups)

Blend together the egg, mustard, vinegar and seasonings. Very slowly, pour in the oil, drop by drop if beating dressing by hand, or in a very slow, steady stream if using a food processor, until the mixture becomes thick and shiny. Taste for seasonings and add more mustard if desired.

ROAST GOOSE WITH ORANGE STUFFING

Although a goose is certainly a fatty bird, don't prick it too much or the meat will become too dry. Pull out all the fat from inside the body cavity (render it and you will have superb cooking fat for weeks to come), and be sure that you cook it only 16 minutes to the pound at 160°C (325°F). An eight-kilogram (16 lb.) goose will feed 12 people well.

1 8-kg (16-lb.) goose
2 L (8 cups) fresh bread cubes
125 mL (½ cup) celery, chopped
125 mL (½ cup) onion, chopped
60 mL (4 tbsp.) butter
250 mL (1 cup) wild rice, cooked
250 mL (1 cup) fresh orange juice
30 mL (2 tbsp.) orange zest, coarsely chopped
250 mL (1 cup) parsley, chopped
2 mL (½ tsp.) ground thyme
2 mL (½ tsp.) ground sage
Dash of salt and pepper

Place the bread cubes in a large bowl. Sauté the celery and onion in the butter until soft. Add to the bread cubes. Add the rest of the ingredients and toss until mixed.

Spoon the dressing into the body cavity, packing it in lightly. Truss the goose and place it on a rack in a shallow baking pan. Roast until the drumstick meat feels soft to the touch and the joint moves easily. It is not necessary to baste, but you may want to remove any excess fat from the baking pan from time to time.

CUMBERLAND SAUCE

This is a wonderful port wine sauce that is often served with wild game and goes well with goose. It is sweet, spicy and a deep red color.

125 mL (½ cup) onions, finely chopped
Boiling water
Zest of 2 oranges and 2 lemons, finely chopped or julienned
Juice of the oranges and lemons
125 mL (½ cup) port
375 mL (1½ cups) red-currant jelly
Pinch of ground ginger
Pinch of dry mustard

Parboil the chopped onions for one minute in boiling water to cover. Drain and set aside. Boil the zest of the oranges and lemons for five minutes in just enough water to cover. Drain and rinse in cold water. Pat dry and set aside.

Place the remaining ingredients into a medium saucepan and heat until jelly melts. Stir in the onions and zest. Reduce heat and simmer for five minutes. Check for seasonings. Add more orange juice if desired. This sauce stores well.

CREAMED POTATOES

This dish can be made ahead and frozen. Reheat in the oven at 180°C (350°F), covered, until hot, about 45 minutes.

12 medium potatoes
125 mL (½ cup) soft unsalted butter
250 mL (1 cup) light cream
125 mL (½ cup) sour cream
Salt, pepper, nutmeg to taste
250 mL (1 cup) green onions, chopped

Peel, cut up and cook the potatoes until soft. Drain and place in a large mixing bowl. Add butter, half of the cream and all of the sour cream. Mash until smooth (a potato ricer is a great help here). Add remaining cream to make a smooth purée. Season to taste. Place in ovenproof casserole. Freeze if making ahead.

An hour before serving time, heat up. Remove the lid, cover the top with chopped green onions and serve.

CONFETTI BROCCOLI WITH RED PEPPERS

Cook the vegetables in the morning and then sauté them in a little butter just before serving time. No need to refrigerate.

2 kg (4 lbs.) broccoli
3 large shallots, minced
2 large red sweet peppers, diced
Butter
Salt and pepper to taste

Cut the broccoli tops into flowerets, then peel and dice the top eight centimetres (3 in.) of the stems. Cook the stems in boiling water until just barely tender, about three minutes, then add the flowerets and continue cooking for another three minutes. Drain and rinse under cold water. Set aside until serving time.

Just before serving, mince the shallots or some green onions, dice the red peppers and melt the butter in a large frypan that will hold all the broccoli.

Sauté the shallots until soft, stir in the red pepper and heat through. Add the broccoli and cook until hot, tossing and stirring. Sprinkle with salt and pepper and toss again. Place in a large serving bowl.

A toast: the mousse with the most, combining three colorful caviars over a creamy base; best served with bubbly.

GINGER BEETS

1 kg (2 lbs.) small beets, trimmed
125 mL (½ cup) seedless raisins
30 mL (2 tbsp.) butter
10 mL (2 tsp.) fresh ginger, finely
  minced
15 mL (1 tbsp.) sugar
5 mL (1 tsp.) red wine vinegar
10 mL (2 tsp.) lime peel, finely
  slivered

Place the beets in a saucepan and
cover with cold water. Bring
slowly to a boil, reduce the heat
and simmer, uncovered, until
barely tender. Use some beet
liquid to cover the raisins in a
small bowl.

Drain the beets and cool under
cold running water. Remove and
discard skins and slice. Drain the
raisins and reserve.

Melt the butter in a large frypan.
Stir in the ginger and cook briefly.
Add the raisins, sugar and vinegar
and stir. Add the beets and cook
until warmed through, tossing and
stirring. This dish may be made
ahead to this point.

At serving time, reheat, sprinkle
with lime peel and serve.

ONION RELISH

2 large onions
90 mL (6 tbsp.) butter
125 mL to 175 mL (½ to ¾ cup)
  white wine

Thinly slice the onions. Melt the
butter in a medium-sized pan and
sauté the onions over medium to
low heat until very soft. Stir
frequently and do not allow to
burn.

Stir in the white wine, scraping
up the onion bits, stirring well.
Simmer until wine is reduced and
onions have absorbed the liquid. It
should be almost a paste.

Store in a small crock. May be
reheated and served warm.

TRADITIONAL STEAMED CHRISTMAS PUDDING

Delicious, old-fashioned and
festive, this pudding is a little
lighter than most.

3 large eggs
250 mL (1 cup) packed brown sugar
60 mL (4 tbsp.) molasses
60 mL (4 tbsp.) rum or brandy
250 mL (1 cup) suet, finely chopped
250 mL (1 cup) carrots, finely grated
125 mL (½ cup) grated apples, peeled
  and cored
125 mL (½ cup) peeled grated
  potatoes, patted dry
125 mL (½ cup) all-purpose white
  flour
2 mL (½ tsp.) baking soda
5 mL (1 tsp.) baking powder
2 mL (½ tsp.) cinnamon
2 mL (½ tsp.) allspice
2 mL (½ tsp.) nutmeg
2 mL (½ tsp.) salt
250 mL (1 cup) raisins
250 mL (1 cup) currants
250 mL (1 cup) fine dry bread crumbs
  (white or brown)

Beat eggs and blend in sugar,
molasses, rum, suet, carrots,
apples and potatoes. In another
bowl, in order given, combine
remaining ingredients and stir into
egg mixture. Spoon into greased
1.5-litre (1½ qt.) pudding mould
or bowl. Cover with buttered
waxed paper and foil, and tie
tightly with string. Place on a rack
in a large pot and pour in boiling
water to halfway up the sides of
the mould.

Cover and steam about four
hours or until a toothpick inserted
in the centre comes out clean.
(Keep the water boiling gently and
add more as needed.)

Unmould when cold and wrap
in foil. The pudding will keep
about three weeks in the
refrigerator. Reheat, wrapped in
foil, in oven or steamer.

To flame before serving: In a
small saucepan, warm 75 millilitres
(⅓ cup) brandy just until it begins
to vaporize. Ignite with a long
match and pour, flaming, over hot
pudding. Serve with brandy butter
(recipe below).

BRANDY BUTTER

This is equally good made with
rum.

125 mL (½ cup) butter
250 mL (1 cup) icing sugar
45 mL (3 tbsp.) brandy
5 mL (1 tsp.) orange rind, grated
5 mL (1 tsp.) lemon rind, grated
5 mL (1 tsp.) orange juice
5 mL (1 tsp.) lemon juice
Pinch of nutmeg

Cream the butter and sugar until
very light. Add the other
ingredients, one at a time. Store
for 25 hours to develop the
flavors.

MINCEMEAT, CRANBERRY AND PUMPKIN TARTLETTES

Each of the fillings makes more
than enough for 12 guests. They
all can be frozen for another
occasion. Make the tartlettes ahead
and freeze, unbaked. The day of
the party, spoon in the fillings and
bake.

Pastry
Makes enough for two dozen tarts,
five centimetres (2 in.) in diameter.

250 mL (1 cup) unsalted butter
75 mL (⅓ cup) white sugar
5 mL (1 tsp.) vanilla
1 large egg
675 mL (2¾ cups) all-purpose white
  flour

Cream the softened butter with the
sugar. Add vanilla and then beat in
the egg. Blend in the flour.

Food processor method: place
dry ingredients in the work bowl.
Cut chilled butter into small pieces
and add to the flour. Process until
crumbly. Mix egg and vanilla in
small bowl. With machine
running, pour egg through feed
tube and process until dough
forms a ball.

Divide pastry into thirds and
shape each into a flat disc. Cover
with plastic wrap and refrigerate at
least four hours. This dough can
be rolled out and cut into shapes
or simply rolled into balls about
the size of a walnut and pressed
into the tart pans.

Fill with appropriate fillings and
bake for 15 minutes at 180°C
(350°F), until pastry is a light
brown. Cool completely.

Mincemeat Filling
This traditional recipe is stored in
the refrigerator or freezer. Pack

into pretty jars and give the extras as gifts.

500 g (1 lb.) suet, finely chopped
750 g (1½ lbs.) currants
750 g (1½ lbs.) raisins
250 g (½ lb.) mixed peel, finely
chopped
750 g (1½ lbs.) Granny Smith
apples, peeled, cored, chopped
125 mL (½ cup) almonds, chopped
500 mL (2 cups) white sugar
Dash of nutmeg
Pinch of allspice
Pinch of mace
5 mL (1 tsp.) salt
15 mL (3 tsp.) ground cloves
125 mL (½ cup) brandy
125 mL (½ cup) port

Combine all these ingredients and mix thoroughly. Pack into jars and refrigerate or freeze until needed.

Cranberry Filling
This is a medium sweet mixture; adjust sugar to your taste.

1.25 L (5 cups) cranberries
625 mL (2½ cups) white sugar
60 mL (4 tbsp.) water

Mix together ingredients in a medium saucepan and cook over low heat, stirring occasionally until a liquid forms on the bottom of the pan. Bring to a high boil and continue to stir for one minute. Turn down the heat and simmer, uncovered, for one minute.
   Cover and simmer, stirring occasionally, until all berries have popped. Store in sterilized jars in the refrigerator. Will keep indefinitely.

Pumpkin Filling
3 eggs, slightly beaten
250 mL (1 cup) canned or mashed
cooked pumpkin
250 mL (1 cup) white sugar
125 mL (½ cup) dark corn syrup
5 mL (1 tsp.) vanilla
2 mL (½ tsp.) cinnamon
Dash of salt
Pecans or walnuts, chopped

Combine the eggs, pumpkin, sugar, corn syrup, vanilla, cinnamon and salt and mix well. Spoon into prepared tart shells. It

will expand a little, so don't fill the shells to the top. Top with chopped nuts.

HOMEMADE CHOCOLATES
These candies are easily made ahead. The recipes are from Au Chocolat in Vancouver.

Grand Marnier Truffles
These will keep, frozen, for one or two months (if no one finds them!). Recipe makes 30 to 35 chocolates.

125 mL (½ cup) whipping cream
250 g (8 oz.) semi-sweet chocolate,
chopped fine
25 mL (1½ tbsp.) Grand Marnier,
Triple Sec or orange brandy
125 mL (½ cup) diced candied orange
peel (optional)
500 g (1 lb.) semi-sweet chocolate for
decoration
250 g (½ lb.) white chocolate for
decoration

Bring cream just to a boil in a heavy saucepan. Remove from heat. Beat chocolate into cream using hand mixer or whisk. Beat until smooth and all chocolate is melted.
   Beat in liqueur and orange peel until mixture is well blended.
   Chill in the refrigerator until firm, approximately one to two hours.
   Scrape spoon or melon ball cutter across surface of mixture, and quickly press chocolate in 2.5-centimetre (1-in.) balls. Freeze well wrapped in plastic. They taste great just as they are.
   To decorate: dip chocolates in melted semi-sweet chocolate and allow to cool completely. Then, holding dipped chocolates between thumb and first finger, dip one half in white chocolate and place on parchment paper to cool.
   Keep hands clean at all times to avoid white fingerprints on the dark chocolate half. These can be stored in the refrigerator for one week if well wrapped.

Pistachios in White Chocolate
This delicious candy can be rolled

in chopped pistachios or spread on a cookie sheet and cut into squares.

500 g (1 lb.) white chocolate
12 egg yolks
500 g (1 lb.) unsalted butter
250 mL (1 cup) pistachios, chopped
250 mL (1 cup) chopped pistachios if
you are making balls or 125 mL
(½ cup) whole pistachios for
decoration on squares
Additional white chocolate for coating
squares
Maraschino cherry bits (optional)

Melt 500 grams (1 lb.) white chocolate carefully over hot, not boiling, water. Whisk in the egg yolks and butter until well incorporated. Stir in the 250 millilitres (1 cup) chopped pistachios until well blended.
   For balls: chill, then roll into balls and roll in the 250 millilitres (1 cup) additional chopped pistachios and top each with a maraschino cherry bit.
   For squares: pour the hot mixture into a parchment-lined jelly-roll pan. Cool in refrigerator. When firm, cut into squares. Decorate with a thin coating of additional white chocolate, whole pistachios and cherry bits.

Cashew-Butter Chocolates
These are a "grownup" version of peanut butter cups. Any nut can be used.

500 g (1 lb.) cashews
500 g (1 lb.) semi-sweet chocolate
125 g (¼ lb.) unsweetened chocolate

In a blender or food processor, blend cashews until you get a chunky butter consistency.
   Roll ground nuts into balls approximately 1 centimetre (½ in.) in diameter.
   Melt the chocolates together carefully over hot, not boiling, water. Dip the cashew balls in the chocolate. For a rough texture, rub the coated balls with hands after coating hands with warm chocolate.
   Let set until firm. These keep for one week in the refrigerator, one to two months in the freezer. □

A Festal Affair

In time-honored holiday tradition, we offer you a formal Christmas dinner, one that will demand your best tablecloth and china. Everything but the main course can be made ahead, and since the beef doesn't need to be fussed over, only the vegetables, gravy and Yorkshire pudding need attention after the guests arrive.

Traditional Yorkshire pudding is not nearly so difficult to make as is often thought. Be sure the ingredients are at room temperature and the oven and baking pan are hot. The pudding can bake while the roast is resting and you are eating the soup.

As a memorable accompaniment to this meal, start a tradition and give your guests a gift — a tiny basket filled with sugar plums, chocolate truffles, candied orange peel, spiced nuts, chocolate walnut fudge and super simple chocolate mint truffles.

MENU (Serves Twelve)
- Appetizer Crêpes
- Tomato Gervaise
- Shrimp and Oyster Bisque
- Cranberry, Chestnut and Pear Salad
- Fillet of Beef with Crab Stuffing
- Mushroom Sauce
- Quick Glazed Onions
- Sweet Potato Croquettes
- Yorkshire Puddings
- Pineapple Beets
- Green Beans Amandine
- Walnut Bread
- Strawberry Pinwheel with Raspberry Sauce
- Chocolate Truffles
- Sugar Plums
- Chocolate Walnut Fudge

APPETIZER CREPES

This recipe makes two stacks of seven crêpes each. Make the crêpes ahead and freeze them until ready to fill for the party. The batter will give you extra crêpes which can be used in other recipes.

Basic Crêpe Batter
Makes 48 15-centimetre (6-in.) crêpes.

425 to 500 mL (1¾ to 2 cups) all-purpose white flour
5 mL (1 tsp.) salt
6 large eggs
750 mL (3 cups) milk, or 375 mL (1½ cups) water and 375 mL (1½ cups) milk
60 to 90 mL (4 to 6 tbsp.) butter, melted and cooled

Blend all the ingredients in a blender. Refrigerate at least two hours. Heat a 15-centimetre (6-in.) frypan. Pour a little batter into the pan and twist to cover the bottom. Cook until small bubbles burst, then turn and briefly cook the other side.

Crab Filling
125 g (4 oz.) fresh crab, or same quantity canned
60 mL (4 tbsp.) mayonnaise
15 mL (1 tbsp.) onion, chopped
Freshly ground pepper

Mix ingredients together in a small bowl.

Cream Cheese Filling
125-g pkg. cream cheese, softened
30 mL (2 tbsp.) mayonnaise
4 strips bacon, crisply cooked and crumbled
15 mL (1 tbsp.) chives or green onion, finely chopped

Mix ingredients together in a small bowl, adding more mayonnaise if needed to make a smooth mixture.

Build two stacks of seven crêpes each, using alternating layers of crab and cheese. Each stack will have three layers of each filling.

Wrap in plastic wrap and refrigerate for several hours. When ready to serve, cut in wedges (12 for each stack). Impale a stuffed olive or gherkin to each wedge with a fancy cocktail pick. Garnish with Tomato Gervaise (see below).

TOMATO GERVAISE

This recipe was developed by the Cordon Bleu Cookery School in London for a luncheon honoring Queen Elizabeth, who loves tomatoes.

14 to 16 small cherry tomatoes, scooped and drained
1 125-g pkg. cream cheese, softened and whipped
Dash of salt
A little milk or cream
15 mL (1 tbsp.) Ranch dressing (French or Catalina are good also)
Seasoned pepper
Baby shrimp or parsley for garnish

Cream all the ingredients together, adding milk as necessary to make a smooth paste. Fill the scooped, drained tomatoes. Top with a tiny shrimp or piece of parsley.

This is nice served in a large tomato and placed on a lettuce leaf for a luncheon. It is very rich.

SHRIMP AND OYSTER BISQUE

May be prepared several hours ahead and reheated just before serving.

500 mL (2 cups) shucked oysters
500 mL (2 cups) shelled, raw shrimp
1 L (4 cups) milk
250 mL (1 cup) whipping cream
125 mL (½ cup) celery, peeled and minced
45 mL (3 tbsp.) shallots, finely minced
15 mL (1 tbsp.) parsley, minced
Pinch of mace
Salt and pepper to taste
45 mL (3 tbsp.) unsalted butter
45 mL (3 tbsp.) all-purpose flour

Finely chop the oysters, reserving any liquid. Chop the shrimp. Place the oysters, liquid and shrimp in a heavy soup pot. Add the milk, cream, celery, shallots, parsley and mace. Simmer for 30 minutes. Cool slightly. Purée in blender or press through a sieve. Season to taste.

Melt the butter in a small saucepan. Stir in flour and cook for a few minutes. Stir a little of the puréed bisque into this roux to make a thin paste. Stir this paste back into the bisque.

Return the bisque to a low heat and stir until slightly thickened.

CRANBERRY, CHESTNUT AND PEAR SALAD

This is an unusual salad that is well worth the trouble. Most of it can be made ahead of time.

250 g (1 cup) fresh chestnuts
375 mL (1½ cups) fresh or frozen
    cranberries
45 mL (3 tbsp.) white sugar
3 pears
Lemon juice
60 mL (4 tbsp.) green onion, minced
10 mL (2 tsp.) Dijon mustard
10 mL (4 tsp.) lime juice
4 mL (¾ tsp.) salt
150 to 250 mL (⅔ to 1 cup) olive oil
1 bunch romaine lettuce
15 mL (1 tbsp.) lime zest, finely
    grated

Make a cross in the rounded side of the chestnuts, being careful not to cut yourself, and place them in a pan of water. Bring to a boil and simmer until they can be peeled easily. (One tin of whole water chestnuts may be substituted, but it's not the same.)

Chop the cranberries coarsely, then place them in a small bowl and toss with the sugar. Chill for at least one hour.

Peel the pears, core and cut into strips. Sprinkle with lemon juice. Mince the green onion.

In a large ceramic or glass bowl, combine the lime juice, mustard and salt. Slowly whisk in the olive oil. Add the pears, chestnuts and green onions. Toss and let marinate, covered, for at least an hour, but not more than four hours.

Line a glass salad bowl or individual salad plates with the romaine, coarse stems removed. Arrange the pear mixture around the edge. Spoon the cranberries into the centre and sprinkle them with the grated lime zest.

FILLET OF BEEF WITH CRAB STUFFING

1 1.2 to 1.5-kg (2½ to 3-lb.) fillet of
    beef (or two, if your guests love
    beef)

Order the fillet well in advance. Make sure the meat is fairly even in thickness, and trim if necessary. Butterfly it by making a deep cut horizontally lengthwise, just about through. Spread open and pound with a mallet to an even thickness of two centimetres (¾-in.). Season with salt and pepper.

Crab Stuffing
75 mL (⅓ cup) tomato juice
15 mL (1 tbsp.) Worcestershire sauce
2 beaten eggs
30 mL (2 tbsp.) lemon juice
2 mL (½ tsp.) salt
250 g (½ lb.) fresh crab
250 mL (1 cup) fine dry breadcrumbs
30 mL (2 tbsp.) parsley, chopped

Combine the tomato juice, Worcestershire sauce, eggs, lemon juice and salt. Add crab, breadcrumbs and parsley. Mix thoroughly. Place lengthwise down centre of roast. Roll the meat up from the long side and tie securely with string. Cover and refrigerate until about two hours before serving.

When ready to roast, brown the meat over high heat in a roasting pan in which some vegetable oil has been heated. The roast may be prepared ahead to this point. Keep at room temperature. When brown, place in oven at 220°C (425°F) for 30 to 40 minutes. Meat should be medium rare (60°C/140°F) on a meat thermometer). Allow the roast to stand 25 minutes before carving. (Cook the Yorkshire puddings at this point.)

MUSHROOM SAUCE

The Shiitaké mushrooms used in this recipe are large, dried mushrooms found in the Chinese section of most good supermarkets.

1 42-g pkg. Shiitaké mushrooms
100 to 125 g (3 to 4 oz.) fresh
    mushrooms, thinly sliced

15 mL (1 tbsp.) vegetable oil
1 L (4 cups) beef stock or canned broth
175 mL (¾ cup) Madeira (or sherry)
20 mL (4 tsp.) cornstarch
20 mL (4 tsp.) cold water

Soak the Shiitaké mushrooms in hot water to cover for 30 minutes. Drain and pat dry. Discard the stems and slice the caps thinly.

In a large saucepan, heat the oil over moderate heat and sauté the fresh mushrooms for one or two minutes. Add the Shiitaké mushrooms and sauté for one to two minutes more. Add the stock, bring the liquid to a boil and reduce to 625 millilitres (2½ cups), about 15 to 20 minutes of boiling.

When the roast has been transferred to the cutting board, add the Madeira to the pan and deglaze the pan over high heat — this means to add liquid to the roasting pan and scrape up the brown bits clinging to the bottom and sides. Boil until the liquid has reduced to about 125 millilitres (½ cup), stirring constantly. Strain into the mushroom sauce.

Dissolve the cornstarch into the water and stir into the mushroom mixture. Bring to a gentle boil and stir until thickened. Season with salt and pepper to taste and transfer to a gravy boat.

QUICK GLAZED ONIONS

8 to 10 medium onions
Beef stock or canned broth to cover
60 mL (4 tbsp.) butter
30 mL (2 tbsp.) brown sugar

Peel the skins from the onions. Cut into halves or quarters, leaving most of the root on to prevent the onion from falling apart. Place in a saucepan and cover with beef stock. Simmer until tender. Drain off stock and set aside until serving time.

Just before serving, melt the butter in a pan and blend in the brown sugar. Heat to boiling. Add the drained onions and toss until well coated and heated through.

SWEET POTATO CROQUETTES

Sweet potatoes are of two types. Some have light tan skin and pale

And to all a good meal: the holiday table groans with goodies, from pineapple beets to sugarplums. Dinner starts with a cranberry, chestnut and pear salad, progressing to crab-stuffed fillet of beef with a mushroom sauce, glazed onions, sweet potato croquettes, beans amandine and Yorkshire pudding flesh, which is similar to a white potato in texture. Others, often called yams, have tan to red-brown skin and sweet, moist, orange flesh. This dish can be baked with the green beans in a hot oven after the Yorkshire puddings have finished.

6 medium sweet potatoes, cooked and
    peeled
45 mL (3 tbsp.) butter
125 mL (½ cup) sour cream
30 mL (2 tbsp.) brown sugar
Dash of cinnamon, nutmeg, salt and
    pepper
Crushed corn flakes

Mash the sweet potatoes and blend in the butter until melted. Add the sour cream, sugar and seasonings to taste. With floured hands, form into fingers about five centimetres (2 in.) long and 2.5 centimetres (1 in.) thick. and roll in the crushed corn flakes. Place on a greased baking sheet and bake until crispy (about 10 minutes). Serve at once.

YORKSHIRE PUDDINGS

Bake these when the roast is resting as the oven temperature is very high.

250 mL (1 cup) milk, room
    temperature
250 mL (1 cup) all-purpose white
    flour
3 large eggs, room temperature
Hot fat from the roast, if any, or
    bacon fat or vegetable oil

Whisk together the milk, flour and eggs, adding a dash of salt. Place five millilitres (1 tsp.) of fat in each cup of a 12-cup muffin tin and place in a 220°C (425°F) oven. When hot and smoking, remove from oven and pour mixture into each cup. Return pan to oven. Bake until puffy and dark golden brown, 25 to 30 minutes.

PINEAPPLE BEETS

Mandarin oranges make a nice alternative to the pineapple, if desired.

30 mL (2 tbsp.) brown sugar
15 mL (1 tbsp.) cornstarch

1 mL (¼ tsp.) salt
1 400-mL can pineapple tidbits
15 mL (1 tbsp.) butter
15 mL (1 tbsp.) lemon juice
2 400-mL cans rosebud beets, drained

Mix together the brown sugar, cornstarch and salt in a medium saucepan. Stir in the pineapple and its syrup. Cook until mixture thickens and bubbles. Add butter, lemon juice and beets. Heat through and serve.

GREEN BEANS AMANDINE

250 to 375 g (1 to 1½ lbs.) whole
    green beans
125 mL (½ cup) sliced almonds
Butter
Breadcrumbs

Remove the tips and rinse the beans under cold water. Bring a large pot of water to the boil and add the beans. Return to the boil and cook until tender, about five to seven minutes. Drain and cool under cold water to stop the cooking. Place in a buttered, ovenproof serving dish and top with breadcrumbs, almonds and a few dots of butter.

About 10 minutes before serving time, place the dish in the oven to heat through and brown the almonds. Serve immediately.

WALNUT BREAD

Walnut oil is found in the food section of specialty food stores. Share the can with a friend; it will make two recipes.

30 mL (2 tbsp.) dry yeast
750 mL (3 cups) water
2 L (8 cups) all-purpose white flour
500 mL (2 cups) chopped walnuts
15 mL (1 tbsp.) salt
250 mL (1 cup) walnut oil

Dissolve the yeast in the water. Stir the salt into 250 millilitres (1 cup) of the flour. When the yeast is bubbling, start whisking in the flour, 250 millilitres (1 cup) at a time, until the batter is too thick to continue. This will take 750 to

1000 millilitres (3 to 4 cups) of flour. Let this mixture stand for 15 to 20 minutes or until it is bubbly.

Stir in the chopped nuts and 60 millilitres (4 tbsp.) of the walnut oil. Add the rest of the flour, 250 millilitres (1 cup) at a time, mixing with a wooden spoon. Once the dough will hold together, turn it out onto a floured board and knead it until smooth. Oil a large bowl with some of the remaining walnut oil and add the dough. Allow to rise until double, about 1½ hours.

Once the dough has risen, pour another 60 millilitres (4 tbsp.) of the walnut oil over it and knead in thoroughly. Again let the dough rise and again pour over 60 millilitres (4 tbsp.) of the oil. Knead it in and then divide the dough into three loaves or rounds. Place in well-oiled baking pans or on a baking sheet and let rise until just less than double.

Brush the loaves lightly with the remaining walnut oil and bake at 220°C (425°F) for 30 to 35 minutes or until they are an even walnut brown.

Let cool before slicing. The interior will be an attractive pinky-brown color.

The bread will freeze well.

STRAWBERRY PINWHEEL WITH RASPBERRY SAUCE

A most elegant dessert, this pinwheel can be partially made weeks ahead and finished off the day before the party.

Cake
6 large eggs, at room temperature
175 mL (¾ cup) sugar
2 mL (½ tsp.) vanilla
250 mL (1 cup) all-purpose white
    flour
90 mL (6 tbsp.) butter, melted and
    cooled
Icing sugar

Preheat oven to 180°C (350°F). Butter and line with parchment, one 25 by 40-centimetre (10 by 15 in.) jelly-roll pan and one 20-centimetre (8 in.) round pan. Butter and dust with flour. Set aside.

Beat eggs and sugar until thick

and light in color, and mixture will form a ribbon when the beaters are raised. Whisk in vanilla. Place flour in a sieve and sift into the egg mixture. Fold in quickly. Fold a few spoonfuls of the flour/egg mixture into the cooled butter, and then pour the whole mixture back into the flour/egg bowl and fold in quickly.

Pour into prepared pans, spreading evenly. Bake 15 to 20 minutes or until light brown and springy to the touch. Turn the cake out onto a wire rack to cool. Sprinkle the top of the jelly roll with icing sugar and turn out onto a sheet of parchment or foil. Cover with another sheet of parchment and a damp tea towel. Let sit for 10 minutes. Trim off the crisp edges and roll, using the bottom parchment as a guide. Let stand until cold.

Filling for Jelly Roll
½ jar seedless raspberry preserves
Dash of cognac or kirsch

Combine the jam with the liqueur, mixing thoroughly. Unroll the cake. Spread the jam over the roll and re-roll lengthwise into a tight jelly roll about 4-cm. (1½-in.) thick. Wrap with foil and freeze. Also freeze the 20-cm. (8—in.) cake layer. Roll is much easier to slice when frozen.

For our presentation we made two jelly rolls. (Freeze and save the cake layer for another time.)

Strawberry Filling for Pinwheel
1 425-g pkg. frozen strawberries in syrup, thawed and drained (reserve 125 g/½ cup of the syrup)
125 mL (½ cup) milk
2 envelopes unflavored gelatin
60 mL (4 tbsp.) sugar
2 egg yolks
15 mL (1 tbsp.) Grand Marnier
375 mL (1½ cups) whipping cream
6 to 8 ice cubes

Place the drained strawberries in a blender. Soften the gelatin in the milk and reserved syrup. Heat gently to dissolve. Pour into blender and process briefly. Add the sugar, egg yolks, Grand Marnier and whipping cream. Process briefly. Add the ice cubes and process until the ice is

incorporated. Pour into a bowl and allow to stand until mixture mounds slightly, about five to eight minutes. Spoon into prepared pinwheel mold.

Either before making the filling or while the filling is standing, prepare the jelly roll. Line a 1½ to two-millilitre (6 to 8-cup) bowl with plastic wrap. Slice the frozen jelly roll into very thin rounds and place over the plastic wrap, beginning with one in the centre and working around until the top of the bowl is reached, pressing them slightly to hold to the sides of the bowl.

When the strawberry mixture mounds slightly, spoon it carefully into the bowl lined with jelly roll. Place the frozen 20 centimetre (8-in.) cake on top, trimming if necessary to make it fit. Trim off any excess jelly roll that extends over the cake.

Cover and chill several hours or overnight.

Raspberry Purée
2 300-g pkgs. whole frozen raspberries, thawed
60 mL (4 tbsp.) sugar or to taste
15 mL (1 tbsp.) cornstarch
30 mL (2 tbsp.) raspberry liqueur

Simmer raspberries over low heat. Blend together the sugar and cornstarch and add. Simmer until slightly thickened. Add liqueur and cool.

A few hours before serving, unmold the pinwheel cake onto a serving platter. Thinly slice the second jelly roll, frozen, and place around the base as garnish. Return to refrigerator until serving time.

Slice and top with raspberry purée.

CHOCOLATE TRUFFLES

In this recipe, candied orange peel, finely chopped, could be substituted for the hazelnuts.

170 g (6 oz.) hazelnuts
300 g (10 oz.) good semi-sweet chocolate
125 g (4 oz.) unsalted butter
30 mL (2 tbsp.) Scotch, rye or bourbon
125 mL (½ cup) unsweetened cocoa

Place the hazelnuts on a baking sheet in a 180°C (350°F) oven for about 10 minutes. Remove and rub between a towel to remove the skins. Return the hazelnuts to the oven for another five minutes to toast them. Chop them finely while still hot.

In the top of a double boiler, or over hot water, melt the chocolate and butter. Add the Scotch with the finely ground hazelnuts. Blend well. Chill briefly in the refrigerator until the mixture holds its shape.

Form into 1 centimetre (½-in.) balls and roll in unsweetened cocoa. For a change of pace the balls could be rolled in coconut or icing sugar, or in a mixture of icing sugar and cocoa.

SUGAR PLUMS

125 mL (½ cup) butter
½ mL (⅛ tsp.) salt
375 mL (1½ cups) icing sugar
5 mL (1 tsp.) orange rind, grated
175 mL (¾ cup) walnuts, finely chopped
Brandy (optional)
2 large pkgs. pitted dates
Granulated sugar

Cream together the butter, salt and icing sugar until very light and fluffy. Add the orange rind, walnuts and a little brandy. Taste and add more sugar if needed.

Use this mixture to fill the pitted dates. Roll in sugar and allow to dry four or five hours before storing.

CHOCOLATE WALNUT FUDGE

500 mL (2 cups) icing sugar
250 mL (1 cup) cocoa
375 mL (1½ cups) butter
375 mL (1½ cups) walnuts, chopped
Walnut halves

Sift together the icing sugar and cocoa. Melt butter in a medium saucepan. Continue cooking until butter is hot and bubbly. Remove from heat. Blend hot butter into cocoa mixture. Stir in chopped nuts. Spread in a greased 2-litre (8-in.) square cake tin. Garnish with walnut halves if desired. Chill until set. Store in refrigerator. □

Festive Pheasant

Pheasant stars in this Christmas meal, and fittingly so, for it is the king of game birds, beloved of epicures for its delicate flavor and tender meat.

For centuries, hunters and chefs have debated the proper treatment of wild pheasant. Some advised removing the feathers immediately after the bird was shot; others believed that exposure to the air robbed the meat of its flavor, and they let the bird age in its fine plumage. Brillat-Savarin advocated hanging a pheasant until the flesh had begun to decompose; Teddy Roosevelt is said to have dangled an undressed brace from his saddle as he rode around in the scorching sun for 48 hours.

Fortunately, none of this is of concern to us. The pheasants we acquire from our butcher or supermarket are farm-raised; they have been plucked and hung and are ready to eat. About five and a half months old when they come to market, farm pheasants have been given a "finish" – that is, they have been fed a diet in their last days that produces a thin layer of fat under the skin. The extra fat and the youth of the birds guarantee tender eating. Farm raised pheasants should be roasted quickly at a high temperature until they are still slightly pink. This will take 45 to 60 minutes – a fact that could make Christmas cooks give up the hours of ruddy-cheeked work required to bring a turkey to the table.

Pheasant meat is also considered nutritionally superior. It is higher in protein and lower in cholesterol than red meat or domestic fowl. A 1.5-kilogram (3-lb.) bird will feed four, with a little bit extra for seconds.

As usual, planning is the key to making this attractive meal as much a pleasure for the cook as it is sure to be for the guests. To make the service somewhat easier, we suggest you let your guests help themselves to the shrimp mousse in the living room. You can then invite everyone to the table for the soup and salad, and offer the main course as a serve-yourself buffet. We have included recipes for a half-dozen hostess gifts, which you may want to present to your guests as you linger over coffee at the end of the meal.

Weeks ahead, if you are that well organized, you can prepare and freeze the curry soup, the Sauce Espagnole for the gravy, and the cake (as indicated in the recipe). A week before, make and refrigerate the dough for the chive rolls. Three to four days before the feast, start marinating the three pheasants and prepare the vegetable pâté. The day before, make the shrimp mousse, wash the spinach and slice the peppers and onion for the salad, and make sure you have bread for the stuffing.

On the morning of the meal, take the soup, sauce and cake out of the freezer, giving the cake five hours in the refrigerator to thaw. Make the balsamic vinaigrette and cook the pheasant giblets for the gravy. Knead the chive into the dough, shape the rolls and leave them to rise. Make and bake the potatoes, being prepared for spills when the milk bubbles over. You'll want to clean up before heating the oven to a high temperature for the pheasant. Prepare the stuffing and put it into its casserole. Several hours before dinner, ice the cake and bake the rolls.

The last stages in your preparation may be easier if you have two ovens, but you can manage quite nicely with one. An hour and a half before you want to eat, put the pheasants and the stuffing into the oven. If the

Cool and creamy: the shrimp mousse appetizer, seasoned with onion, olives, dill and Tabasco, set in a scallop shell mould; best served with a hearty black bread.

pheasants take longer than 45 minutes, remove the stuffing and keep it warm. Prepare the salad and reheat the soup. When the pheasants are done, cover them with foil (and several bath towels, if you like). Reduce the heat in the oven to 180°C (350°F) and reheat the vegetable terrine and the potatoes for 30 minutes. While the gravy simmers, serve the soup with the chive rolls, and then the salad. As your guests sip on the Gewürztraminer, carve the pheasants, proceeding as you would for a turkey. Make the breast slices nice and thin. Place pheasant, potatoes, vegetable terrine and gravy on the sideboard, breathe a deep sigh and say, "God bless us, everyone."

MENU *(Serves Twelve)*

- Shrimp Mousse
- Curried Nut Soup
- Chive Rolls
- Spinach Salad with Balsamic Vinaigrette
- Pheasant with Rice and Fruit Stuffing
- Potatoes in Tarragon Cream
- Hot Vegetable Pâté
- Brazil Nut Genoise with Cranberry/Raspberry Glaze

SHRIMP MOUSSE

A delicate variation of our favorite salmon pâté, this mousse will serve 12 easily as an hors-d'oeuvre. It also makes a nice, light luncheon dish. Make it at least one day ahead of serving.

1½ envelopes unflavored gelatine
250 mL (1 cup) water, divided
30 mL (2 tbsp.) fresh lemon juice
15 mL (1 tbsp.) onion, finely chopped
10 mL (2 tsp.) dill weed, dried
Dash of Tabasco (one or two drops)
Pinch of salt
300 g (10 oz.) shrimp, freshly cooked
175 mL (¾ cup) mayonnaise
60 mL (4 tbsp.) celery, finely chopped
60 mL (4 tbsp.) pimiento-stuffed green olives, finely chopped
125 mL (½ cup) whipping cream

Sprinkle gelatine over 125 millilitres (½ cup) cold water in a medium bowl. Let stand a few minutes to soften. Pour on 125 millilitres (½ cup) boiling water. Stir until gelatine is dissolved. Add lemon juice, onion, dill weed, Tabasco and salt. Stir to blend. Refrigerate until slightly thickened, about 15 minutes.

Process half the shrimp in a food processor or blender, or finely chop them. Add the mayonnaise and blend until thoroughly mixed. Stir the shrimp mixture into the gelatine and add the celery, olives and remaining shrimp, reserving a handful for garnish.

Beat the whipping cream until soft peaks form, and fold into the mixture. Spoon into an oiled 1½-litre (1½-qt.) mould and chill until set, about three to four hours. Before serving, unmould and garnish with extra shrimp. Serve with black bread triangles.

CURRIED NUT SOUP

A fine beginning to a festive meal, this curry-scented soup has a rich nutty flavor. It can be made ahead and frozen. Choose punch cups or small bowls for this soup, which will provide about 125 millilitres (½ cup) for each guest.

1 medium onion, chopped
2 green apples, peeled and chopped
60 mL (4 tbsp.) butter
2 cloves garlic, finely chopped
10 mL (2 tsp.) curry powder, or to taste
2 mL (½ tsp.) salt
1 L (4 cups) chicken stock or canned broth
250 mL (1 cup) nut butter (see note)

Sauté the onion and apple in the butter until soft. Add garlic, curry powder and salt. Cook two to three minutes more. Add chicken stock and simmer for 10 minutes. Cool slightly. Purée in blender, in batches if necessary, gradually adding the nut butter. The soup may be frozen at this point. At serving time, reheat but do not boil.

For nut butter:
Grind 500 millilitres (2 cups) of toasted nuts (cashews, almonds, peanuts or hazelnuts with skins removed) in a food processor or blender until coarse in texture. With the machine running, add 15 millilitres (1 tbsp.) vegetable oil and continue to process until smooth.

CHIVE ROLLS

The following recipe makes enough dough for four dozen rolls. The dough can be refrigerated for a week. We've used a quarter of the dough for a dozen chive rolls.

550 mL (2¼ cups) lukewarm water
30 mL (2 pkgs.) yeast
90 mL (6 tbsp.) butter
10 mL (2 tsp.) salt
125 mL (½ cup) sugar
3 eggs, beaten
2 L (8 cups) all-purpose white flour
125 mL (½ cup) chives, chopped

Measure 250 millilitres (1 cup) water at 40° to 43°C (105° to 110°F) into a large bowl. Dissolve 10 millilitres (2 tsp.) sugar in the water and add the dry yeast. Let stand 10 minutes and blend. To the remaining 300 millilitres (1¼ cups) of water add the butter, salt, sugar and beaten eggs. Blend well and add to the dissolved yeast.

Add flour to the liquid ingredients 250 millilitres (1 cup) at a time, mixing until the dough comes away from the sides of the bowl. Turn out onto a floured board and knead for only a few more minutes, adding in a little more flour. Place the dough in a large greased bowl. Brush the top with melted butter and cover with well-greased paper and a tight-fitting lid (a large dinner plate is good). This will prevent a crust forming on the dough. Place the dough in the refrigerator; it may be used after eight hours or within a week.

To make a dozen chive rolls, use a quarter of the dough. Knead in thoroughly 125 millilitres (½ cup) chopped chives. Grease medium muffin tins. With a rolling pin, roll out the dough to form a 30 by 25-centimetre (12 by 10-in.) rectangle, half a centimetre (¼ in.) thick. Loosen the dough from the board several times during the rolling to make sure it does not shrink. With a sharp greased knife, cut the dough lengthwise into five strips, each five centimetres (2 in.) wide. Brush the top of each strip with melted butter. Pile the strips evenly on top of one another, buttered side up. With a sharp, greased knife, cut the pile into 12 even pieces, using a quick, heavy stroke. Place in greased muffin pans cut-side down, separating the slices slightly on top. Cover and let rise until doubled (about 30 minutes to an hour). Bake for 20 minutes in a preheated 190°C (375°F) oven. Turn out onto a rack and brush the tops with melted butter.

SPINACH SALAD WITH BALSAMIC VINAIGRETTE

The day before, prepare the spinach, slice the red pepper and red onion and keep all chilled in plastic wrap. Make the dressing earlier on the day of the dinner so that flavors can meld.

4 bunches fresh spinach, or romaine or
*   other firm lettuces*
2 red peppers
1 large red onion
1 clove garlic, unpeeled
15 mL (1 tbsp.) Dijon mustard
45 mL (3 tbsp.) balsamic vinegar
*   (sherry vinegar is good also)*
Pinch of salt
A few grinds of black pepper
250 mL (1 cup) good olive oil

Wash and trim the spinach or lettuce. Core the peppers and cut or slice into chunks. Peel and slice the onion into rings. Set aside in a cool place.

Cut the garlic in half and set aside. Whisk the mustard and vinegar together in a medium bowl. Add salt and pepper to taste. Dribble the oil into the bowl in a slow steady stream, whisking constantly, until all the oil has been incorporated. The vinaigrette will be thick and creamy. Taste and adjust seasoning. Add whole garlic pieces, and let stand at room temperature for flavors to blend. Remove garlic and whisk again before serving.

Arrange spinach leaves on individual serving plates or a large flat platter. Scatter on red pepper and onion rings. Spoon some dressing over all; serve extra dressing separately.

PHEASANT WITH RICE AND FRUIT STUFFING

Pheasant should be cooked at a high temperature and should be slightly underdone when removed from the oven. Let it rest at least 10 minutes before carving. It is best to cook the stuffing separately rather than overcook the bird. A one-kilogram (2-lb.) pheasant yields two to three servings; a 1.5-kilogram (3-lb.) pheasant yields four generous servings.

750-mL bottle dry red wine
1 onion, chopped finely
2 bay leaves
Pinch each of rosemary, thyme, black
*   pepper*
5 to 6 juniper berries, crushed
30 mL (2 tbsp.) vinegar
125 mL (½ cup) oil
3 1.5-kg (3-lb.) pheasants

Mix together the wine, onion, bay leaves, rosemary, thyme, pepper, berries, vinegar and oil. Place the pheasants in a large bowl and add the marinade, or put each bird in a ziploc bag and add a third of the marinade. Marinate, refrigerated, for up to four days, turning at least once a day. The wine will stain the skin of the birds.

To cook, drain off the marinade, reserving 250 millilitres (1 cup) of the liquid. Pat the birds dry with a paper towel. Tie back the wings and wrap string around the legs to hold a snug shape. Roast in a preheated 220°C (425°F) oven for 45 minutes to one hour, or to an internal temperature of 70°C (160°F). Let stand for 10 minutes before carving.

Serve with stuffing and brown gravy.

Pheasant Gravy
A delicious gravy for any poultry, this is one you will want to keep on hand in the freezer.

500 mL (2 cups) Sauce Espagnole
*   (recipe follows)*
250 mL (1 cup) reserved marinade
Giblets, cooked and chopped

In a medium saucepan, bring the sauce espagnole, marinade and giblets to a boil. Reduce heat to a simmer and cook until gravy is thickened and smooth, about 15 minutes. Taste and adjust seasonings. Strain into a gravy boat.

Sauce Espagnole (Brown Sauce)
1 clove garlic, chopped
1 medium onion, chopped
1 carrot, chopped
60 mL (4 tbsp.) butter
60 mL (4 tbsp.) all-purpose white
*   flour*
750 mL (3 cups) beef stock or canned
*   broth*
75 mL (⅓ cup) tomato paste
Pinch of thyme
½ bay leaf, crumbled
Salt, pepper to taste

Sauté the garlic, onion and carrot in the butter over low heat until golden. Stir in the flour and also cook until golden. Gradually whisk in the beef stock, and then the tomato paste, thyme and bay leaf. Stirring constantly, cook until the sauce simmers and is thickened.

Cook gently and stir occasionally for 45 minutes to an hour until the sauce is reduced to about 500 millilitres (2 cups). Strain out the vegetables and season lightly. The sauce may be frozen at this point.

Stuffing
A useful rule of thumb in judging the amount of stuffing needed is to allow 125 millilitres (½ cup) for each pound of bird.

6 slices of day-old bread, cubed
250 mL (1 cup) wild rice, cooked, or
*   a mixture of white and brown rice*
125 mL (½ cup) raisins
60 mL (4 tbsp.) currants
250 mL (1 cup) dried apricots,
*   chopped*
30 to 45 mL (2 to 3 tbsp.) wine,
*   sherry or brandy*
1 medium onion, chopped
45 mL (3 tbsp.) butter
Herbs such as parsley, sage, thyme
Salt and pepper to taste

Place the bread cubes and rice in a large bowl. In a smaller bowl place the raisins, currants and apricots.

Add brandy to barely moisten the fruit. Let stand.

Place the onion and butter in a small pan and sauté until tender. Add to the bread mixture. Add the fruit and brandy. Toss lightly. If too dry, melt a little more butter and stir in. Season with the herbs, salt and pepper to your own taste.

Place in a greased casserole, cover and bake 30 to 40 minutes at 220°C (425°F) or until hot through.

POTATOES IN TARRAGON CREAM

This is best made the day of the party. It may be baked ahead and reheated for 30 minutes at 180°C (350°F) before serving. You may need two large casserole dishes to hold all the potatoes. Instant-blending flour is best for this dish.

12 potatoes, peeled and sliced thinly
90 mL (6 tbsp.) flour
125 mL (½ cup) butter
30 mL (2 tbsp.) chives, chopped
60 mL (4 tbsp.) fresh tarragon (or
  parsley or basil), finely chopped
10 mL (2 tsp.) salt
Freshly ground pepper
Paprika
500 to 750 mL (2 to 3 cups) light
  cream or milk for each casserole

Layer the potatoes in a baking dish to within a centimetre (½ in.) of the top. Dot each layer with butter, and sprinkle on flour, a few chives, herbs, salt, pepper and paprika. Pour over enough cream or milk to almost cover. The potatoes will sink lower as they bake. Bake, covered, for one hour at 180°C (350°F), then uncover and bake for a further half-hour or until potatoes are tender and golden.

HOT VEGETABLE PATE

This dish must be made a few days ahead of the party to give it time to firm. Do not freeze. Without a blender or food processor, making

Fair game: the pheasant, well marinated in wine, juniper berries and herbs, roasted to perfection and served with vegetable pâté, spinach salad and potatoes in tarragon cream.

a terrine or pâté is a time-consuming business. If you plan carefully, you will not have to rinse your work bowl between steps.

1 medium onion, finely chopped
60 mL (4 tbsp.) olive oil
2 medium cloves garlic, chopped
800-mL can whole tomatoes
7 mL (1½ tsp.) oregano
7 mL (1½ tsp.) basil
Salt and pepper to taste
350 g (¾ lb.) cauliflower florets
    (1 small head)
Pinch of cayenne
30 mL (2 tbsp.) butter
1 medium onion, chopped
1 clove garlic, minced
2 300-g pkgs. frozen spinach, thawed
    and squeezed dry
Pinch of nutmeg
1 whole chicken breast, approx. 250 g
    (½ lb.)
2 egg-whites
Salt and pepper
175 mL (¾ cup) whipping cream
Oil for preparing pan
1-L (1-qt.) jar grapevine leaves

Place one chopped onion in medium frypan and add olive oil. Sauté until onions are transparent. Add garlic. Cook for about one minute and add tomatoes, oregano, basil and a little salt and pepper. Cook over high heat, stirring from time to time. The fast cooking will help to reduce the sauce and make it thick. In about 15 minutes, when it has thickened, remove from heat, taste for seasonings and cool. Set aside.

Boil the cauliflower in water in a medium saucepan for about eight minutes, or until tender. Cool under cold running water. Purée in blender until smooth. Season with a pinch of cayenne. Set aside.

Melt the butter in a medium frypan and sauté the second onion until soft. Add the garlic and cook another two to three minutes. Add the spinach and cook briefly. Cool. Purée in blender until smooth. Season with a pinch of nutmeg. Set aside.

Cut the chicken into small chunks, place in food processor or blender and chop coarsely. Add the egg-whites and purée until smooth. With the machine running, add whipping cream.

Season lightly with a little salt and pepper. Divide the mixture into thirds and stir into the three vegetable mixtures. Chill until ready to bake.

Oil a 1.5-litre (6-cup) loaf pan or terrine mould (or shape of your choice), and line the bottom and sides with a single layer of grape leaves, shiny side facing pan and extra hanging over edges.

Spoon the tomato mixture into the prepared pan. Spread the spinach mixture over, and then spoon on the cauliflower mixture. Fold the grape leaves over the top and add a few more leaves, if necessary.

Cover the pan with parchment or foil and place in a larger baking pan. Pour hot water into the second pan to come halfway up the sides of the terrine.

Bake at 150°C (300°F) for one and a half hours, to an internal temperature of 65°C (150°F). Remove from oven and take off foil. Cool to room temperature in the same water bath. Drain the moisture that accumulates around the terrine and remove it from its pan. Wrap it well in foil and refrigerate for at least 24 hours, and up to four days. Bring to room temperature before reheating. Replace the foil-wrapped terrine in its baking pan. Heat at 180°C (350°F) for 20 to 30 minutes or until heated through.

BRAZIL NUT GENOISE WITH CRANBERRY RASPBERRY GLAZE

This cake can be made and frozen, leaving only the icing of the sides to be done on the day of the party. Serve with a little raspberry sorbet or ice cream.

6 large eggs, at room temperature
175 mL (¾ cup) sugar
2 mL (½ tsp.) vanilla
250 mL (1 cup) cake flour, sifted
90 mL (6 tbsp.) butter, melted and
    cooled
350 g (12 oz.) Brazil nuts, toasted,
    half finely ground and half coarsely
    chopped
Sugar syrup
Cranberry-raspberry glaze (recipes
    follow)
125 mL (½ cup) whipping cream

Preheat oven to 180°C (350°F). Grease and flour, or use parchment paper on, a 30 by 40-centimetre (12 by 15-in.) cookie sheet with sides.

Beat eggs and sugar until thick and light in color, about eight minutes. The mixture should make a thick ribbon. Whisk in vanilla. Place flour in a sieve and sift onto the egg mixture. Fold in quickly. Pour in the cooled butter and the finely ground Brazil nuts. Fold thoroughly. Pour into prepared pan and bake about 15 minutes or until cake is lightly browned and springs back to the touch. Cool on wire racks.

Turn out onto the counter and cut into thirds lengthwise. Brush each layer with a little sugar syrup and spread with glaze. Freeze at this point.

Allow to thaw in the refrigerator about five hours before icing with whipped cream and decorating with coarsely chopped nuts.

Sugar Syrup
Any syrup left over will keep in the refrigerator for about four weeks.

125 mL (½ cup) water
125 mL (½ cup) sugar
60 mL (4 tbsp.) liqueur, such as
    Kirsch

Bring water and sugar to a boil. Stir to dissolve sugar. Boil without stirring for five minutes. Cool. Stir in liqueur. Brush onto surface of cake. Do not soak the cake.

Cranberry-Raspberry Glaze
This glaze will keep, refrigerated, for about four weeks.

170 g (6 oz.) fresh cranberries
Juice of 1 lemon
125 mL (½ cup) sugar
425-g pkg. frozen raspberries in syrup
60 mL (4 tbsp.) cornstarch
30 mL (2 tbsp.) butter
15 mL (1 tbsp.) liqueur, such as
    Kirsch

Cook cranberries, lemon juice and 60 millilitres (4 tbsp.) sugar in medium saucepan over low heat until berries are soft and pop. Stir frequently.

Drain raspberries into a small

Happy endings: the brazil nut genois with cranberry-raspberry glaze, washed down with coffee and cognac.

bowl and press out as much liquid from the berries as possible. Discard pulp.

When cranberries are soft, press juices through a sieve into the raspberry juice. Discard pulp. Press juices again through a very fine sieve. Discard pulp. There should be 500 millilitres (2 cups) liquid. Pour into a medium saucepan.

Mix together the remaining sugar and cornstarch. Stir into juices. Cook over medium heat, stirring constantly, until thick and bubbly. Remove from heat and stir in butter and liqueur. Cool thoroughly. May be stored in the refrigerator at this point.

Reserve about 60 millilitres (4 tbsp.) of the glaze for the sides. Spread the remaining glaze over the three oblongs of cake. Stack the layers, keeping the neatest one for the top. May be frozen at this point.

Once the cake has thawed, and a few hours before serving time, whip 125 millilitres (½ cup) whipping cream until soft peaks form, fold in the reserved glaze and whip again until smooth. Spread along the sides and pipe into rosettes along the edges. Press the reserved, coarsely chopped nuts into the sides. ☐

Five Courses to Midnight

There are eight of you, good friends who like food and wine and who agree that the best way to approach the beginning of a new year is to sit together around a table, eating slowly, talking about the old year, pulling the cork on yet another bottle, toasting tomorrow.

You'll begin this New Year's Eve dinner at eight, leisurely shedding the outside world as you give in to the group and the evening. In the living room in front of the fire, there'll be champagne, because nothing is more festive and nothing more stimulating.

About nine, you'll move to the table for the first of five courses – a lobster, caviar and endive salad. Perfect with more champagne. By now the conversation is easy, familiar, and it's time to make this a party, to pause in the eating and drinking, to put on whatever music you all love – and to dance.

The second course looks seasonal and innocent – a red pepper timbale on a bed of puréed spinach – but it has a spicy bite that won't allow it to be taken for granted. The red wine is open now. Stéphane Grappelli and Yehudi Menuhin are whipping out old Fred Astaire tunes. Everyone dances.

Time then to pause, to rest, to prepare for the main course with a champagne sorbet. Just a few scoops in tiny, frosty glasses.

Then, the main course – chicken and julienned vegetables and rice – sautéed ahead of time and needing only reheating at the last minute, so that the cook can wear her best silk dress without fear. In the space of a few Sinatra ballads, it's ready.

Dessert comes before midnight. Something spectacular but light for people who don't often indulge. A fragile, deliquescent apricot

but there are no points for neatness now.

There is only the approaching hour. The chilled Sauternes. The tin horns. The paper streamers. The kisses. The toasts. And the momentarily unblemished newness of the new year.

MENU *(Serves Eight)*

- Lobster, Caviar and Endive Salad
- Hazelnut Oil Vinaigrette
- Red Pepper and Tomato Timbale with Spinach Purée
- Champagne Sorbet
- Breast of Chicken in Herbed Wine Sauce with Julienne of Leeks and Carrots
- Two-Rice Pilaf
- Meringue Cake with Apricot Cream

LOBSTER, CAVIAR AND ENDIVE SALAD

For the sweetest taste, choose small oval heads of Belgian endive that are as white as possible. Make the salad early in the day and keep chilled.

2 lobsters, 750 g (1½ lbs.) each or
*   500 mL (2 cups) fresh lobster meat*
30 mL (2 tbsp.) fresh parsley
1 bay leaf
5 to 6 heads Belgian endive
250 mL (1 cup) watercress, washed
*   and trimmed*
125 mL (½ cup) hazelnut oil
*   vinaigrette (see recipe below)*
40 mL (8 tsp.) salmon caviar

Cook the lobsters in boiling, salted water with the herbs until done, about 15 minutes. Cool in cold water. Drain, crack and remove the meat from the shells.

Trim the stems of the endive and separate into leaves. Drizzle endive and watercress with vinaigrette and place on serving plates. Garnish with lobster meat and caviar. Pass extra dressing.

Serve chilled with crispy crackers.

HAZELNUT OIL VINAIGRETTE

Hazelnut oil can usually be found in gourmet sections of specialty stores. It is expensive and perishable, and so should be kept refrigerated. To give extra flavor to any basic dressing recipe, just add a tablespoon or two. If you can't find hazelnut oil, use a regular oil and vinegar dressing with an extra touch of lemon juice.

45 mL (3 tbsp.) fresh lemon juice
250 mL (1 cup) hazelnut oil
Salt and pepper to taste

Whisk the lemon juice and oil together. Add salt and pepper and taste for seasonings.

RED PEPPER AND TOMATO TIMBALE WITH SPINACH PUREE

A timbale is a vegetable or meat custard made in individual or large moulds, turned out to serve, and often coated or set on a sauce. As fresh tomatoes are not very nice in winter, use a canned sauce.

2 red bell peppers
1 213-mL can tomato sauce
250 mL (1 cup) half-and-half cream
4 eggs
2 mL (½ tsp.) paprika
2 mL (½ tsp.) cayenne (or to taste)
Salt and pepper to taste

Remove the skin of the peppers by placing them on a foil-lined baking sheet and broiling until blackened and blistered on all sides. Place in a paper bag to steam for five to 10 minutes. Peel and seed under cool running water. Purée.

Mix together the puréed peppers and the remaining ingredients.

The big countdown begins with a lobster, caviar and endive salad and a red pepper and tomato timbale.

A refreshing champagne sorbet to cool the palate, followed by deboned breast of chicken in a wine sauce, with pilaf, leeks and carrots.

Pour into buttered individual moulds or one large mould, filling only two-thirds full. Place in a large container with enough very hot water to cover the bottom half of the moulds (à bain-marie).

Bake at 160°C (325°F) for 30 to 60 minutes depending on the size of the mould. The water should never boil. The timbales are done when a thin knife inserted just off centre comes out clean. Remove from the hot-water bath to cool.

The timbales may be made ahead to this point. At serving time, reheat them either in the microwave at 50 per cent power (medium) for one to two minutes or covered, in a hot-water bath, at 180°C (350°F) for 10 minutes. Gently run a knife around the edge of the mould and turn out on a warm serving plate. Spoon the heated spinach purée (recipe follows) around the base. Or, you may place the purée and the timbale on a serving plate and heat both in the microwave at 50 per cent (medium) power for one to two minutes.

Spinach Purée
With its delightful texture and flavor, this purée can be served on its own.

2 300-g pkgs. of frozen chopped
  spinach, thawed and drained
1 medium onion, finely chopped
30 mL (2 tbsp.) butter or oil
1 clove garlic, finely chopped
Freshly grated nutmeg
Salt and pepper to taste
125 mL (½ cup) chicken stock or
  canned broth
250 mL (1 cup) whipping cream or
  half-and-half cream (or more, if
  desired)

Squeeze all the moisture from the spinach and set aside. Sauté the onion in the butter until soft, add the garlic and cook for one or two minutes. Add the spinach and season with nutmeg, salt and pepper. Stir and cook for one minute. Add the chicken stock and mix thoroughly.

Purée the mixture, adding 125 millilitres (½ cup) of the cream, until very smooth. Add enough of the remaining cream to make a thick sauce. Adjust the seasonings.

Reheat gently in a pan to serve with the red pepper timbale or follow the microwave instructions above.

CHAMPAGNE SORBET

A wonderfully refreshing, between-courses palate cleanser that will clear your taste buds. Do not serve too much. A scoop or two in a tiny cup, small wine glass or even a plain egg cup will do.

300 mL (1¼ cups) sugar
125 mL (½ cup) fresh lemon juice
  (about 3 lemons)
150 mL (⅔ cup) pink champagne
2 egg-whites

Dissolve 250 millilitres (1 cup) of the sugar in 300 millilitres (1¼ cups) of water. Bring to a boil and remove from the heat. Stir in the lemon juice and champagne. Transfer to a medium bowl. Cover and chill.

In a small saucepan, dissolve the remaining sugar in 30 millilitres (2 tbsp.) water. Bring to a boil and cook for one minute. Remove from the heat.

Beat the egg-whites until foamy. Gradually beat the hot syrup into the whites in a thin, steady stream. Continue to beat for three to five minutes or until the egg-whites are stiff. Quickly stir the champagne syrup into the egg-whites. They will remain separate. Pour into the container of an ice-cream maker and freeze according to the manufacturer's instructions.

Turn the sorbet, which will be soft, into a covered container and place in the freezer until firm, about four hours or overnight.

BREAST OF CHICKEN IN HERBED WINE SAUCE WITH JULIENNE OF LEEKS AND CARROTS

Cilantro adds an interesting flavor to this easy and elegant dish. There is no need to refrigerate the partially prepared chicken or vegetables if the final dish is made within two to three hours.

60 mL (4 tbsp.) butter
30 mL (2 tbsp.) oil

4 whole chicken breasts, boned and
  halved (may be skinned if desired)
4 leeks, white part only, finely
  julienned
8 carrots, cut into julienne to match the
  length of the leeks
375 mL (1½ cups) white wine or
  chicken stock or canned broth
250 mL (1 cup) whipping cream
60 mL (4 tbsp.) fresh herbs such as
  cilantro or parsley or 10 mL (2
  tsp.) dried herbs such as basil,
  thyme or rosemary
Salt and pepper to taste

Heat the butter and oil in a large frypan until very hot. Add the chicken, skin side down, and reduce the heat to medium high. Sauté until golden, about five minutes. Turn and sauté the other side for two to three minutes. Remove from the pan and set aside.

Sauté the leeks and carrots for two to three minutes in the same pan. Add the wine and simmer until the vegetables are just tender-crisp, about five minutes. May be made ahead to this point.

To serve, reheat the vegetables in the liquid and add the chicken. Cover with a lid or foil and steam for three to five minutes or until the chicken is done. Remove the chicken to heated serving plates. Remove the vegetables with a slotted spoon and divide among the plates.

Bring the wine to a hard boil and cook until reduced by half. Add the cream and bring to boiling again. Boil, stirring, until of a saucelike consistency. Add the herbs and seasonings. Spoon over the chicken. Serve with Two-Rice Pilaf and pass extra sauce.

TWO RICE PILAF

An interesting dish that can have many variations. Make this a day or two ahead and reheat in the oven or microwave.

250 mL (1 cup) each of two kinds of
  rice such as pecan, long grain
  brown, long grain white, basmati
250 mL (1 cup) jumbo Thompson
  seedless raisins (found in health food
  stores)
250 mL (1 cup) whole almonds,
  toasted and coarsely chopped

*60 mL (4 tbsp.) parsley, finely
  chopped
Salt and pepper*

Place the rice in a medium
saucepan and add water, covering
by at least 2.5 centimetres (1 in.).
Bring to a boil, turn the heat
down, cover and simmer until
tender, about 10 to 15 minutes,
depending on the kind of rice
used. Drain off excess water. Place
in an ovenproof serving dish. Add
the raisins, almonds, parsley and
salt and pepper to taste. Cover
until ready to serve.

At serving time, reheat in the
oven or microwave (on medium
high). Moisten with chicken stock
if desired.

MERINGUE CAKE WITH APRICOT CREAM

A melt-in-your-mouth dream
dessert that will earn you raves.
Make the meringues a few days
before and store in an airtight
container until ready to use. For a
melting texture, put the cake
together up to six hours before
serving.

*6 large egg-whites
250 g (8 oz. or 1½ cups) fine berry
  sugar
Pinch of salt*

The hour is near, spirits are rising. It is time to serve the meringue.

Beat the egg-whites in a clean
mixing bowl until frothy. Add the
sugar, 30 millilitres (2 tbsp.) at a
time, along with the pinch of salt,
until the sugar is dissolved and the
mixture is stiff.

Line a large baking sheet with
parchment paper. Form two 20-
centimetre (8-in.) circles of the
meringue on the paper, keeping
enough meringue to pipe rosettes
around the outside rim of one of
the rounds, which will be the top
layer.

Bake in a cool oven 150°C
(300°F) for about 50 to 60 minutes
or until very lightly colored and
quite dry. Turn the oven off and
leave for one hour. Remove from
the oven and cool on racks. The
meringues can be stored for several
weeks in a tight tin or in the
freezer. They will looked cracked;
it is a characteristic of a meringue.

When ready to serve, spoon
some apricot cream onto the
bottom layer. Put the top layer on
and either add more apricot cream
or leave it plain. Chill until serving
time.

Apricot Cream
This is a delightful dessert on its
own as well as a wonderful filling
for meringues.

*250 g (8 oz.) dried apricots, soaked
  overnight in enough water to cover
120 mL (8 tbsp.) sugar
Juice of 1 lemon
30 mL (2 tbsp.) apricot brandy
500 mL (2 cups) whipping cream
60 mL (4 tbsp.) icing sugar*

Place the soaked apricots and their
soaking liquid in a medium pot,
add the sugar and the lemon juice,
cover and simmer gently until soft
enough to purée. This can be done
in the microwave. Do not drain
off the liquid.

Purée the apricots and their
liquid until smooth. Place in a
medium bowl. Stir in the brandy.

Whip the cream with the icing
sugar until soft peaks form. Fold
into the apricot purée. Chill until
ready to use. ☐

Mid-Winter Nibblies

January being one of the year's coldest months, we are wont to seek out the fireside after a day outdoors, and to warm our chilled souls with snacks of substance. That being the case, we have prepared a potpourri that includes a hearty meal in a pouch imported from the United Kingdom.

Wherever there were mines in America the miners of Cornwall and Wales could be found, with their now-famous "lunch" of Cornish pasties (pronounced past-ees): large rounds of pastry filled with cooked or uncooked cubed or chopped meat, onion, potatoes and a root vegetable (usually carrots or turnips), all moistened with a rich, thick gravy. Usually, the pastry was made with a heavy dough so that the miners could wrap the pasties in cloth or newspaper, tuck them into a pocket and go down into the mines to work.

In addition to those already mentioned, fillings can include ground meat, firm-fleshed fish, canned tuna or shellfish and are best if moistened with gravy or even a little soup, as the pasties are apt to be a bit dry. Try making them in small rounds about five to eight centimetres (2 to 3 in.) in diameter and serving them as cocktail bites.

It's not likely that many readers will be down in the mines when they partake of the pasties in this menu, but fireside on one of winter's frigid evenings should serve just as well.

MENU *(Serves Four)*

- Deluxe Travellers' Mix
- Creamy Carrot Soup
- Cornish Pasties
- New York-Style Cheesecake
- Hot Mexicana Chocolate

DELUXE TRAVELLERS' MIX

This recipe is for backpacking, school lunches or premeal snacks. We have it courtesy of Earth's Good Harvest natural-food store, out of their secret-recipe file.

125 mL (½ cup) whole, unblanched almonds
125 mL (½ cup) cashews
125 mL (½ cup) raisins
125 mL (½ cup) honey-glazed papaya, coarsely chopped
125 mL (½ cup) honey-glazed pineapple, coarsely chopped
60 mL (4 tbsp.) pumpkin seeds
60 mL (4 tbsp.) sunflower seeds

Mix ingredients together, adding other nuts and seeds of your choice, if desired. If you would like this to form into bars, add some cut-up dates, figs or apricots and press into rolls.

CREAMY CARROT SOUP

This is a basic soup recipe in which any vegetable can be substituted for the carrot. Makes approximately 1½ litres (6 cups).

30 mL (2 tbsp.) butter
1 finely sliced onion
2 cloves garlic, crushed
1 L (4 cups) sliced carrots
1¼ L (5 cups) beef stock or canned broth
250 mL (1 cup) whipping cream
Salt and pepper
Parsley for garnish

Melt the butter in a heavy saucepan and add onion and garlic. Sauté until onion is soft but not brown. Be careful not to burn the garlic. Add carrots and cook, covered, for about 10 minutes. Add the beef stock and simmer over low heat about 30 minutes. The vegetable should be very soft.

Remove soup from heat and let cool slightly. Purée in a blender or food processor. The whipping cream can be added either lightly whipped or as is. Season with salt and pepper.

Serve hot or chilled. Top with a dollop of additional whipped cream, if desired, or just a sprig of parsley.

CORNISH PASTIES

Makes six 15-centimetre (6-in.) pasties.

250 g (½ lb.) round steak, boneless chuck or ground meat cut into 1-cm (½-in.) cubes
1 small potato, peeled and cut into 1-cm (½-in.) cubes
1 small onion, peeled and cut into 1-cm. (½-in.) cubes
1 carrot, peeled and cut into 1-cm (½-in.) cubes
1 small turnip (optional), peeled and cut into 1-cm (½-in.) cubes
5 mL (1 tsp.) salt
2 mL (½ tsp.) freshly ground pepper
15 mL (1 tbsp.) Worcestershire sauce
15 mL (1 tbsp.) parsley, chopped
125 to 175 mL (½ to ¾ cup) thick, rich gravy or soup
1 egg mixed with 15 mL (1 tbsp.) water (for glaze)

Mix together all the ingredients, except the egg glaze, adding enough gravy to bind the mixture together.

On a lightly floured board, roll out the dough (recipe follows) and cut it into 15 to 18-cm (6 or 7-in.) rounds (a plate makes a good guide) about 3 mm (⅛ in.) thick.

For each pasty put about 30 mL (2 tbsp.) of the filling in a strip down the centre of each round. Dampen the edges with a little of the egg glaze. Fold one side of the round up over the filling. Then turn up the other side of the round and press the edges of the dough together snugly, starting at one end and forming a thick band of dough about 1 cm (½ in.) wide along the seam. With your finger, crimp the band into a decorative rope or scalloped fluting. The pasties may be refrigerated or frozen at this point.

When ready to bake, brush the pasties with egg glaze and place carefully on an ungreased baking sheet. Bake at 230°C (450°F) for 10 to 12 minutes. Then reduce the heat to 180°C (350°F) and bake for a further 30 minutes or until a dark golden color. Serve hot or at room temperature. Any extra gravy can be served on the side.

Pastry
Use your favorite pastry recipe or try this one. Weighing ingredients means that the results will be the same every time.

400 mL (approx. 1⅔ cups) all-purpose white flour or wholewheat pastry flour
Pinch of salt
120 mL (8 tbsp. or 4 oz.) butter, frozen and coarsely chopped
60 mL (4 tbsp. or 2 oz.) Crisco or lard, frozen and coarsely chopped
125 mL (approx. ½ cup) water,

Sift the flour and salt into a mixing bowl. Cut in the butter with two knives or a pastry cutter until the mixture resembles small peas. Or place the flour and salt in the work bowl of the food processor and pulse briefly. Add the butter and Crisco and process for five to 10 seconds or until the mixture resembles small peas. Turn out into a large bowl.

Make a well in the centre, add two-thirds of the water and mix quickly with a round-bladed knife. Add additional water as necessary until the dough forms a ball.

Turn out on a floured board and knead lightly until smooth. Form into two flat discs, wrap in wax paper and chill for at least one hour.

NEW YORK STYLE CHEESECAKE
Creamy, rich and delicious, a small piece of this cake goes a long way. Slice at home and place each piece in individual containers for travelling. Makes one 25-centimetre (10-in.) cake. The crust is crumbly to make but will smooth together as you work at it with your hands. If it's still a little crumbly after chilling and won't roll out, just break off pieces and press them into the pan, as you would a cookie crust. The pan must be at least 25 centimetres (10 in.) in diameter, as this is a lot of filling.

Shortbread Crust
375 mL (1½ cups) all-purpose white flour
75 mL (⅓ cup) white sugar
1 large egg yolk
125 mL (½ cup) butter, softened
125 mL (½ cup) carob or chocolate chips (chocolate mint makes a tasty change)

Mix the flour and sugar together. Add the beaten yolk and butter and blend well. Knead until as smooth as possible. Shape into a ball and chill.

Press into a 25-centimetre (10-in.) springform pan. Spread the carob chips over the crust. Bake at 200°C (400°F) for 10 to 15 minutes or until golden and the chips are melted. Remove from the oven and spread the chips evenly over the crust. Cool.

Filling
5 250-g pkgs. cream cheese
425 mL (1¾ cups) white sugar
45 mL (3 tbsp.) all-purpose white flour
2 mL (½ tsp.) grated orange rind
2 large egg yolks
5 large eggs
60 mL (4 tbsp.) whipping cream

Beat the cream cheese until light and fluffy. Add the sugar and flour and beat until smooth. Add the grated rind, yolks and eggs, one at a time, beating until thoroughly blended. Stir in the cream and mix briefly.

Pour into prepared pie crust and bake 15 minutes at 250°C (450°F), then reduce the oven to 100°C (200°F) and bake for one hour. When the cake is done, turn off the oven and let it cool slowly – in the oven – for one more hour. There will be a few cracks in the crust. Remove from oven and cool to room temperature. Chill. Cut with a hot knife.

Fruit Sauce
This is a lovely addition to the cheesecake. The best fruits are raspberries or blackberries.

300 g (10 oz.) frozen berries, thawed and strained
60 mL (4 tbsp.) sugar, or to taste
15 mL (1 tbsp.) cornstarch
15 mL (1 tbsp.) kirsch, brandy or raspberry liqueur

Place the strained berry juice in a small pot. Mix together the sugar and cornstarch and stir into the juice. Heat over medium heat until the sugar is dissolved. Cool. Stir in the liqueur. Chill.

HOT MEXICANA CHOCOLATE
A thick, exotic brew that is wonderful on a winter picnic. It should be served frothy, but don't shake your thermos, since the hot mixture may cause the lid to pop off. Whisk it up before serving. This mixture can be mixed half and half with hot coffee to create a special taste. Serves four.

60 g (2 oz.) semi-sweet chocolate, coarsely chopped or grated
500 mL (2 cups) milk
250 mL (1 cup) whipping cream
45 mL (3 tbsp.) white sugar
5 mL (1 tsp.) cinnamon
Pinch of cloves (optional)
Pinch of salt
1 egg
5 mL (1 tsp.) vanilla

In a medium saucepan, melt the chocolate in the milk and cream. Add the sugar, spices and salt. Whisk the mixture over medium heat until it comes to a boil, and then lower the heat and cook for five minutes, whisking continuously.

In a small bowl, beat the egg and vanilla together until frothy. Slowly add a little of the hot chocolate to the egg to warm it up, then return the egg mixture to the hot chocolate mixture, whisking all the time.

Whisk for another three minutes and serve at once. This mixture can be reheated and whisked up again successfully.

For variation, try these: Choc-Ole, adding 60 mL (4 tbsp.) instant coffee with the spices; Choco-Mint, adding 60 mL (4 tbsp.) mint liqueur and stirring with a candy cane; or Choco-Rum, adding 60 mL (4 tbsp.) rum and stirring with a cinnamon stick. □

Cozy cuisine: travellers' mix and vegetable sticks to munch on; creamy carrot soup, hot Mexicana chocolate and cornish pasties to warm the soul; cheesecake for good luck.

The Salad in Winter

It's a difficult beast — a winter salad. Nine-tenths of the time it's made of snoozy iceberg lettuce, and we wonder, as we tear up yet another head and pour on Paul Newman's bottled dressing, why we're bothering. What makes us keep trying to create a salad when good greens are impossible to find? It's the piquancy, of course, the kick to the palate that a tangy dressing gives. The problem, then, when the sorrel and chive are buried under the snow and when there's no arugula or mâche at the market, is to find an intriguing base to carry the dressing.

Our winter salads are built with hearty ingredients — beans, rice, potatoes, pasta and poultry. We add readily available extras — nuts, raisins and winter vegetables. We season with a variety of vinaigrettes, made with wonderful oils and vinegars, and we serve these filling winter salads warm.

Beyond the neutral and bland corn and sunflower oils that we so often choose for salad dressing, there's a range of salad-enhancing oils. You might try a costly French walnut oil; buy it in small quantities and use it up soon because it is perishable. Or a delicate almond oil, equally expensive and perishable.

But once you have tried it, you will find yourself turning most often to extra-virgin olive oil. Extracted in the first, cold, stone pressing of hand-picked olives, extra-virgin olive oil has a flavor that can lift an ordinary salad to the sublime. The Italians pick their olives semi-ripe and produce an oil that is golden green in color with a fruity flavor; the French use ripe

Salads of substance: cubed potatoes cooked in mustard; corkscrew pasta with radishes and green onions in a balsamic vinaigrette; and a Sicilian medley of beans with winter vegetables.

black olives to get the sweeter, golden oil they prefer. If you get your hands on a good Olio Extravergine d'Oliva, keep it in the dark in a cool place, and use it in ways that allow its flavor to prevail.

You can enliven ordinary oils by infusing them with herbs: add 60 millilitres (¼ cup) of chopped fresh herbs to 500 millilitres (2 cups) of oil and let stand, tightly capped, for two weeks, shaking the bottle from time to time. Strain out the herbs through cheesecloth and use the oil within three months.

These days, the choice of salad vinegars is wide and varied. Cider, white and malt vinegars are simply too sharp-tasting for salads. Try instead wine or champagne vinegars. Red wine vinegar combines well with olive oil to make a dressing bold enough to stand up to tangy greens; white wine vinegar is a good match for milder greens; and sherry vinegar goes nicely with nut oils.

Herb and fruit vinegars are easy to make at home. Combine one litre (1 qt.) white wine vinegar and 125 millilitres (½ cup) of chopped herbs in a non-metallic container and let steep for a month, stirring at half time with a wooden spoon. Strain out the herbs through cheesecloth and store the vinegar in sterilized jars. Fruit vinegars require 500 millilitres (2 cups) of bruised (but not crushed) fruit to one litre (1 qt.) of wine vinegar. After steeping for two days, heat the vinegar to the boiling point, strain out the fruit and store your vinegar in sterilized bottles.

RICE MEDLEY

A salad variation of the pilaf we featured in our New Year's Eve supper last month, this recipe makes an elegant luncheon when topped with bright pink hand-peeled shrimp. You can double the recipe, but to keep the salad light don't increase the amount of barley. For the rice, use basmati, cajun or the wonderful Country Wild Rice found at health food stores. This blend contains long-grain brown rice, a California rice

called wehani and an unusual small black rice of the japonica type. Serves four.

125 mL (½ cup) raw rice
125 mL (½ cup) barley
125 mL (½ cup) raisins
125 mL (½ cup) whole almonds, toasted and coarsely chopped
30 mL (2 tbsp.) parsley, finely chopped
Vinaigrette dressing
Lettuce or romaine for garnish

Place the rice and barley in a medium saucepan and add water to cover by 2.5 centimetres (1 in.). Bring to a boil, turn down the heat, cover and simmer until tender, about 10 to 15 minutes depending on the type of rice used. Drain off excess water.

Place in a serving bowl, add the raisins, nuts and parsley and toss with a few spoonfuls of your favorite dressing. Serve at room temperature on a lettuce leaf and pass extra dressing.

SICILIAN SALAD

Warm beans topped with marinated winter vegetables make a filling dish for cold days. Serves four.

375 mL (1½ cups) small white beans
250 mL (1 cup) chicken stock or canned broth
1 onion, finely chopped
30 mL (2 tbsp.) parsley, finely chopped
15 mL (1 tbsp.) oregano, finely chopped
Freshly ground pepper
30 mL (2 tbsp.) vinaigrette
3 carrots, peeled and sliced
1 small turnip, peeled and sliced
1 small cauliflower, broken into florets
1 medium tomato, cut into small chunks
Vinaigrette
Lettuce or romaine for garnish

Cover the beans with five centimetres (2 in.) of water and let stand overnight. Drain. Place in a saucepan and cover with the same quantity of fresh water. Bring to a boil and simmer until barely tender. Drain. Add the chicken broth, onion, parsley and oregano. Stir well. Bring to a boil and cook

until the liquid has just evaporated. Spoon into a bowl to cool. Season with pepper to taste and stir in 30 millilitres (2 tbsp.) vinaigrette.

Cook the carrots, turnips and cauliflower until tender crisp. Place in a bowl, add the tomato and toss with vinaigrette to coat.

When ready to serve, gently reheat the beans. Place on a leaf of lettuce and top with the vegetables. Pass extra dressing.

NOUVELLE POTATO SALAD

For this salad, a wonderfully flavored mustard is cooked with potato cubes, which are served warm or at room temperature. The salad is spectacular by itself but could have finely diced ham scattered over top. We used Sable & Rosenfeld's Black Peppercorn Mustard, but we suggest you also try Stone County Specialities' Beer Mustard. Depending on the size of the potatoes, plan on serving two per person when making this recipe as a salad course.

30 mL (2 tbsp.) mustard
125 mL (½ cup) water
4 potatoes, peeled and cut into 2.5-cm (1-in.) cubes
Lettuce for garnish

Place the mustard and water in a medium saucepan. Bring to a boil and add the potato pieces. Stir well. Cook until the potatoes are tender, stirring often, about 10 minutes. Serve at once, or at room temperature, on a lettuce leaf.

PASTA SALAD

Colorful fusilla pasta, found dried in bulk-food and health-food stores, is used with a balsamic vinaigrette to create an interesting flavor.

375 mL (1½ cups) dried fusilla pasta or small macaroni
5 or 6 radishes, sliced
3 or 4 green onions, sliced
Balsamic vinaigrette (see below)

Cook the pasta or macaroni until tender, about 20 minutes. Toss with radishes, green onions and a few spoonfuls of the vinaigrette. Serve on a lettuce leaf, warm or at room temperature. Pass extra dressing.

WHICH CAME FIRST SALAD

For a different salad, try any poultry – chicken, turkey, duck or pheasant – with a sweet and sour dressing. Serves four.

8 slices grilled, poached or roasted poultry
1 medium red onion, finely chopped
2 green onions, coarsely chopped
4 hard-boiled eggs
Toasted sesame seeds
Sweet and sour vinaigrette (see below)
Buckwheat noodles, vermicelli or sautéed shredded red cabbage

Slice the meat into thin rounds or shred into strips. Toss with the onions. Arrange over the noodles, vermicelli or cabbage and spoon over the dressing. Garnish with slices of hard-boiled egg and sprinkle with sesame seeds.

As a variation, mix the chicken and onions in the dressing and let stand for half an hour. Place over the cabbage and garnish with egg slices and sesame seeds.

SWEET AND SOUR VINAIGRETTE

Blend together:
250 mL (1 cup) light vegetable oil
175 mL (¾ cup) white vinegar
125 mL (½ cup) sugar
30 mL (2 tbsp.) soy sauce
2 mL (½ tsp.) dry mustard
1 mL (¼ tsp.) freshly ground black pepper

BALSAMIC VINAIGRETTE

75 mL (⅓ cup) balsamic or sherry vinegar
5 mL (1 tsp.) lemon juice
Pinch of dry mustard
1 small shallot, minced
Finely minced thyme, to taste
Salt and freshly ground pepper
250 mL (1 cup) olive oil

In a small bowl, mix together the vinegar, lemon juice, mustard, shallot, thyme, salt and pepper.

Slowly whisk in the olive oil to make a creamy vinaigrette.

ITALIAN VINAIGRETTE

Blend together:
250 mL (1 cup) vegetable oil
60 mL (4 tbsp.) fresh lemon juice
60 mL (4 tbsp.) white wine vinegar
2 cloves garlic, crushed
10 mL (2 tsp.) seasoned salt
5 mL (1 tsp.) dry mustard
2 mL (½ tsp.) salt
1 mL (¼ tsp.) dry red chilies, crushed (optional)

FRENCH VINAIGRETTE

Blend together:
175 mL (¾ cup) mixed vegetable and olive oils
60 mL (4 tbsp.) white wine vinegar
1 clove garlic, chopped
Pinch of dry mustard
1 mL (¼ tsp.) each oregano and basil
Salt and pepper to taste

Add chopped fresh parsley to mixture, if desired.

RED WINE VINAIGRETTE

Blend together:
125 mL (½ cup) olive oil
75 mL (5 tbsp.) red wine vinegar
1 clove garlic, crushed
5 mL (1 tsp.) oregano
5 mL (1 tsp.) dried dill
Salt and pepper to taste

MUSTARD VINAIGRETTE

Blend together:
125 mL (½ cup) olive oil
75 mL (5 tbsp.) red or white wine vinegar
15 mL (1 tbsp.) Dijon mustard, or to taste
Salt and pepper to taste

BASIL VINAIGRETTE

Use basil or any favorite herb.

Blend together:
75 mL (⅓ cup) red wine vinegar
1 mL (¼ tsp.) dry mustard
Salt and pepper to taste
15 mL (1 tbsp.) fresh basil, chopped or 5 mL (1 tsp.) dried
Whisk in:
150 mL (⅔ cup) olive oil

LEMON FRENCH DRESSING

Blend together:
45 mL (3 tbsp.) lemon juice
2 mL (½ tsp.) salt
1 mL (¼ tsp.) pepper
1 mL (¼ tsp.) sugar
1 mL (¼ tsp.) dry mustard
125 mL (½ cup) vegetable oil

WALNUT OIL DRESSING

Mix together:
60 mL (4 tbsp.) red or white wine vinegar
15 mL (1 tbsp.) Dijon mustard
Salt and pepper to taste

Whisk in:
125 mL (½ cup) vegetable oil
60 mL (4 tbsp.) walnut oil □

Breakfast for Lovers

This special feature celebrates the day of hearts, flowers and romance. Saint Valentine, a Roman priest and martyr who died circa 269, would no doubt approve of his day, though the customs associated with it have no relation to his life. Our tradition of exchanging affectionate cards on February 14 originated in ancient Rome, where boys drew girls' names from a love urn on February 15. The Christian church adopted this popular pagan custom and made it part of St. Valentine's feast day on February 14. In the sixteenth century, people began sending each other the paper greeting cards that we are familiar with today.

St. Valentine is known as the patron of lovers, and it is to them that we dedicate this elegant breakfast. It should be enjoyed in a leisurely fashion, with no thought given to clocks. If St. Valentine's Day falls on a weekday, arrangements will have to be made with the office regarding your late arrival.

MENU *(Serves Two)*

- Champagne Framboise
- Double Melon Salad
- Shrimp Soufflé Roll
- Quick Croissants
- Apricot Pineapple Conserve
- Judy's Rhubarb Marmalade
- Apple Butter

CHAMPAGNE FRAMBOISE

Place 15 millilitres (1 tbsp.) of raspberry (framboise) liqueur in the bottom of a champagne flute and fill up with champagne. Or try a spoonful of undiluted, frozen raspberry cocktail instead.

DOUBLE MELON SALAD

Melon should be served cold and is extra delicious if marinated in wine, rum or sherry.

1 cantaloupe, peeled
500 mL (2 cups) honeydew melon balls
Springs of mint for garnish
Fruit Dressing (recipe follows)

Slice the cantaloupes into rings about 2.5 centimetres (1 in.) thick and remove seeds. Place on a plate and sprinkle with a little sherry. Place the melon balls into a bowl and sprinkle with a little sherry. Chill both cantaloupe and honeydew melon balls well.

When ready to serve, place the ring on a small plate and fill the centre with the balls. Garnish with mint and serve with Fruit Dressing.

Fruit Dressing

1 egg, beaten
30 mL (2 tbsp.) white sugar
60 mL (4 tbsp.) sherry
Dash of salt
10 mL (2 tsp.) butter
60 mL (4 tbsp.) orange juice
30 mL (2 tbsp.) lemon juice
60 mL (4 tbsp.) whipping cream

Combine all the ingredients except the whipping cream in a heavy saucepan or double boiler and cook until slightly thickened, stirring constantly. Chill. At serving time, whip the cream and fold in. Serve with fruits.

SHRIMP SOUFFLE ROLL

Although this is a soufflé mixture, it is cooked in a jelly-roll pan, and is foolproof. It is best served immediately, but still is very good if refrigerated and reheated the next day. Store it in foil and reheat for about 30 minutes at 180°C (350°F).

60 mL (4 tbsp.) fine dry breadcrumbs
30 mL (2 tbsp.) butter
30 mL (2 tbsp.) all-purpose white flour
250 mL (1 cup) milk
2 mL (½ tsp.) salt
2 mL (½ tsp.) dry mustard
Dash of pepper, freshly ground
8 large eggs, separated
125 mL (½ cup) parmesan cheese, grated

Grease a two-litre (10 by 15-inch) jelly-roll pan, line with parchment paper or foil and grease again. Sprinkle with the breadcrumbs.

In a medium saucepan, melt the butter and stir in the flour. Cook for two or three minutes. Whisk in the milk and cook until the mixture is smooth and comes to a boil. Whisk in the seasonings.

Beat the egg yolks lightly and whisk a little of the hot mixture in to warm them up. Then return the egg mixture to the sauce, whisking all the time. Cook one minute longer. Stir in one-half of the parmesan cheese. Cool.

Beat the egg-whites until stiff but not dry. As with all soufflés, stir one-quarter of the beaten whites into the cooled yolk mixture to lighten it, then fold in the remaining whites gently but thoroughly. Spread evenly in the prepared pan. Bake at 200°C (400°F) for 20 minutes or until golden and firm to the touch.

When the soufflé roll is done, remove from the oven and sprinkle with the remaining parmesan cheese. Cover with wax paper, then a clean tea towel and invert onto the counter. Carefully remove the parchment from the bottom. Spread with filling (recipe follows) and roll up from the long side. It may also be rolled from the narrow end, if desired. Place seam-side down on a serving platter. Slice into eight generous pieces and garnish each with cheese sauce and a tiny shrimp.

Shrimp Filling and Cheese Sauce

While the soufflé is baking, prepare the sauce.

90 mL (6 tbsp.) butter
60 mL (4 tbsp.) all-purpose white flour

625 mL (2½ cups) milk
5 mL (1 tsp.) salt
2 mL (½ tsp.) dry mustard
1 mL (¼ tsp.) nutmeg, grated
Dash of white pepper and cayenne
pepper
500 mL (2 cups) white cheddar cheese,
shredded
60 mL (4 tbsp.) parmesan cheese,
grated
125 mL (½ cup) whipping cream
250 g (1 cup) cooked shrimp,
reserving some for garnish
30 mL (2 tbsp.) parsley, chopped

In a medium saucepan, melt the butter and stir in the flour. Cook for two or three minutes. Whisk in the milk and cook until the mixture is smooth and comes to a boil. Whisk in the seasonings. Let the mixture simmer for two or three minutes.

Stir in the cheeses, mixing until smooth. Stir in the cream.

Place the shrimp and the parsley in a medium bowl and add one-third of the cheese sauce, remembering to keep a few shrimp for the garnish. Mix together gently. Taste for seasonings. Use remaining cheese sauce for garnish.

QUICK CROISSANTS

250 mL (1 cup) warm water, about
43°C (110°F)
5 mL (1 tsp.) sugar
30 mL (2 tbsp.) Rapidmix yeast
160-mL can evaporated milk
7 mL (1½ tsp.) salt
75 mL (⅓ cup) white sugar
1.25 L (5 cups) all-purpose white
flour
125 mL (½ cup) unsalted butter,
melted
250 mL (1 cup) unsalted butter,
frozen, coarsely chopped

Dissolve the yeast in the water with the 15 millilitres (1 tsp.) of sugar. Let stand 10 minutes until dissolved. Stir well. Add the milk, salt, sugar and 250 millilitres (1 cup) of the flour. Beat to a smooth batter. Blend in the melted butter. Set aside.

In a large bowl or food processor, cut the frozen butter into the remaining one litre (4 cups) of flour until the size of dried kidney beans. If using the processor, turn out the mixture

into a large bowl. Pour the yeast batter over top and blend until the liquid is absorbed. Form into a ball – no need to knead it – and place in a medium bowl. Cover with plastic wrap and refrigerate. Chill the dough mixture for four hours before using. This dough will keep in the refrigerator for up to four days and in the freezer up to six months. Thaw in the refrigerator.

To form tiny croissants: remove one-quarter of the dough from the bowl. Knead briefly, then roll out into a 30-centimetre (12-in.) circle and cut the dough into 12 triangles. (For large croissants, cut the dough into six or eight triangles.) Roll each wedge towards the point, pulling the large end a little to even it out. Shape into crescents and place on parchment on a baking sheet. Let rise until puffy, about 1½ hours. Brush with a mixture of one egg beaten with 15 millilitres (1 tbsp.) of water.

Bake at 160°C (325°F) for 25 to 30 minutes or until golden brown. Baked croissants will freeze well. Reheat on baking sheets at 180°C (350°F) for 10 minutes.

Jams, butters and pastes are purées of increasing density. Preserves, marmalades and conserves are bits of fruit cooked to a translucent state in a heavy syrup. These and the jams, all of which need only one cooking, take patience and careful stirring. The following jams are made with dried, frozen and canned fruit and can be made all year long.

APRICOT PINEAPPLE CONSERVE

This is a very soft jam that needs to be kept in the refrigerator.

500 mL (2 cups) dried apricots,
chopped
300 mL (1¼ cups) water
375 mL (1½ cups) white sugar
1.25 L (5 cups) canned crushed
pineapple

Cook the apricots in the water until the fruit is pulpy and disintegrates easily when stirred

with a wire whisk.

Add the sugar and stir until dissolved. Add the pineapple. Bring the mixture to a boil, reduce heat and simmer until thickened. Pour into sterilized jars. Keep refrigerated.

JUDY'S RHUBARB MARMALADE

1 kg (2 lbs.) rhubarb, (frozen or fresh
– there should be 1.75 L (7 cups),
coarsely chopped
1.5 L (6 cups) white sugar
3 whole lemons, thinly sliced
4 large oranges, thinly sliced

Discard the seeds and the thick end pieces of the lemons and oranges. Place all the ingredients in a large bowl and chill for at least 24 hours. Place in a large saucepan and bring to a boil, stirring constantly until sugar is dissolved. Simmer until thick, about 1½ hours. Place in sterilized jars and let cool. Cover with a thin coating of wax. Makes about 2.5 litres (4 pints).

APPLE BUTTER

Use fresh apples if you can in this recipe, but frozen will give a nice result as well.

2 kg (4 lbs.) apples, cored, stemmed
and quartered
500 mL (2 cups) water or cider
10 mL (2 tsp.) cinnamon
7 mL (1½ tsp.) cloves
2 mL (½ tsp.) allspice
Grated rind and juice of 1 lemon

Cook the apples in the water slowly, until soft. Press the fruit through a strainer or push through a food mill. For each cup of pulp add 125 millilitres (½ cup) white sugar. Over medium heat, stir until sugar is dissolved. Add the cinnamon, cloves, allspice and the grated lemon rind and juice. Continue to cook, stirring frequently, until the mixture is thick and rich. It is done when a small quantity is placed on a plate and it remains solid, with no liquid separating from it. Store in sterilized jars in the refrigerator. ☐

Wake up and smell the soufflé: champagne framboise to open your eyes; melon salad to arouse your appetite; shrimp soufflé roll with croissants and conserve to start your day

One for the Heart

It was in a small restaurant in Santa Barbara that we first encountered heart symbols on a menu. These dietary valentines, we were told, indicated a dish low in cholesterol and sodium, and they were sprinkled on the menu at the suggestion of the American Heart Association.

We haven't yet seen little hearts on western Canadian restaurant menus, but dishes that are kind to your cardiovascular system are available. The Four Seasons hotel chain, for instance, introduced an "alternative cuisine" in their dining rooms and on their room-service menu. These meals are low in cholesterol and sodium and will add fewer than 650 calories to your daily deposit.

In keeping with this trend, we have prepared a tasty, light meal of our own. We have not been puristic; small quantities of butter, egg and cream are called for in some dishes. But if you are resolved to cut out animal fats, simply omit the offending ingredients and pass on the cookies.

Part of the appeal of our alternative meal is visual: its bright colors please the eye. Another is in the taste: its intriguing ingredients will charm your palate and make you forget that you are being abstemious. But its chief appeal is to your health. Award it a heart.

MENU (Serves Four)

- Papaya and Pepper Salad
- Crispy Flatbread
- Fresh Sole on a Purée of Watercress
- Spaghetti Squash with Sun-dried Tomatoes and Wild Mushrooms
- Chinese Long Beans

PAPAYA AND PEPPER SALAD

This refreshing combination is served as the vegetable accompaniment to broiled red snapper at Amsterdam's, a New York bistro. Tossed with a flavorful vinaigrette, it makes a wonderful salad. The vinaigrette can also be used on poached fish, pasta or a vegetable terrine.

½ papaya, peeled and seeded
½ medium red pepper, seeded
2 green onions
½ English cucumber, peeled and seeded
Salad greens
Egg Vinaigrette

Dice the papaya, pepper, onion and cucumber into small pieces and place in a medium bowl. Make the vinaigrette and toss some of it with the vegetables. Place the salad greens on chilled salad plates. Spoon on the diced mixture. Drizzle on a little more dressing or pass it at the table. Serve with crackers.

Egg Vinaigrette
Makes 250 millilitres (1 cup).

1 egg
5 mL (1 tsp.) Dijon mustard
1 clove garlic, mashed
30 mL (2 tbsp.) wine vinegar
120 mL (8 tbsp.) olive oil
30 mL (2 tbsp.) parsley, dill or tarragon, minced
15 mL (1 tbsp.) capers
1 mL (¼ tsp.) salt
Freshly ground black pepper

Hard boil the egg. Chill, peel and cut it in half. Remove the yolk and mash it with the mustard and garlic. Mix in the vinegar and then dribble in the oil, whisking constantly until thickened. Add the

Lite delights: diced papaya and pepper salad with herb and caper vinaigrette; crispy flatbread; sole on a purée of watercress with spaghetti squash and Chinese beans.

parsley, dill or tarragon and the capers. Dice the white of the egg and add it to the sauce, seasoning to taste with salt and pepper.

CRISPY FLATBREAD

Similar to pita, this is a bread best eaten the day it is made. It is often softened with a little water and used as a rolled casing for fillings such as chicken or pork.

10 mL (2 tsp.) yeast
250 mL (1 cup) warm water
Pinch of sugar
10 mL (2 tsp.) vegetable oil
675 to 750 mL (2¾ to 3 cups) all-purpose white flour
5 mL (1 tsp.) salt
Sesame seeds

Sprinkle the yeast over the water and let stand until bubbly. Add the pinch of sugar and the oil.

Place the flour and salt in a medium bowl or the work bowl of a food processor. Whisk in the yeast mixture, stirring until the mixture forms a ball and pulls away from the sides of the bowl. Turn out onto a floured board and knead until smooth and silky.

Place in a lightly greased bowl, cover and let rise for one hour. Punch the dough down and knead gently. Cut the dough into 12 equal pieces, form each piece into a ball and let rest, covered, for 15 minutes.

Preheat the oven to 240°C (475°F). Roll out the balls as thinly as possible. Sprinkle with sesame seeds and roll again. Prick all over with a fork. Transfer the rounds to a cookie sheet and bake two to three minutes; turn the bread and cook again for two to three minutes or until lightly browned. The bread will crisp as it cools.

FRESH SOLE ON A PUREE OF WATERCRESS

If watercress is not available, use any greens – such as spinach, romaine, sorrel, peas, parsley or a combination thereof.

4 pieces of sole
1 shallot or green onion, chopped
1 clove garlic, chopped

Pinch of nutmeg
125 mL (½ cup) white wine
300 mL (1¼ cups) chicken stock or canned broth
Bunch of watercress, washed and patted dry
Whipping cream

Fold the sole into thirds with the smooth side out. Place in a greased pan and bake at 230°C (450°F) until done, about 10 to 15 minutes. The fish will be white and will flake easily.

As the sole bakes, add the shallot, garlic and nutmeg to the wine and stock and bring to a boil. Boil until reduced by half. Cool slightly. Place watercress in a blender and purée. Add enough of the wine and stock until you have a thick, smooth mixture. Taste for seasonings and add salt and pepper if needed. Stir in a little cream.

Place a large spoonful of the purée on a heated serving plate. Top it with the sole and arrange the vegetables on the side.

SPAGHETTI SQUASH WITH SUN DRIED TOMATOES AND WILD MUSHROOMS

Regular tomatoes and mushrooms can be substituted with only a slight variation in flavor.

4 large dried mushrooms, such as boletus, porcini, cep, shiitaké
1 spaghetti squash
2 whole, sun-dried tomatoes
30 mL (2 tbsp.) butter
30 mL (2 tbsp.) oil

Cover the mushrooms with hot water to soften. Cut the spaghetti squash in half and place the pieces cut-side down on a baking sheet. Bake at 180°F (350°F) until tender when pierced with a skewer, about 45 minutes. Remove from the oven and let cool slightly. Scrape out the meat of the squash (it will look like strings of fine spaghetti) and place in a bowl.

Sliver the sun-dried tomatoes. Drain the mushrooms and pat dry. Discarding any tough stems, sliver the mushrooms.

Just before serving time, heat butter and oil in a large frypan or spray with vegetable spray. Add

the squash, tomatoes and mushrooms. Toss and cook until heated through. Serve as a vegetable side-dish.

CHINESE LONG BEANS

If you cannot find these long, interesting beans in a Chinese grocery store, use ordinary green beans. Slice the beans on a long diagonal for a professional look. Bring water to a boil and add the beans, cooking only until tender. Drain and cool under cold running water.

Just before serving time, toss and heat in a small teflon-coated frypan. □

Minestrone!

This is a good time for color, for hearty, for nutritious, for basic. Practically all the fuels a winter-weakened body needs to face the chilblain night are found in one, thick, piquant, tomatoey minestrone. This soup is absolutely loaded – with beans, lentils, celery, noodles, carrots, onions, squash, potatoes, basil, oregano and garlic. Marry a bowlful to a chunk of wholewheat sourdough bread, tangy and tender, and you have a meal that is not only delicious but also entirely defensible before the board of gurus and bwanas at the local natural-foods depot. For dessert, fetch a large jar of homemade yoghurt and drop in carrot shreds, fresh apple sauce, walnuts, chopped dried fruit, the frozen berries of last summer or a purée of papaya and pineapple.

IL MINESTRONE DI ROMA

Makes lots. A meal.

60 mL (4 tbsp.) butter
125 mL (½ cup) olive oil
1 medium onion, finely chopped
4 medium carrots, finely chopped
2 leeks, finely chopped
2 stalks celery, finely chopped
1 clove garlic, minced
2 medium potatoes, peeled and diced
1 796-mL can of ground tomatoes
250 mL (1 cup) peeled and diced
    squash, such as winter, yellow,
    hubbard, crookneck or zucchini
30 mL (2 tbsp.) fresh parsley, finely
    chopped
5 mL (1 tsp.) dried oregano
10 mL (2 tsp.) dried basil
1 398-mL can red kidney beans (or
    garbanzo or white beans),
    undrained
250 mL (1 cup) dried lentils
250 mL (1 cup) broken spaghettini,
    fine noodles or small macaroni
1.5 to 2 L (1½ to 2 qt.) chicken
    broth or canned stock, depending
    upon how thick you want the end
    result – it will thicken on standing
Salt and pepper to taste
Cayenne pepper to taste

In a large heavy pot, melt the butter and olive oil together. Add the finely chopped onion, carrots, leeks, celery, garlic and potatoes and cook, covered, until the vegetables have absorbed most of the butter/oil mixture, about 20 minutes.

Add the tomatoes, diced squash, parsley, oregano, basil, beans, lentils, spaghettini and chicken broth. Stir well to mix. Bring to a boil, turn down the heat and simmer until the lentils and spaghettini are tender, about 30 minutes.

Season to taste and serve with a hearty bread. This soup freezes, but the vegetables tend to become soft upon reheating from the frozen state. It will keep several days, refrigerated. It does thicken as it stands and it may be necessary to add more broth.

SOURDOUGH BREAD

As with all yeast breads, there are two methods of making sourdough breads: straight dough and sponge. The sponge method is preferable, because the long rising time improves the flavor. If you begin the night before, you can have bread out of the oven by mid-morning the next day. Also, a starter replenished from a sponge is of better consistency, livelier and tastier.

In this recipe, the addition of baking soda is optional. The soda makes the bread a little lighter, but it reduces the sourness of the starter and makes the bread less tangy, with a milder sourdough flavor.

To make a smooth sponge, sprinkle the flour into the milk or water and beat hard with a wire whisk. Then add the starter, stirring with a wooden spoon.

To Make the Starter:

500 mL (2 cups) warm water or milk
500 mL (2 cups) all-purpose
    unbleached white flour
30 mL (2 tbsp.) sugar
15 mL (1 tbsp.) Rapidmix yeast

If you use milk, which will make a stronger-tasting starter, let it stand at room temperature for 24 hours, then mix in the flour, yeast and sugar. Put mixture in a suitable container (never metal, as it will affect the flavor) and cover with cheesecloth. Keep at room temperature until mixture bubbles. This will take from two to three days. Stir often. When ready, cover and refrigerate.

Every month or so, add a spoonful of sugar to your starter. Freeze your starter when you go on vacation. Defrost at room temperature, and when it starts to bubble, it is ready to use again. If it takes on a pinkish tinge, throw it away.

How to Care for Starter:

Starter cannot stand as high a temperature as active dry yeast. Heat over 35° C (95° F) will kill it. It works fastest at 30° C (85° F), but room temperature is good, since it gives the dough time to develop flavor. Starter becomes dormant when cold and so will keep well in the lower part of the refrigerator. In fact, it will keep indefinitely there if refreshed at least every two weeks. Refresh it by removing half your starter (give it away or freeze it) and replacing it with the *same amount* of a mixture of one-half flour and one-half water (this is in addition to its regular monthly sugar feedings). Leave it at room temperature until it bubbles, stirring occasionally. When you have taken out some of the starter to make a sponge, replace it the next morning with the same amount from the sponge that has stood overnight, before the remaining ingredients have been added to it. Stir in thoroughly. A starter will thrive for years this way.

The best container for starter is a crock, but heavy glass or plastic will do. It should hold at least a litre (1 qt.). Do not fill it more than two-thirds full, leaving room for expansion, and do not cap

tightly, particularly if you are using a glass container, for an enthusiastic starter might shatter it. Label it, so that no one will consider it just a smelly mess and throw it out.

To Make the Sponge:
In the evening before making the bread, mix together in a large bowl:

500 mL (2 cups) all-purpose
  unbleached white flour
375 mL (1½ cups) lukewarm water
  or milk
250 mL (1 cup) starter

Let rise overnight, covered with plastic wrap, in a warm place. In the morning stir and return 250 millilitres (1 cup) of the sponge to the starter. To the remaining sponge add:

30 mL (2 tbsp.) very soft butter
30 mL (2 tbsp.) molasses or brown
  sugar
15 mL (1 tbsp.) yeast dissolved in
  60 mL (4 tbsp.) warm water
10 mL (2 tsp.) salt
5 mL (1 tsp.) baking soda (optional)
375 mL (1½ cups) all-purpose
  unbleached white flour
375 mL (1½ cups) wholewheat,
  graham or rye flour (more or less)

Stir in the butter, molasses, dissolved yeast, salt and baking soda. Mix well. Add the white flour and beat well. Beat in the wholewheat flour, 250 millilitres (1 cup) at a time, until the dough pulls away from the sides of the bowl. Turn out onto a floured board and knead until smooth and silky, about 10 minutes. Form into a ball and place in a well-greased bowl, turning to grease the dough. Let rise in a warm place for 1½ hours.

Punch down and knead the dough again for two or three minutes. Let rest for 10 minutes. Divide into three medium or two large loaves and shape as desired. Place in greased pans, or on a greased cookie sheet sprinkled with a little cornmeal if you are making freeform loaves. Let rise until just doubled.

Bake at 190° C (375° F) for 10 minutes, then reduce heat to 180° C (350° F) for 20 minutes or until the bread is golden and sounds hollow when tapped on the bottom.

For a smooth, shiny crust, use a milk glaze before baking.

This makes a very soft loaf that will not slice easily until the next day.

HOMEMADE YOGHURT

You don't need to buy a yoghurt machine to make yoghurt; the best alternative is a wide-mouth thermos. If you have a kitchen-corner or a register that maintains an even temperature of about 43° C (110° F), it will work too. The bacteria will multiply in a culture that is between 32° C (90° F) and 48° C (120° F).

Put one litre (1 qt.) of milk in a heavy pot and heat until it is about to boil. Stir to prevent a skin formation. Turn the heat off and let milk cool until it is 43° C (110° F). If you don't have a thermometer, cool it until you *think* it's 43° C. (One book says you should be able to stick your finger in the milk for a slow count to 10 without it hurting. This method works.) Then put 30 millilitres (2 tbsp.) of pure, unflavored yoghurt in a small bowl, add a bit of the hot milk and whisk until yoghurt is liquid. Pour yoghurt mixture into the pot of milk and whisk until completely mixed in. Pour milk into a wide-mouthed thermos and place thermos, closed, in a warm place for six hours. Then put thermos in the fridge. When cool, the yoghurt is done.

You can also put the milk in a covered bowl and put the bowl in a place of sufficient, constant warmth until yoghurt is set.

The thickness and richness of the yoghurt will depend on the milk used. Skim-milk yoghurt is watery, two per cent is the thickness of heavy cream and yoghurt made with whole milk sets quite firmly.

Save 30 millilitres (2 tbsp.) of this batch to use as starter for the next batch. Every once in a while, use a new starter. ☐

The meal in a bowl: an Italian country favorite, combining nutritious ingredients — from chick peas to chicken — in a hearty and colorful dish; on the side, a loaf of sourdough, straight from the oven, and a dollop of homemade yoghurt.

Thali

Not long after she came to Canada from Kenya with her husband and children in 1972, Sharin Sondhi began teaching Indian cooking through the Adult Education office of the North Vancouver School Board. Simply put, she wanted to spread good will through good cooking. A nice idea.

Few who eat Sondhi's chutneys, samosas and carrot halva can help but be impressed by her renderings of the classic dishes of Indian cuisine. We may speculate that the anonymous Mogul poet who said in 1640, "If there is a paradise on the face of the earth, it is this, oh! it is this, oh! it is this!" might not, in fact, have been talking about the fabled Red Fort of New Delhi, as is commonly believed, but about its kitchens. Perhaps he had simply taken three bites of *makhani murgh*, the sublime Mogul dish of chicken, cream and spices that Sondhi has interpreted for our Thali menu. Having seen the Red Fort *and* tasted *makhani murgh*, we favor the latter as a hint of paradise – a place where all will have enough to eat and where every morsel will be perfectly spiced, perfectly cooked and served in perfect Mogul splendor.

Sondhi was born in Kenya and learned to cook from her mother, sister and friends. She brought a thorough knowledge of the ingredients and fundamentals of Indian cooking with her, and then discovered the food processor. To someone who cooks a lot of Indian food, the food processor offers a kind of liberation. "If my house was on fire and I had to run," Sondhi jokes, "I'd run with my Cuisinart. I use it all the time, for everything." The traditional mortar and pestle has been tossed

Sondhi's samples: lemon and carrot pickles, cauliflower and broccoli bhaji, paratha, yoghurt salad, mung dhal, tandoori chicken, samosas and basmati rice; carrot halva for dessert.

aside in favor of an electric coffee grinder used exclusively to grind fresh spices. "That's another thing I'd run with."

The cupboards in Sondhi's large, well-appointed kitchen seem to contain all the bounty of an Indian spice and dry-goods market. She keeps quantities of whole spices in airtight containers. Because she uses them frequently, she keeps them in a cupboard and grinds them when needed. "In Canada, they will keep a long time. When I was in Kenya, they would get something like cobwebs over them," she says. She recommends that occasional cooks keep their spices in the refrigerator, and advocates grinding up large quantities of ginger root and garlic and storing them in the freezer.

If there is any secret to Indian cooking, it is, of course, using authentic ingredients. Thankfully, this is less of a problem now than ever before. Not only Indian shops, but many health-food stores, specialty stores and even supermarkets are selling whole spices, lentils, fresh herbs and other essential ingredients. (For those simply unable to acquire the needed spices locally, the mail-order option exists. An excellent source is Patel Discount Bulk Foods in Vancouver. Call (604) 255-8151/6729.

This meal is Punjabi, and Punjabi food is not as hot as southern Indian food. The perfumed subtleties of cardamom, coriander, cinnamon, cloves and cumin pervade these dishes and would be overpowered by an excess of chilies. Sondhi suggests that pickled or chopped fresh chilies be served alongside the meal for diners who prefer more fire.

With the exception of the samosas and the mint and tamarind chutneys, which make an excellent appetizer, the meal should be served all together, preferably from a buffet. The traditional style of service, shown in the photograph, is on a *thali*, which consists of several small containers and a tray for each diner – a kind of deluxe TV dinner. The traditional method of eating is with the fingers and thumb of the right hand.

As indicated in the recipes, the tandoori chicken can be marinated overnight, and its sauce made a day ahead. The chutneys and pickles improve if made ahead (especially the pickled lemons, which require a couple of weeks to develop), and the carrot halva will keep for many days in the refrigerator. Make the dhal and raita a few hours before serving. The vegetables in the cauliflower dish can be cut and readied for cooking ahead of time. The ingredients and doughs of the samosas and parathas can be made ahead, but final assembly and cooking should be done shortly before the meal is served.

MENU *(Serves Six)*

- Punjabi Garam Masala
- Punjabi Vegetarian Samosas
- Mint Chutney
- Tamarind Chutney
- Fresh Carrot Pickle
- Pickled Lemons
- Dahi Raita
- Tandoori Chicken in Butter and Cream Sauce
- Cauliflower and Broccoli Bhaji
- Bhasmati Rice
- Paratha
- Carrot Halva
- Spiced Tea

PUNJABI GARAM MASALA

Garam masala is simply a mixture of freshly ground spices. There are many kinds in India, and they vary tremendously. Pre-mixed garam masalas are available in many spice stores, but for these recipes it's important to use the Punjabi type. Of course, it's best to make your own. If you cannot get whole spices, pre-ground will do. Use garam masala from this recipe whenever garam masala is called for below. Store leftover spice mixture in a tight jar in the fridge.

20 g (¾ oz.) brown cardamom seeds
20 g (¾ oz.) cinnamon
7 g (¼ oz.) whole cloves
7 g (¼ oz.) black cumin seeds (see below)
7 g (¼ oz.) white cumin seeds (see below)
A good-sized pinch of ground nutmeg
A good-sized pinch of ground mace

Cardamom seeds usually come in small, round seed-packets that must be broken open by hand and discarded. Black cumin seeds, called *kala zeera*, are not true cumin. Their shape is similar to that of caraway seeds. They add a pungent flavor to the garam masala that cannot be duplicated. If unavailable, leave out. White cumin seeds (*sufaid zeera*, the only kind of cumin available in some Indian stores) are actually grey. They are usually roasted in an oven until brown before being crushed or ground. Some recipes below call for crushed cumin, which delivers a different flavor than finely ground cumin. To crush, grind coarsely in a coffee grinder or in a mortar.

To make the garam masala, grind spices to a fine powder in a coffee grinder or mortar and store in an airtight container.

PUNJABI VEGETARIAN SAMOSAS

Samosas are fried triangular packets of pastry filled with vegetables or meat and spices. A wok is an ideal instrument for deep-frying, requiring far less oil than other pans because of its shape. Use a small pool of oil and fry one or two samosas at a time. If you don't overcook them, they won't absorb much oil.

Filling
125 mL (½ cup) oil
5 mL (1 tsp.) whole white cumin seeds
3 medium potatoes, peeled and diced very small
250 g (½ lb.) fresh (or frozen) peas
6 mL (1¼ tsp.) salt
Juice of 1 lemon
10 mL (2 tsp.) garam masala
2 mL (½ tsp.) black pepper
2 mL (½ tsp.) white cumin seeds, crushed
1 large onion, finely chopped
5 mL (1 tsp.) fresh ginger root, finely chopped
1 or 2 hot green chili peppers, chopped
125 mL (½ cup) fresh coriander (cilantro), chopped
Pastry (recipe below)

Heat oil in a large frypan. Add whole cumin seeds. When they brown, add potatoes and fresh peas. Stir for one minute, cover and cook on low heat for about seven minutes, until soft. Frozen peas should be added four minutes after the potatoes.

Add salt, lemon juice, garam masala, pepper and crushed cumin. Mix well and remove from heat. Cool.

Mix in onions, ginger, green chili and coriander leaves. Adjust seasonings. This mixture will be slightly overspiced to compensate for the bland pastry. Set filling aside.

Pastry
300 mL (1¼ cups) all-purpose white flour
2 mL (½ tsp.) salt
60 mL (4 tbsp.) oil
About 60 mL (4 tbsp.) water

Mix flour, salt and oil in a food processor until the mixture is crumbly, or mix by hand. Work in a few tablespoons of water at a time to form a fairly soft dough. Knead until smooth, cover and let stand in a warm place for 30 minutes or more.

Divide dough into eight balls. Roll balls into thin (⅓-cm/⅛-in.) circles about the diameter of a dessert plate. Cut each circle in half. Wet edges of pastry, then place a small spoonful of filling on pastry. Pinch pastry until pastry packet is sealed.

To cook, pour some vegetable oil into a wok or frypan and heat over a medium burner. The oil is ready when a cube of bread dropped into the oil quickly turns toasty brown.

Deep-fry samosas a few at a time, turning frequently to brown evenly. Drain on paper towels. Serve with mint and tamarind chutney or wedges of lemon.

MINT CHUTNEY

250 mL (1 cup) fresh mint leaves
1 hot green chili pepper
2 mL (½ tsp.) fresh ginger, sliced
1 mL (¼ tsp.) cumin seeds, crushed
1 medium tomato
Salt to taste
2 mL (½ tsp.) sugar
Juice of 1 lemon

Place all ingredients in a blender or food processor and process until smooth. Fresh coriander leaves — sometimes called cilantro or Chinese parsley — are often more readily available than fresh mint and can be substituted. If you use coriander, you can add a small quantity of dried mint.

TAMARIND CHUTNEY

Tamarind, called *imli* in Hindi, is the sour red pulp of the fruit of the tamarind tree and is available in most Indian specialty stores. Its flavor cannot be duplicated. Leftover tamarind can be refrigerated.

125 mL (½ cup) tamarind pulp
500 mL (2 cups) water
125 mL (½ cup) brown sugar
5 mL (1 tsp.) salt
5 mL (1 tsp.) cayenne powder
1 mL (¼ tsp.) cumin, crushed (optional)
15 mL (1 tbsp.) vinegar

Wash tamarind pulp, then soak in water for half an hour. Bring mixture to a boil and add brown sugar, salt, cayenne powder, crushed cumin and vinegar. Simmer for five minutes. When cool, rub through a sieve and store in a jar in the refrigerator.

FRESH CARROT PICKLE

250 g (½ lb.) carrots, peeled and cut into thin sticks
5 mL (1 tsp.) salt
2 mL (½ tsp.) coarsely ground mustard seeds or 2 mL (½ tsp.) mustard powder
1 mL (¼ tsp.) ground turmeric
2 mL (½ tsp.) cayenne powder
A few small green chillies, slit in half
10 mL (2 tsp.) vinegar

Mix all ingredients together and leave for at least an hour before serving. This pickle will keep in the refrigerator for up to two weeks.

PICKLED LEMONS

The lemons should pickle for at least two weeks before serving.

12 fresh lemons
45 mL (3 tbsp.) pickling salt
15 mL (1 tbsp.) turmeric
15 mL (1 tbsp.) cayenne power
Lemon juice

Slice lemons into quarters, then slice each quarter into three or four slices. In a bowl, toss lemons, salt, turmeric and cayenne powder until lemons are well coated. Place lemons in a jar and leave overnight. Next day, the salt will have drawn some of the juice out of the lemons. Add lemon juice until lemons are completely covered. Leave jar on top of the refrigerator, where you can see it. Let lemons stand in juice for two or three weeks, turning the jar once a day to circulate the pickling mixture.

DAHI RAITA

This yoghurt salad is a deliciously cool dish.

500 mL (2 cups) thick, whole-milk yoghurt
15 mL (1 tbsp.) raisins, soaked in 10 mL (2 tsp.) water
15 mL (1 tbsp.) onion, chopped
1 tomato, chopped
2 mL (½ tsp.) salt
2 mL (½ tsp.) ground cumin
1 small potato, boiled and diced (optional)
Chili powder to taste
Fresh coriander leaves

Stir yoghurt with a fork. Add all other ingredients and mix well. Garnish with more cumin, paprika and chopped coriander.

MAKHANI MURGH
(Tandoori Chicken in Butter and Cream Sauce)

This is a dish in the royal Mogul style, in which Tandoori chicken is bathed in a rich sauce of cream and spices.

Tandoori chicken, one of India's most famous dishes, is traditionally roasted in a special, very hot clay oven, but many of the same flavors can be achieved at home. Food coloring, called for in this recipe, is also used in India to produce a brilliant orange effect. If you are unhappy about using it, leave it out; a dash of paprika will also achieve similar results.

The uncooked chicken should marinate overnight. Some of the steps involved in making the sauce can also be taken a day ahead. Finish the sauce while the chicken is roasting in the oven.

Tandoori Chicken

1.5 kg (3 lbs.) chicken breasts or legs, skinned
5 mL (1 tsp.) salt
1 medium onion
5 mL (1 tsp.) fresh ginger, finely chopped
2 mL (½ tsp.) fresh garlic, finely chopped
5 mL (1 tsp.) ground coriander seeds
5 mL (1 tsp.) garam masala
5 mL (1 tsp.) cayenne powder, or two hot green chili peppers
250 mL (1 cup) yoghurt
Juice of 1 lemon
A few drops of red and yellow food coloring, in a ratio of 2 red to 1 yellow, or a dash of paprika (both optional)
15 to 30 mL (1 to 2 tbsp.) melted butter or oil
Freshly ground pepper

Cut breasts in half, leave legs whole. Cut two gashes in each piece on both sides and rub with salt.

Make a marinade by blending or processing until smooth the onion, ginger, garlic, coriander seeds, garam masala, cayenne powder or chilies, yoghurt, lemon and optional food coloring.

Lay chicken in a large container and spread on the marinade. Let sit overnight in the refrigerator, covered tightly.

Heat oven to its maximum temperature. Shake off marinade from chicken pieces and arrange on a baking sheet. Brush with oil and sprinkle with pepper. Bake for 15 to 20 minutes, or until cooked and brown. While chicken is cooking, finish the sauce.

Sauce

60 mL (4 tbsp.) tomato paste
250 mL (1 cup) water
2.5-cm (1-in.) piece of fresh ginger
1 hot green chili
5 mL (1 tsp.) garam masala
3 mL (¾ tsp.) salt
1 mL (¼ tsp.) sugar
5 mL (1 tsp.) ground cumin
15 mL (1 tbsp.) fresh coriander, chopped
300 mL (1¼ cups) whipping cream
125 mL (½ cup) unsalted butter

Place tomato paste and water in a large bowl and stir well. Grind ginger and chili into a paste and add to tomato mixture. Stir in garam masala, salt, sugar, cumin, coriander and cream. The mixture may be made ahead to this point and refrigerated.

Just before serving, melt butter in a large saucepan and add tomato/spice/cream mixture. Bring to a simmer, stirring constantly. Cook for two minutes. Add chicken and coat with sauce. Heat through and serve with parathas or rice.

CAULIFLOWER AND BROCCOLI BHAJI

Indian vegetable dishes are often severely overcooked, by Western standards. Shirin Sondhi prefers to cook them for less time in order to preserve their texture.

80 to 125 mL (⅓ to ½ cup) vegetable oil
1 medium onion, sliced
5 mL (1 tsp.) ginger, chopped
1 green chili, chopped
Salt to taste
1 mL (¼ tsp.) ground black pepper
2 mL (½ tsp.) ground turmeric
2 mL (½ tsp.) garam masala
5 mL (1 tsp.) lemon juice
1 medium cauliflower, divided into sprigs and sliced
1 bunch broccoli, divided into sprigs and sliced
1 large potato, diced into 2.5-cm (1-in.) cubes

In a large frypan which has a lid, heat oil and fry onions until soft. Add ginger and green chili and fry another minute. Add salt, pepper, turmeric, garam masala and lemon juice and stir well.

Add vegetables and stir to coat with spice mixture. Put lid on pan, and cook vegetables over medium heat for 10 or 15 minutes, until vegetables are tender but crisp.

MUNG DHAL
(Green Dhal Curry)

250 mL (1 cup) mung beans
30 mL (2 tbsp.) oil
1 small onion, sliced
1 mL (¼ tsp.) whole white cumin seeds (sufaid zeera)
5 mL (1 tsp.) fresh garlic, chopped
5 mL (1 tsp.) fresh ginger, chopped
5 mL (1 tsp.) salt
15 mL (1 tbsp.) ground coriander
5 mL (1 tsp.) ground cumin
1 mL (¼ tsp.) ground turmeric
2 mL (½ tsp.) garam masala
1 medium tomato, chopped
5 mL (1 tsp.) tomato paste
Juice of 1 lemon
15 mL (1 tbsp.) yoghurt
Fresh coriander leaves
Pinch of garam masala

Soak mung beans for two hours in plenty of water. Drain, place in a pot and add water until water is five centimetres (2 in.) above the beans. Boil until tender, about 10 to 20 minutes, adding a little more water if beans get dry. Set aside.

Fry onions in oil until golden brown, adding whole cumin, garlic and ginger, and fry for one more minute.

Add all other spices, tomato, tomato paste and lemon juice and fry until oil oozes up. Add yoghurt and boiled beans with their water. Simmer for 10 minutes.

Garnish with chopped coriander and a little garam masala.

BHASMATI RICE

Bhasmati rice is a special long-grain rice with a wonderful aroma all its own. More expensive than plain rice (but worth the price), it is available in specialty stores and some health food stores.

500 mL (2 cups) bhasmati rice
10 mL (2 tsp.) oil
5 mL (1 tsp.) whole white cumin seeds, or a mixture of 2 whole cinnamon sticks, 2 whole cloves, 2 whole peppercorns and 2 whole cardamom pods
10 mL (2 tsp.) onion, chopped
1 L (4 cups) water
10 mL (2 tsp.) salt

Wash rice and soak in plenty of cold water for 30 minutes (if you soak it longer, cook with less water or it will get soggy). Drain.

Heat oil, add cumin or spices and onion and fry for just a minute, taking care that the onion does not brown.

Add 500 millilitres (2 cups) water and salt and bring to a boil. Add drained rice. The water level should be 2.5 centimetres (1 in.) above the rice. Cover. After five minutes, lower the heat and simmer rice until water is absorbed and the rice cooked, about 30 minutes.

PARATHA
(Flaky Flat Bread)

250 mL (1 cup) wholewheat flour
250 mL (1 cup) all-purpose white
    flour
2 mL (½ tsp.) salt
15 mL (1 tbsp.) vegetable oil
150 mL plus 30 mL (⅔ cup plus
    2 tbsp.) hot water
125 mL (½ cup) oil
Extra white flour

Mix together wholewheat flour, white flour, salt and vegetable oil to make a fairly stiff dough. Knead in hot tap water. Cover and put aside for a half-hour or up to six hours.

Divide dough into 12 balls. Keep them covered while you work one ball at a time.

Flatten the ball, dust with flour and roll into an even 15-centimetre (6-in.) round. Dust work surface with flour as necessary.

Spread one millilitre (¼ tsp.) oil over paratha. Sprinkle with flour and fold in half. Again spread on a little oil, sprinkle with flour and fold. This gives you a triangle. Roll this into a larger triangle with about 18 centimetre (7-in.) sides.

Brush hot frypan with a little oil and fry the paratha for about a minute or two, until the bottom is brown and cooked. Brush top of the paratha with oil and turn over. Fry until second side is done. Serve hot or cover with foil and serve later.

GAJJAR HALVA
(Carrot Pudding)

The addition of cardamom and saffron gives this very sweet pudding a delicate, perfumed character.

175 mL (¾ cup) oil
A few cardamom seeds
1.25 kg (2¾ lbs.) carrots, peeled and
    shredded
1 small tin evaporated milk
250 mL (1 cup) sugar
A little saffron soaked in 15 mL
    (1 tbsp.) milk
A few almonds
Silver leaf (optional, see below)

Heat oil and fry cardamom seeds for one minute. Add carrots and fry for half an hour, stirring now and then over medium heat. (A non-stick pan is best, otherwise watch out for scorching.)

Add evaporated milk and stir until dry, about five minutes. Add sugar and saffron. Keep stirring until halva leaves sides of pan, about 20 minutes.

Remove onto a serving dish and garnish with almonds and silver leaf. Serve warm.

Note: if you've visited an Indian sweets store, you may have observed that many desserts appeared to be covered with a thin layer of silver. It is, indeed, silver leaf, so thin that it disappears on the tongue; it is entirely safe to eat. This leaf is called verak and is available in packets of 10 sheets at some Indian grocery stores. Each sheet is packed between two sheets of paper. To put verak on halva, remove the top sheet of paper carefully, then pick up the bottom sheet with the verak on it. Gently turn this sheet of paper over and hold it over the halva. Press the sheet into the halva, then carefully remove the paper. The silver should stick to the dessert. Verak must be stored in an airtight tin or it will tarnish.

MASALA CHAI (Spiced Tea)

This recipe makes four cups.

1 L (4 cups) water
250 mL (1 cup) milk
10 mL (2 tsp.) tea leaves, or two tea
    bags
1 stick cinnamon
4 cardamom pods, still in their white
    hulls but split on top
4 whole cloves

4 black peppercorns
1 mL (¼ tsp.) ginger powder

Bring the water, milk and tea to a boil in a large pan. Add the cinnamon, cardomom, cloves, peppercorns and ginger. Simmer for five minutes, strain into a teapot and serve with sugar, if desired. □

The rights of spring: a delightfully delicate meal, from the hearts of romaine salad to the fresh strawberry dessert; in between, quenelles of pike mousseline with red pepper purée and a risotto dish with wild mushrooms.

From Sorrel to Strawberries

When we first got our food processor, a model that now stands like a Nash Metropolitan beside the powerful off-road vehicles manufactured by Cuisinart and Robot Coupe, my wife and I ate a lot of puréed, shredded and thinly sliced foods; so much so that you might have thought we both lacked good teeth. Then came disillusionment and a renewed interest in well-made, hefty knives and other hand tools. I began to feel like the abacus user who would challenge any computer user to a short-order calculation. Then came reconciliation, the final stage of the adoption process, when we realized that the food processor, like any machine, is suited to some jobs and merely interferes with others. One thing it does superlatively is make the fancy little French dumpling called a quenelle.

A few years ago, an American food writer named Jinx Morgan, in the somewhat florid prose style which, like dyspepsia, is an occupational hazard among food writers, described the quenelle as "an ethereal pleasure that appears on your plate for a fleeting moment and then dissolves like a cloud on your tongue." In other words, the sort of insubstantial candy-floss morsel that restaurants often charge substantially for; the sort of delicacy not often attempted at home because everyone knows it involves laborious kitchenwork.

Enter the above-mentioned machine. As Morgan pointed out, the food processor blade can do in seconds what takes the hand 30 minutes of pounding, stirring and sieving. With quenelles, the idea is to make an entirely smooth mixture that can be poached to yield a fluffy, delicate creation, one which is, indeed, the most deliciously insubstantial of dumplings.

The process of pounding meat or fish until it loses its fibre and then binding it for poaching is not restricted to haute cuisine, however. I once ate a soup at a bus-stand in Jakarta called *mie bakso tennis*, so named because the quenelle-like balls of poached fish floating in broth were almost as big as Slazengers. In Jakarta the dumplings were boiled until you wondered if the word "tennis" actually referred to their ability to perform well on clay surfaces. The lesson there is, don't boil your dumplings overlong. Quenelles are, in fact, gently simmered. They should float to the surface of the broth while cooking and are done shortly thereafter.

Quenelles of Pike Mousseline, at the centre of this menu, is a classic quenelle recipe. It is served here on a brilliant purée of red peppers and surrounded by fresh vegetables, with risotto on the side. The meal opens with a subtle sorrel and lettuce soup. Salad follows the entrée in French fashion, and strawberry shortcake ends a meal that is a delightful tribute to springtime. *—Scott Mowbray*

MENU *(Serves Six)*

- Sorrel and Lettuce Soup
- Quenelles of Pike Mousseline with Red Pepper Purée
- Risotto with Wild Mushrooms
- Hearts of Romaine with Homemade Croutons
- Old-Fashioned Strawberry Shortcake with Devon-Style Cream

SORREL AND LETTUCE SOUP

Sorrel, sometimes called sour grass, has always been popular with central European cooks. If fresh sorrel is not available, substitute spinach and the juice of one lemon.

60 mL (4 tbsp.) unsalted butter
1 small onion, sliced
125 g (¼ lb.) sorrel
125 g (¼ lb.) lettuce (any kind will do)
375 mL (1½ cups) fresh parsley
1 medium potato, peeled and sliced
750 mL (3 cups) chicken stock or canned broth
125 mL (½ cup) light cream
Salt
Freshly ground pepper

Buy the sorrel and lettuce by weight, or weigh it at the store and note how much you will need for this soup. Wash and dry the sorrel, lettuce and parsley. Chop roughly. Melt the butter and add onion. Simmer for two to three minutes. Add the sorrel, lettuce and parsley. Simmer gently for a few minutes, covered, then add potato and stir until well mixed. Add stock and cover. Simmer for 25 minutes or until potato is soft. Cool.

Purée in a blender — potatoes become a bit sticky if puréed in a food processor.

For a silkier texture, press the purée through a sieve or food mill to remove any coarse pieces.

Reheat gently and add cream and seasonings.

Do not boil.

QUENELLES OF PIKE MOUSSELINE WITH RED PEPPER PUREE

A purée of white fish (or poultry or shellfish), egg-white and cream is a mousseline. When poached in a flavorful broth, it becomes a quenelle, airy and delicate. Quenelles can be made ahead and frozen. When ready to be reheated, place quenelles on a buttered dish, cover with buttered parchment or buttered wax paper and bake at 180°C (350°F) for 25 or 30 minutes, until heated through (heating time is about the same for frozen or chilled quenelles). The quenelles can also be steamed for about 20 minutes or microwaved for three minutes (for six quenelles).

750 g (1½ lb.) skinned and boned pike, trout, sole, flounder or halibut

meat, cut into 2.5-cm (1-in.) pieces
2 egg-whites
Freshly ground white pepper
Pinch of cayenne
Pinch of nutmeg
Dash of cognac or brandy
Pinch of tarragon or savory
250 mL (1 cup) whipping cream

Place the fish in the food processor and chop with several on/off motions. Add the egg-white and seasonings and process until the mixture is smooth. With the machine running, pour in the whipping cream and process a few seconds longer. The mixture should be smooth and creamy, with the thickness of porridge. (This can also be done by first grinding the fish two or three times with a meat grinder, then combining it with the egg-white and seasonings in an electric blender. Then add the whipping cream. You might want to force this mixture through a sieve. Either way, the mixture *must* be completely smooth.)

Quenelles can be shaped in several ways. Little balls or ovals can be shaped by hand or with a spoon. The mixture can also be moulded in buttered moulds or piped from a pastry bag. Shape the prepared mixture and place the quenelles on a greased tray. Refrigerate for at least two hours.

To poach, use chicken broth, fish stock or a combination of wine and broth. Slip the quenelles into simmering liquid or pour hot liquid into the pan in which they have been placed. The liquid should just cover them.

Simmer gently — the liquid should near the boiling point but not meet it — for 10 to 12 minutes, depending on the size of the quenelles. Quenelles should rise off the pan when almost done. Gently assist those that don't. Turn the quenelles over and cook for the remaining time.

Transfer cooked quenelles to a rack set over a plate to drain. Just before serving time, reheat as directed above for frozen quenelles.

When ready to serve, place a few spoonfuls of red pepper purée on a plate, arrange a few quenelles on top and garnish with seasonal

vegetables.

The risotto is served in a small bowl to one side of the main dish.

Red Pepper Purée
Quenelles have a delicate flavor that is perfectly emphasized by the appropriate sauce. This red pepper sauce is outstanding. The same method could be used for spinach or watercress. Add a pinch of freshly grated nutmeg to the green sauce.

45 mL (3 tbsp.) olive oil
1 medium onion, sliced
1 clove garlic, chopped or crushed
1 kg (2 lbs.) sweet red bell peppers, seeded and chopped
2 mL (½ tsp.) salt
Pinch of cayenne
2 to 5 mL (½ to 1 tsp.) thyme
Juice of ½ lemon

Heat the oil and sauté the onion until it begins to soften. Add the garlic and cook for one minute. Add the peppers and the remaining ingredients and simmer, covered, until very soft, about 45 to 60 minutes.

Cool slightly. Purée in a food processor or blender until smooth. Press through a sieve or food mill to remove any bits of skin that remain. Taste and adjust seasonings.

This purée may be refrigerated up to two weeks or frozen up to six months. It makes about three cups.

Just before serving, reheat to boiling.

RISOTTO WITH WILD MUSHROOMS

A classic Italian dish, risotto has recently become popular in western cooking. It should be served as soon as it is done. It is easy to make, but it does need a bit of watching.

Use fresh wild mushrooms if they are available. Morel, shiitaké and Japanese tree oyster mushrooms are often in the markets and health food stores. Packaged porcini mushrooms are readily available in Italian delicatessens.

If dried mushrooms are being

used, crumble 30 grams (1 oz.) into a glass or cup, cover with hot tap water and let them soak at least 20 minutes.

45 mL (3 tbsp.) unsalted butter
15 mL (1 tbsp.) olive oil
1 small onion
Soaking liquid from mushrooms, if available
500 mL (2 cups) Italian short grain rice
125 mL (½ cup) dry white wine or vermouth
2 mL (½ tsp.) salt
Dash of freshly ground black pepper
About 1.25 L (5 cups) chicken stock
Mushrooms, coarse stems removed, sliced
30 mL (2 tbsp.) butter
125 mL (½ cup) parmesan cheese, freshly grated

Melt the butter with the oil and sauté the onion until soft, but not brown. Add the soaking liquid and the rice and stir constantly for about three minutes. Add the wine, salt and pepper and stir well.

When the liquid has been almost entirely absorbed, add enough chicken stock to just cover the rice. Stir again. Simmer steadily, stirring frequently. When the liquid level falls below the rice, add more stock. The stock should be added gradually and the rice kept at a constant simmer. Halfway through, add the mushrooms.

The rice should take about 18 to 20 minutes to cook. It will start to look creamy. When finished, it probably will have absorbed about 1.25 litres (5 cups) of liquid.

The mixture should be creamy, but stiff enough to be eaten with a fork.

Stir in the butter and the parmesan cheese.

Taste for salt and pepper. Serve immediately in a small bowl.

HEARTS OF ROMAINE WITH HOMEMADE CROUTONS

Arrange the delicate romaine lettuce hearts on a chilled serving plate. Drizzle on a little vinaigrette and add a few croutons. Pass additional dressing and croutons separately.

Vinaigrette

125 mL (½ cup) olive oil
75 mL (5 tbsp.) red wine vinegar
1 clove garlic, crushed
5 mL (1 tsp.) dried or 15 mL
   (1 tbsp.) fresh oregano
2 mL (½ tsp.) dried dill
Pinch of salt
Freshly ground black pepper

Place all ingredients in a jar and shake well. Adjust seasonings. Do not refrigerate or the olive oil will thicken. Allow to stand for a few hours for the flavors to blend and mellow.

Croutons

3 or 4 slices of white bread, preferably
   day-old
90 mL (6 tbsp.) unsalted butter
Crushed garlic and/or chopped herbs of
   your choice

Trim the crusts off the bread. Cut into small cubes. Melt butter in a frypan, add garlic and/or herbs and cook for one minute. Add the bread cubes and toss until well coated with the flavored butter. Fry until crisp and drain on paper towels. Store in an airtight container.

OLD FASHIONED STRAWBERRY SHORTCAKE WITH DEVON-STYLE CREAM

Delicate little biscuits filled with homemade Devon cream and a generous number of the first strawberries of the season yield a rich dessert; don't make the shortcakes too large.

90 mL (6 tbsp.) soft butter
60 mL (4 tbsp.) sugar
125 mL (½ cup) sour cream
1 egg
375 mL (1½ cups) all-purpose white
   flour
10 mL (2 tsp.) baking powder
2 mL (½ tsp.) salt
1 mL (¼ tsp.) baking soda
1 L (1 qt.) strawberries
250 mL (1 cup) Devon cream

Cream the butter and sugar until smooth, beat in the sour cream and egg. Mix together the flour, baking powder, salt and baking soda and stir into the butter mixture. Stir until just moistened.

Turn the mixture onto a floured board and pat into a circle about 1.25 centimetres (½ in.) thick. With a medium-sized glass or round cutter, cut out circles and place on a greased baking sheet, gently reforming and patting the dough until it is all used. There should be eight rounds.

Bake at 200°C (400°F) for 12 to 15 minutes or until golden brown. Cool on a wire rack.

Carefully split shortcakes, fill with cream and strawberries and top with additional cream and one strawberry.

Devon-Style Cream

Devon cream can be found in the dairy section of most supermarkets, but it's very costly. This homemade version duplicates the flavor and texture of the real thing.

250 mL (1 cup) whipping cream
30 mL (2 tbsp.) light brown sugar
125 mL (½ cup) sour cream

In a small bowl, combine the whipping cream and sugar. Stir to dissolve. Whip the mixture until stiff peaks form. Fold in the sour cream. Refrigerate for several hours to allow flavors to blend. □

Earl Grey & All That

Afternoon tea as it should be: Father is just back from the stables, Rover still frisky at his heels, and Biff and Sissy are lounging on the lawn after a rousing match of tennis. Suddenly Mother appears on the veranda, resplendent in her summer silks and festive straw bonnet, pushing a tea-wagon laden with the Empire's finest china and tiniest sweets.

This isn't, as you might expect, a high tea. That term is reserved for a working class supper of sausage, meat pies, eggs and other heavies, washed down with the deepest, darkest tea that a spoon ever stood up straight in. *Afternoon* tea, by comparison, is light, delicate and pretty. Its roots are Victorian, and its rightful home is your own gracious parlor (er, living room). There you can dwell in history to the hilt, or chuck it in favor of your original teatime twists. But you'd be wise to observe certain time-tested rules:

When brewing tea, use china (silver is also acceptable) that has been washed in a baking-soda solution rather than soap, which leaves a residue; use loose tea, strained through stainless steel or bamboo but not aluminum, which has a taste; serve milk at room temperature (not cream, which is too heavy for delicate teas); and offer sugar, not honey.

But the crucial ingredient for a successful Victorian tea is the sweet tray, whose offerings should balance richness and delicacy. Scones, tea biscuits, crumpets and cakes are the heart of it, and our taste panel has narrowed its choices to the very best of these traditional goodies.

CREAM SCONES

Popular because they can be made quickly, scones require a gentle touch to get a flaky texture. Because of the addition of eggs, they are richer than ordinary tea biscuits. Try brushing any of the following scones with a sherry glaze, consisting of 15 millilitres (1 tbsp.) melted butter blended with five millilitres (1 tsp.) sherry and five millilitres (1 tsp.) sugar. Cake flour should be used in this recipe for best results.

500 mL (2 cups) sifted cake flour
10 mL (2 tsp.) baking powder
15 mL (1 tbsp.) sugar
2 mL (½ tsp.) salt
60 mL (4 tbsp.) butter, at room temperature
2 eggs, beaten
75 mL (1/3 cup) whipping cream

Mix together the flour, baking powder, sugar and salt. Cut in the butter with a pastry blender or lightly rub between your cool fingers until the mixture looks like rough sand. (Cool your fingers by holding them under cold water.)

Stir in the eggs and cream and combine with a few strokes, mixing until just blended.

If the dough is to be cut into shapes, place on a lightly floured surface and gently roll or pat into a circle about two centimetres (¾ in.) thick. Cut into desired shapes and place on a greased baking sheet.

If the dough is to be left whole, place it on a greased baking sheet and pat or gently roll into a 20-centimetre (8-in.) circle about two centimetres (¾ in.) thick.

Brush with a little egg-white, yolk or milk and sprinkle with sugar.

Bake at 220°C (425°F) for 15 minutes, or until golden.

YEAST SCONES

An easier dough to handle, this is our version of a delicious recipe published by the *Vancouver Sun*.

5 mL (1 tsp.) sugar
125 mL (½ cup) warm water
15 mL (1 tbsp.) dry yeast
1 L (4 cups) all-purpose white flour, more or less

30 mL (2 tbsp.) sugar
10 mL (2 tsp.) baking powder
5 mL (1 tsp.) salt
60 mL (4 tbsp.) soft butter
300 mL (1¼ cups) buttermilk, warmed

Dissolve the five millilitres (1 tsp.) of sugar in the warm water. Sprinkle on the yeast. Let stand until dissolved, about 10 minutes.

Mix 750 millilitres (3 cups) of the flour, the remaining sugar, baking powder and salt. Rub in the butter with cool fingers (see instructions for cream scones). Stir in the yeast and buttermilk. Add enough of the remaining flour to make a moderately stiff dough.

Knead for a few seconds on a lightly floured surface. Divide the dough into two pieces.

Form into shapes as directed in cream scones. Let rise in a warm place until almost doubled, about 45 to 60 minutes.

Bake at 220°C (425°F) for 12 to 15 minutes or until golden.

CRUMPETS

Moist and chewy, crumpets freeze well. Pop into the toaster for a quick thaw. It's difficult to mix in the baking soda by hand or with a hand-held electric beater, and so We recommend using an electric mixer. If you see small brown spots in the baked crumpets, you will know that the soda wasn't thoroughly incorporated. Makes 8 to 10.

5 mL (1 tsp.) sugar
175 mL (¾ cup) warm water
15 mL (1 tbsp.) dry yeast
125 mL (½ cup) milk, at room temperature
30 mL (2 tbsp.) butter, melted
5 mL (1 tsp.) salt
300 mL (1¼ cups) all-purpose white flour
2 mL (½ tsp.) baking soda
15 mL (1 tbsp.) hot water

In the large bowl of an electric mixer, dissolve the sugar in the

water and sprinkle on the yeast. Let stand until dissolved, about 10 minutes. Add the milk, butter, salt and flour. Beat at medium speed for three to four minutes. Leave in the same bowl, cover and let stand in a warm place until double, about one hour. In a small bowl, stir the soda into the hot water. Stir into the batter and return the bowl to the mixer. Beat on medium speed until thoroughly blended. Let rise again for one hour.

Lightly grease a griddle or skillet and the muffin rings, or use 198-gram tuna cans with tops and bottoms removed. Arrange the rings on the skillet, not touching. Preheat over medium heat until a drop of water sizzles on the surface.

Spoon batter into the rings, about one centimetre (½ in.) deep. Cook over medium heat about five to seven minutes or until the surfaces appear dry. Lift the rings from the pan and remove the crumpets, which should have pulled away from the sides of the rings. You may need to use a knife to free them, but be careful, the rings are hot. Turn the crumpets and lightly brown the other side, about three minutes. Repeat with remaining batter, cleaning and greasing the rings between batches. Serve warm. Toast without splitting.

ENGLISH MUFFINS

Makes about 20 wonderful muffins.

5 mL (1 tsp.) sugar
250 mL (1 cup) warm water
15 mL (1 tbsp.) dry yeast
250 mL (1 cup) buttermilk, warmed
5 mL (1 tsp.) salt
30 mL (2 tbsp.) sugar
60 mL (4 tbsp.) butter, very soft
1.25 to 1.5 L (5 to 6 cups) all-
    purpose white flour
Cornmeal

Dissolve the sugar in the warm water and sprinkle on the yeast. Let stand until bubbly, about 10 minutes.

Combine the buttermilk, salt, sugar and butter in a large bowl. Beat to blend, add yeast and beat in 750 millilitres (3 cups) of flour. Gradually add 500 to 750 millilitres (2 to 3 cups) more flour to form a stiff dough. Turn out onto a lightly floured board and knead for eight to 10 minutes until dough is smooth and silky. Place in a greased bowl and let rise until doubled, about one hour.

Punch down the dough and turn out onto a floured board. Roll out to about one-centimetre (½-in.) thickness. Fold in half and roll out again to the same thickness. Because of this folding and rolling, the baked muffins will break naturally in the centre. Cut with a floured 7.5 or 10-centimetre (3 or 4-in.) round cutter. Place on baking sheets sprinkled with cornmeal. Brush the tops with water and sprinkle on more cornmeal.

Cover and let rise until doubled, about 35 minutes. Bake in a preheated 230°C (450°F) oven five to eight minutes on each side.

Or fry over low heat, in a lightly greased frypan, for five to eight minutes on each side. These muffins freeze well.

WELSH CAKES

These fried currant cakes are a sweeter, dense version of a baking powder biscuit. Makes 36 to 48 cakes, depending on the size of the rounds.

750 mL (3 cups) all-purpose white
    flour
7 mL (1½ tsp.) baking powder
2 mL (½ tsp.) baking soda
5 mL (1 tsp.) salt
250 mL (1 cup) sugar
5 mL (1 tsp.) nutmeg
250 mL (1 cup) cold butter
250 mL (1 cup) currants
2 eggs
90 mL (6 tbsp.) milk

In a large bowl, stir together the flour, baking powder, baking soda, salt, sugar and nutmeg. With a pastry cutter or two knives, cut

The traditional sweets of an afternoon tea: a scone, sliced and spread with homemade jam and heavy cream, shortbread cookies and bite-sized, raisin-laden Banbury tarts.

in the butter until the size of peas. Add the currants.

Beat the eggs and milk together. Add to the dry mixture, blending well.

Turn out onto a floured surface and roll out to about one centimetre (½ in.) thick. Cut into four or five-centimetre (1½ or 2-in.) rounds. Bake on a frypan over low heat (150°C or 300°F in an electric pan) for 10 to 12 minutes on each side.

ECCLES CAKES

Make these ahead and freeze before baking. Makes about 20 to 24 little cakes.

Pastry for single-crust pie or a 215-g
  pkg. frozen puff pastry
30 mL (2 tbsp.) soft butter
30 mL (2 tbsp.) brown sugar
60 mL (4 tbsp.) mixed peel, finely
  chopped
45 mL (3 tbsp.) currants
1 egg-white
Sugar

Make the pastry and chill or thaw the frozen pastry.

Beat the butter and brown sugar together until pale and fluffy. Add the peel and currants.

Roll out the chilled pastry thinly, about three millimetres (1/8 in.) thick. Cut into rounds with a 7.5-centimetre (3-in.) cutter.

Put a scant five millilitres (1 tsp.) of the filling in the centre of each round and draw the edges together to cover the filling completely. Pinch to seal. Reshape each cake into a round and turn over, sealed side down. With a lightly floured rolling pin, roll over the top of each gently to flatten and until the currants just show through the pastry.

With the tip of a knife make three slits across the top of each cake. Let rest, refrigerated, until baking time. Or freeze at this point.

Just before baking, brush with egg-white and sprinkle on the sugar. Bake at 220°C (425°F) for 15 minutes or until golden.

CHERRY ALMOND CAKE

Made like a Christmas cake, this cherry almond cake is a good keeper and freezes well. It can be made in one large round, if desired, but increase the baking time by about 20 to 30 minutes.

625 mL (2½ cups) all-purpose white
  flour
10 mL (2 tsp.) baking powder
2 mL (½ tsp.) salt
500 g (1 lb.) glacé maraschino
  cherries, lightly rinsed
250 mL (1 cup) unsalted butter
5 mL (1 tsp.) vanilla
5 mL (1 tsp.) almond flavoring
25 mL (1½ tbsp.) lemon juice
250 mL (1 cup) sugar
4 eggs
60 mL (4 tbsp.) milk

Grease and line two standard loaf pans.

Stir 125 millilitres (½ cup) of the flour into a small bowl containing the cherries. Blend together the remaining flour, baking powder and salt.

In another bowl, beat the butter until light and fluffy. Add the vanilla, almond flavoring and lemon juice. Gradually add the sugar, beating until creamy. Beat the eggs and add to the butter mixture along with the milk.

Stir in the flour mixture and then the cherries. Fold until well combined. Turn into prepared pans, filling two-thirds full and spreading the batter evenly. Bake at 150°C (300°F) for one hour and 10 minutes, or until golden brown and a tester inserted slightly off centre comes out clean. The cake will split a little down the centre.

Allow to stand in the tins for five minutes, then turn out onto a rack to cool.

POPPY SEED CAKE

Often just called seed cake, this is a firm, moist cake with a nutty flavor. It will become a family favorite. You might make it in two small *kugelhopf* pans and serve one fresh and freeze the other.

175 mL (¾ cup) poppy seeds
75 mL (1/3 cup) honey

250 mL (1 cup) soft butter
375 mL (1½ cups) white sugar
4 eggs, separated
250 mL (1 cup) sour cream
5 mL (1 tsp.) vanilla
625 mL (2½ cups) all-purpose white
  flour
5 mL (1 tsp.) baking soda
5 mL (1 tsp.) salt

In a small saucepan, cook poppy seeds with honey and 60 millilitres (4 tbsp.) water for five to seven minutes. Cool.

Cream the butter and sugar until light and fluffy. Add the poppy-seed mixture. Add yolks, one at a time, beating well after each addition. Blend in sour cream and vanilla.

Sift together the dry ingredients. Gradually add to the moist ingredients, beating well after each addition.

Beat the egg-whites until soft peaks are formed. Stir one-quarter of the egg-whites into the poppy-seed mixture, and then fold in the remaining whites.

Pour the batter into a lightly greased and floured 22-centimetre (9-in.) tube pan. Bake at 180°C (350°F) for one hour and 15 minutes (35 to 45 minutes for two smaller pans) or until done and a cake tester comes out clean. Cool in the pan for 10 minutes. Remove the cake and cool on rack. Frost if desired.

SHORTBREAD

Rich and smoothly flavored shortbread is a must at any tea. Make rounds and oblongs in the traditional style.

125 mL (½ cup) icing sugar
250 mL (1 cup) soft butter
500 mL (2 cups) all-purpose white
  flour

Cream the butter with the sugar and add the flour. It may be necessary to blend the mixture with your hands.

Turn out onto a floured surface and roll out about 6 millimetres (¼ in.) thick. Cut into shapes.

Place on a baking sheet and prick the cookies with a fork.

Bake at 150°C (300°F) until

light brown, about 20 minutes. Cool on a rack.

Shortbread stores well, and unbaked cookies may be frozen. Let thaw before baking.

BROWN SUGAR SHORTBREAD WITH CHERRIES AND ALMONDS

Crisp, yet chewy, this is a wonderful cookie. You can freeze the dough in logs, and then slice off what is needed. The cookies will taste bitter if they are overcooked and become too dark.

250 mL (1 cup) soft butter
250 mL (1 cup) light brown sugar
500 mL (2 cups) all-purpose white
  flour
125 mL (½ cup) glacé cherries,
  washed and chopped
125 mL (½ cup) almonds, peeled and
  slivered

Beat together the butter and sugar. Stir in the flour and blend in the cherries and almonds. Mix together well.

Shape into two long rolls, about five centimetres (2 in.) in diameter. Place on waxed paper and chill. May be frozen at this point. Thaw before using.

Slice into rounds about 6 millimetres (¼ in.) thick. Bake at 160°C (325°F) for about 10 to 20 minutes or until very lightly golden on the bottom. Cool on racks. These cookies are best eaten the day they are made.

BANBURY TARTS

Reminiscent of mincemeat tarts and wonderfully flavored with lemon, Banbury tarts are often served as turnovers. Make the tiniest tart shells you can for bite-sized servings.

30 mL (2 tbsp.) soft butter
125 mL (½ cup) sugar
1 egg, well beaten
30 mL (2 tbsp.) very fine cracker or
  cookie crumbs
250 mL (1 cup) raisins or 125 mL
  (½ cup) each raisins and currants
Grated rind of 1 lemon, finely minced
Juice of 1 medium lemon

60 mL (4 tbsp.) candied peel or fruit,
  finely chopped
Pinch of nutmeg and cinnamon
18 to 24 mini pastry shells
Whipped cream for topping

Place the first nine ingredients in a medium saucepan. Bring to a boil, reduce the heat and cook and stir these ingredients until the sugar is dissolved, about five minutes. Remove from the heat and cool thoroughly. Spoon into the baked tart shells and top with a dollop of whipped cream.

The filling will keep but does harden upon storage. Bring it to room temperature to restore it to a working consistency.

CREME FRAICHE

Served over fruits in France, this naturally matured, slightly sour-flavored cream makes a very good substitute for Devonshire cream. It is often used in cooking because it does not break down as sour cream does.

250 mL (1 cup) whipping cream
250 mL (1 cup) sour cream

Blend the two creams together and warm to body temperature. Let stand for 18 hours at warm room temperature. Stir and refrigerate. Use chilled.

Or:

250 mL (1 cup) whipping cream
30 mL (2 tbsp.) buttermilk

Blend together and warm to body temperature. Let stand as above and chill. □

Meal from Morocco

Just after the Second World War, the pasha of Marrakech decided that he was weary of feeding a constant parade of palace guests, so he approached two French women with a gift. He offered Suzy Larochette and her mother a woman from his harem. The woman was a cook. The pasha proposed that Ms. Larochette and her mother take advantage of the gift and open a fine Moroccan restaurant, which, in a country where good cooking happened only at home, would be the city's first. He knew the Larochettes had the credentials to run such an establishment, since he had been, years before, to their well-known restaurant in Paris.

La Maison Arabe became world-famous, and Suzy Larochette not only still runs it but also recently opened a small pension next door. As the name suggests, the restaurant is found in an authentic Arab house in the old section of the city. Polished copper tables are cozily located in the corners and alcoves of small, airy rooms. A courtyard opens to the stars. The lower sections of walls are tiled; above the tiles hangs Moroccan craftwork.

Ms. Larochette is a quintessentially elegant Frenchwoman with a reputation for treating her guests coolly. However, she warms to questioning, recalling the time she travelled to New York and cooked in Craig Claiborne's kitchen, and the occasions much before that when her restaurant served the likes of Winston Churchill, the Queen Mother of Denmark, Adlai Stevenson and Orson Welles. Stevenson she remembers as "very agreeable." Orson was a trial: "He eats three chickens at one time, and at the same time he says, 'Do this! Do this! Do this!' It was something terrible."

At La Maison Arabe we had the dish considered to be Morocco's culinary triumph, *bstilla*. Bstilla is a complex layering of 50 leaves of papery thin pastry with squab, ground nuts and spices. Lines of powdered sugar and cinnamon are arranged in latticework design on top. The dish is rich, light, sweet and savory, eaten with the hands and served dangerously hot. The pastry, unique to Morocco, can take a practised cook an hour for each bstilla.

The dish internationally known and associated with Morocco is couscous. Real couscous is not at all like the boxed variety found in supermarkets in the West. Laborious and repeated steaming and working of the couscous with the hands plumps the semolina grains to perfection without rendering them soggy. This is an art many Moroccan chefs say is beyond them.

But there is more to Moroccan food than these two difficult dishes. *Tagines* — Moroccan stews — are found all over the country, and vary sharply from region to region. Salads are also a common beginning to a Moroccan meal. Moroccan salads often consist of cooked vegetables — zucchini, eggplant, green pepper — served cold with a spicy sauce.

Most of the recipes here came from a unique source — a young Arkansas woman who learned Arabic while learning to cook in her Moroccan mother-in-law's kitchen. Cheryl Lamghara is an enthusiastic, gracious native of Little Rock who happens to be married to a Moroccan hotelier. He works in the grand La Mamounia hotel in Marrakech, while she manages the hotel's art shop. Since moving to Morocco, Cheryl has become fluent in both Arabic and French, which she speaks with a gentle southern

Marrakech moods: beef brochettes with Moroccan bread; chicken with preserved lemons; minced tomato and bell-pepper salad; and a fruit plate with rosewater.

accent. Her in-laws, she says, are a delight, and she has collected a small book of authentic Moroccan recipes from her mother-in-law. The families live a few houses apart, and food flies in both directions: "We have a little deal, and when she [her mother-in-law] makes a dish, she sends me part of it. When I make a pizza or fried chicken, I send her part of it."

MENU *(Serves Six)*

• Chicken with Preserved Lemons
• Brochettes and Kefta
• Tagine of Brochettes
• Moroccan Bread
• Tomato and Bell Pepper Salad
• Fruits with Rose Water

CHICKEN WITH PRESERVED LEMONS

None of the dishes in this meal are difficult, but the lemons used with the chicken require a month, and preferably more, of preservation. They lend a superb and unique flavor to all sorts of entrées, and may be addictive. Moroccans will always warn you not to eat too much preserved lemon; they say it leads to an unquenchable thirst.

2 chickens, whole or cut into serving pieces
10 to 12 cloves of garlic
5 mL (1 tsp.) powdered ginger
5 mL (1 tsp.) string saffron
60 mL (¼ cup) vegetable oil
Several small pieces of preserved lemon (recipe follows)
500 to 750 mL (2 to 3 cups) chicken stock or canned broth
250 mL (1 cup) Greek olives

In a few spoons of melted butter, brown the chicken on both sides but don't completely cook it. Set chicken aside in a covered bowl. You can drain some of the fat from the pan but leave the brown bits for flavor. Press the livers of the chickens through a sieve or garlic press (this dish is even better if you use a few extra livers). Crush half of the garlic cloves and leave the rest whole. Add the garlic, ginger and saffron to the liver, along with the hearts and gizzards of the chickens. Add oil and liver mixture to frypan and

cook over low heat. Add remaining garlic, preserved lemon, chicken stock, olives (the closest thing to Moroccan olives is sharp-tasting, purple-black Greek or Italian olives that are preserved in olive oil with their pits in; don't use the jarred variety) and spices. Increase heat and reduce the sauce mixture until almost thick, then add chicken and cook until chicken is done and sauce is thick. (Remove hearts and gizzards, or eat them if you wish.)

Preserved Lemons

Slice fresh, medium-sized, smooth-skinned lemons so that you have quarter sections attached at the bottom by a small amount of peel. Take about 60 millilitres (¼ cup) of rock salt (not too coarse) and sprinkle the lemons with salt, then gently press the lemons to close them. Put a small palmful of salt on the bottom of a large sterile mason jar, then pack in the lemons to fill it; this will squeeze out a bit of the juice. Cover the lemons with fresh-squeezed lemon juice and close the jar (you can also add a bit of olive oil). Leave a little air in the jar. Because of the large amount of salt and acid in this mixture, you don't have to heat it before sealing the jar. In her book *Couscous and Other Good Food from Morocco*, Paula Wolfert says the jar must be stored in a warm place for at least 30 days and turned over every few days. The lemons are "done" when the skin gets soft; they will last for up to a year. To use, remove the inside of the lemons and slice the skin into thin pieces.

BROCHETTES

500 g (1 lb.) tender lamb or beef fillet
½ grated onion and juice
5 to 10 mL (1 to 2 tsp.) cumin
5 mL (1 tsp.) powdered ginger
2 to 5 mL (½ to 1 tsp.) string saffron
5 mL (1 tsp.) paprika
Several garlic cloves, crushed with fresh coriander (cilantro)
5 mL (1 tsp.) black pepper, freshly ground
Salt to taste

Mix the spices, garlic, onion and salt. Cut the meat into bite-sized

cubes. With hands, rub the meat in the spice mixture until thoroughly coated. Put meat on skewers and roast over charcoal or just under broiler until rare.

KEFTA

500 g (1 lb.) regular ground beef
5 to 10 mL (1 to 2 tsp.) cumin
2 to 5 mL (½ to 1 tsp.) powdered ginger
2 to 5 mL (½ to 1 tsp.) string saffron
5 to 10 mL (1 to 2 tsp.) paprika
5 mL (1 tsp.) ground chilies
15 mL (1 tbsp.) crushed fresh garlic, with small palmful of fresh coriander
½ onion, grated
5 mL (1 tsp.) ground black pepper
Salt to taste
Dash or two of cinnamon

Mix all ingredients except beef. Spread the meat on a plate, sprinkle with the spice mixture, and then work the meat by hand for a few minutes until spices are mixed in. Don't work it until meat is gluey. To cook over charcoal, put a small palmful of meat mixture in your hand and work the meat around a small skewer. Pinch the ends of the meat. Don't use too much meat or it will fall off during cooking. Grill over charcoal until just done – cook fast over high heat to seal in the juices.

KEFTA SAUCE

You can serve kefta with a side-sauce of puréed tomatoes mixed with fresh parsley, fresh coriander, salt and a red chili sauce (or ground red chilies). Add a bit of oil. Don't mix this in a blender or it will become foamy. Vary the ingredients to taste. This sauce is not cooked.

TAGINE OF BROCHETTES OR KEFTA

A tagine is a Moroccan stew.

½ large onion, diced
10 medium to large tomatoes, peeled and chopped (or canned tomatoes)
2 to 5 mL (½ to 1 tsp.) string saffron
2 to 5 mL (½ to 1 tsp.) powdered ginger

2 mL (½ tsp.) black pepper
2 sticks of cinnamon or 2 to 4 mL
   (½ to 1 tsp.) powdered cinnamon
30 mL (2 tbsp.) vegetable oil
Palmful of parsley and fresh coriander,
   chopped and mixed
375 mL (1½ cup) water or tomato
   juice
Brochettes or kefta
4 eggs
Lemon juice

If you use brochettes in this recipe, cook them first over charcoal as described above. If you use kefta, prepare the meat and spice mixture but do not cook. A third alternative is to served grilled brochettes or kefta on the side, and use only eggs in the tagine.

Put the onion, tomatoes and oil in a heavy pot with water or tomato juice. Cook it down to chili thickness. Add saffron, ginger, pepper, cinnamon, coriander and parsley about 10 minutes before tagine is thick. If using cooked brochettes, add them now, and then crack the whole eggs directly into the sauce. Cover pot to steam the eggs, but do not overcook eggs – the yolks should be liquid.

If using kefta, make small meatballs with the beef mixture and drop them into the sauce to cook. After a few minutes, add the eggs and finish cooking.

This tagine can be made with eggs only. Pour plenty of fresh lemon juice over the tagine just before serving.

MOROCCAN BREAD

This is a heavy bread that is easy to make and is wonderful for sopping up the delicious sauces.

250 mL (1 cup) warm water
15 mL (1 tbsp.) dry yeast
5 mL (1 tsp.) sugar
750 mL (3 cups) all-purpose white
   flour
250 mL (1 cup) wholewheat flour
10 mL (2 tsp.) salt
125 mL (½ cup) lukewarm milk
15 mL (1 tbsp.) sesame seeds
15 mL (1 tbsp.) ground aniseed
Cornmeal

Dissolve the sugar in the warm water and sprinkle on the yeast.

Let stand until dissolved and bubbly, about 10 minutes.

Mix together, in a large bowl, the white flour, wholewheat flour and salt. Stir in the dissolved yeast and warm milk. Add the sesame seeds and aniseed. Turn the dough onto a lightly floured board and knead until smooth and silky, about 10 minutes.

Form the dough into two equal balls and let rest for five minutes.

Grease a baking sheet and sprinkle it with cornmeal.

Gently press the balls of dough into a flattened disc about 15 centimetres (5 in.) in diameter with a slightly raised centre. Grease dough. Place on baking sheet and let rise until not quite double, about one hour.

Preheat oven to 200° C (400° F). With a fork, prick the bread around the sides. Place in the hot oven and bake for 12 minutes. Reduce heat to 150° C (300° F) and bake for 30 to 40 minutes more or until the loaf sounds hollow when tapped on the bottom.

Cool. Cut in wedges for serving or allow diners to break pieces with their hands.

TOMATOES WITH BELL PEPPERS

6 tomatoes, peeled, skinned and seeded
2 large green peppers
½ onion, chopped
Salt and pepper to taste
Juice of 1 lemon
30 mL (2 tbsp.) vegetable or olive oil
15 mL (1 tbsp.) fresh coriander,
   chopped

Seed the tomatoes by squeezing them by hand. Take the peppers and place over a fire and burn until solid black. Another method is to preheat the broiler to its highest setting, line the broiler rack with foil and place foil about 10 centimetres (4 in.) from the heat. Broil peppers, turning them, until evenly charred.

When peppers are charred, wrap them in a tea towel or put in a paper bag and set them aside. Let them steam under their own heat for 10 minutes, then rinse the peppers under running cold water. The pepper skins will slide off.

Slice peppers and tomatoes and mix with onion, oil, lemon juice, salt and pepper. Serve cold or at room temperature. Use red, green and yellow peppers for additional color.

SEASONAL FRUIT WITH ROSEWATER

A delightful aromatic ending to the meal. Rosewater and other perfumed waters are often used in Moroccan sweets. They are available at Middle Eastern specialty stores.

½ honeydew melon
2 cantaloupes
Pomegranate
Salt
3 large peaches
125 mL (½ cup) white sugar
75 mL (5 tbsp.) lemon juice
75 mL (5 tbsp.) rosewater

Peel melons and cut into cubes, or make balls with melon baller. Put in deep bowl, pour any melon juice over and toss with salt. Peel peaches and cut into thin slices. Add to melon, along with other ingredients, and gently mix. Cover tightly and refrigerate for at least two hours.

This dish can be garnished with finely chopped pistachios and a sprinkling of cinnamon. □

A Delicate Meal for May

That May is a month that can go either way — dumping snow on the prairies and bucketfuls of rain on the West Coast, or opting instead to mimic July's heat — is an indication of how far north of the regions of reasonable climes we are. But often the month behaves itself, and there are days when you walk out onto the balcony or porch and stare at the sky and remark that, well, summer is almost upon us, and it seems a not unduly optimistic remark. A superb day in May is a gift — relish on the bun of summer.

It was with optimism about May that this meal was conceived. It is a meal to be eaten, if not right out on the back lawn, at least on a covered deck, or in a room with the windows flung open and a glass of Gewürztraminer in hand to toast the nascent season.

A *blanquette* is a traditional French dish of chicken, veal or lamb which is poached in stock and served with a sauce derived from the stock. Chicken is superbly tender and juicy cooked this way. Select plump, fresh birds and debone the breasts carefully or ask for fresh, deboned breasts from your butcher. The *blanquette* with curry mayonnaise, detailed below, is versatile — excellent served on a hot day or hot on a cool evening. The cold vegetables in vinaigrette to accompany the chicken are equally light and refreshing.

Those who have been shying away from attempting to make puff pastry can ease into the task by trying the easy method featured

Cool cuisine: creamy brie all dressed up in puff pastry; a delicate blanquette of chicken with curry mayonnaise and vegetable vinaigrette; a refreshing dish of kiwifruit ice.

in the Brie en Croute recipe. The timing and the butter temperature are less critical in this version. If you substitute store-bought frozen puff pastry dough, try to find a brand that contains butter. Some contain margarine, shortening or lard, and the flavor and texture are inferior. We have also heard that friendly neighborhood bakers will sell puff pastry dough to those who make special enquiries.

MENU *(Serves Eight)*

- Brie en Croute
- Blanquette of Chicken with Curry Mayonnaise
- Vegetables Vinaigrette
- Kiwifruit Ice
- Madeleines

BRIE EN CROUTE

Brie is superb all dressed up. Brioche dough or phyllo pastry are alternatives to the jacket of puff pastry described here.

⅓ to ½ of a 22-cm (9-in.) wheel of firm Brie (approx. 400 g)
½ puff pastry recipe below, or two 215-g pkgs. frozen puff pastry
1 egg yolk, beaten

Roll out pastry into two rounds, one large enough to encase the Brie across the bottom and up the sides. Roll out the second round to cover the top and sides completely. Brush the edges of the pastry with egg yolk and stick the two pastry sheets together, encasing the cheese and pinching the pastry edges. Brush the entire package with egg glaze. Use the scraps of pastry to make a decoration if desired and brush again with glaze.

Place on a baking sheet, which has sides to catch any drips, and bake at 180°C (350°F) for 20 to 30 minutes or until golden.

This recipe may be made ahead and refrigerated until serving time. Brush with egg glaze again just before baking.

Julia's Quick Puff Pastry
Both Julia Child and Jacques Pepin lay claim to versions of this recipe. It is a very good method for making puff pastry the easy way.

This recipe makes 750 grams (1½ lbs.).

500 mL (2 cups) all-purpose white flour
7 mL (1½ tsp.) salt
375 mL (12 oz., or 1½ cups plus 2 tbsp.) chilled unsalted butter
125 mL (½ cup) ice water, more or less

Place the flour and salt in a bowl, mixer or food processor. Cut the butter into one-centimetre (½-in.) cubes and add to the flour. Blend rapidly until pieces are about the size of kidney beans. Turn out into a large bowl.

Add the ice water until the dough will hold together, mixing with a round-bladed knife. Do not add too much water.

Turn out onto a floured board and quickly roll into a rectangle about 30 by 35 centimetres (12 by 14 in.). Fold the bottom third so that the fold of the "book" of pastry is on your left. Roll and fold as before three more times. Wrap in parchment or waxed paper and chill 40 minutes. Roll and fold as described above two more times. Chill for 30 minutes. Dough is now ready to use or to store in the freezer.

Note: any good margarine can also be used; just decrease the quantity of salt accordingly. If at any time the butter starts to become too soft, pat a little more flour over the sticky areas and continue rolling and folding, or place the dough into the fridge until the butter firms up.

BLANQUETTE OF CHICKEN WITH CURRY MAYONNAISE

Four large chicken breasts
1 large carrot, sliced
1 onion, sliced
2 stalks of celery, sliced
1 bay leaf
2 mL (½ tsp.) thyme
5 mL (1 tsp.) salt
Freshly ground black pepper
250 mL (1 cup) dry white wine
750 mL (3 cups) chicken stock or canned broth
Fresh parsley, finely chopped

Skin, bone and cut the chicken breasts in half.

In a large pot, place the carrot, onion, celery, bay leaf, thyme, salt, pepper, wine, stock and parsley. Bring to a boil. Add the skin and bones from the chicken and simmer for 30 minutes. Add the chicken breasts to the liquid and arrange so they are spread flat. Simmer gently for 20 minutes. Do not overcook as they will become dry. Remove from the stock and cool thoroughly. Strain cooking liquid and reserve.

While the chicken breasts are cooling, make the curry mayonnaise.

Curry Mayonnaise
1 small onion, finely chopped
1 clove garlic, minced
30 mL (2 tbsp.) butter
30 mL (2 tbsp.) curry chutney or 15 mL (1 tbsp.) curry powder
5 mL (1 tsp.) tomato paste
60 mL (4 tbsp.) reserved chicken stock or canned broth
30 mL (2 tbsp.) orange marmalade
375 mL (1½ cups) mayonnaise (recipe below)
60 to 120 mL (4 to 8 tbsp.) additional chicken stock or canned broth

Sauté the onion in the butter until soft, adding the garlic for the last few minutes of cooking. Add curry and cook a few minutes longer. Stir in the tomato paste and chicken stock and cook about five minutes. Add marmalade and mix together well. Cool and strain. Add the curry liquid to the mayonnaise, adding the additional chicken stock if necessary. The sauce should be the consistency of sour cream. Taste and add more seasoning if desired.

This dish can be served hot, at room temperature or cold. If it is to be served hot, reheat the stock to a simmer and warm the chicken breasts in it for about five minutes. Place a few pieces of butter lettuce on individual serving plates or on one large platter. Arrange the meat on the lettuce and gently spoon the curry mayonnaise over the chicken to just blanket it. Serve additional sauce on the side.

Homemade Mayonnaise
This mayonnaise recipe, which makes 375 mL (1½ cups), will keep up to 10 days in the fridge.

1 large egg
5 mL (1 tsp.) Dijon mustard
5 mL (1 tsp.) fresh lemon juice
5 mL (1 tsp.) red or white wine
* vinegar*
375 (1½ cups) oil, a mixture of 45
* mL (3 tbsp.) olive oil and the rest*
* vegetable oil*

In a blender or food processor, whirl together the egg, mustard, lemon juice and vinegar. With the machine running, very slowly pour in the oil until the mixture becomes thick and shiny.

There should be no need to season, but a tiny dash of salt and/or pepper could be added, if desired.

VEGETABLES VINAIGRETTE

Choose three or four kinds of young, tender spring vegetables for this colorful presentation. Cut them all to approximately the same size. Bring a large pot of water to a boil and cook the vegetables, one kind at a time, until crisp but tender to the bite. Remove vegetables and cool rapidly under cold running water. This will stop the cooking and preserve the color. Place in a large bowl, adding the remaining vegetables as they are done.

Toss the cooked vegetables in the vinaigrette (recipe below) until they are thoroughly coated. This can be done several hours before serving time, but store the coated vegetables at room temperature. Taste for seasonings and add more salt, pepper or oregano as needed.

Arrange the vegetables around the chicken breasts.

Vinaigrette
Makes about 175 mL or ¾ cup.

125 mL (½ cup) olive oil
75 mL (5 tbsp.) red wine vinegar
1 clove garlic, crushed
5 mL (1 tsp.) oregano
60 mL (4 tbsp.) fresh dill, snipped
2 mL (½ tsp.) salt
Freshly ground pepper to taste

Place all the ingredients in a jar with a tight-fitting lid and shake until well mixed. Allow to stand

for a few hours to mellow flavors. Shake just before using.

KIWIFRUIT ICE

This ice is a glorious green color and has a refreshing tartness.

60 mL (4 tbsp.) sugar
125 mL (½ cup) water
6 large kiwifruit
Juice of four oranges, about 175 mL
* (¾ cup)*
Juice of one lime
1 egg-white
Sprig of mint

Simmer the sugar and water together for five minutes. Cool. Peel and purée the kiwifruit. Strain out as many of the little black seeds as possible. Combine the pulp with the orange juice, lime juice and sugar syrup. Place in a shallow container and freeze for three hours or until almost solid. Whisk the egg-white until stiff. Beat in the frozen ice by spoonfuls. Return to the freezer and freeze until firm. Scoop into serving dishes and top with a few slices of mint.

Note: The kiwifruit from New Zealand, which comes into the markets in May, have a much more intense green flesh than the kiwifruit from California. If the color of your kiwi seems pale, you can add one or two drops of food coloring when you are combining the juices and pulp.

MADELEINES

To bake these, you need a special pan with shell-shaped indentations. Made in France of a single sheet of metal, the pan will hold a dozen cakes, each about eight centimetres by five centimetres (3 in. by 2 in.). Lightly dust these delicate morsels with icing sugar and serve them like cookies, with tea or coffee and the kiwifruit ice. They do not keep well, so plan to eat them the day they are made.

3 large eggs
75 mL (⅓ cup) white sugar
1 mL (¼ tsp.) vanilla
125 mL (½ cup) all-purpose white
* flour*
45 mL (3 tbsp.) butter, melted and
* cooled*

Preheat the oven to 180°C (350°F). Using part of the melted butter, lightly brush the moulds, making sure to get butter in all of the indentations. For a crispy texture, lightly sugar the mould, tossing out the excess.

Beat the eggs with the sugar until they are thick and light and a ribbon forms when the beater is raised. Stir in the vanilla. Shake the flour through a sieve onto the batter and quickly stir it in. Add the butter rapidly.

Drop the batter by large tablespoons into the pan. Bake until light brown, about 10 to 15 minutes. Remove from pan and turn shell-side up. When cool, sprinkle with icing sugar.

To make a second batch, wash pan and rebutter before using. □

Fancy Fish

One cannot help but marvel that fish with succulent flesh are often spectacularly ugly. With its ferocious maw gaping wide, the monkfish scours the sea bottom, angling for food. It is grotesque, but it has sweet meat so like lobster it's hard to tell the difference. Skate, with its bat-like wings and sinister tail, is the only fish that gets better two or three days after it has been caught. The meat of its wings is often compared to scallops and may even be cut in circles to masquerade as such. For ophidiophobes, eels may be as threatening as snakes, but their flesh is nutritious, delicate and sweet, and they have inspired an amazing variety of recipes. Our recipes for swordfish, shark, monkfish, plaice and skate are interchangeable; these fish can be poached, baked, broiled, grilled or fried, and served with any of the sauces we suggest. If you can't find the fish you want, Canada Safeway says, "If it swims, we'll get it."

PERIWINKLES

Periwinkles are similar to land snails and can be treated as you would mussels and clams. They can also be eaten raw. As an appetizer or first course, allow about 250 grams (½ lb.) per person. This recipe serves six.

1.5 kg (3 lbs.) fresh periwinkles
60 mL (4 tbsp.) dry white wine
1 shallot, thinly sliced
6 thin slices of carrot
Pinch of thyme
Small piece of bayleaf
Stalk of parsley

Wash the periwinkles in several changes of water until clean. Place in a large pot and add the

Brandishing the sword: firm-fleshed swordfish steaks, grilled and daubed with basil butter, lightly peppered and garnished with fresh dill.

Cool under cold running water.

The periwinkles are removed from their shells with a long pin, skewer or lobster fork and then dipped into a sauce. Any dipping sauce that you like for escargots can be used. Serve with thinly sliced baguette or French bread that has been buttered and sprinkled with parmesan cheese and lightly broiled.

Try the following black bean sauce if you are looking for a new idea.

BLACK BEAN SAUCE

This sauce is rich and goes far.

10 mL (2 tsp.) shallots or green onions, finely chopped
5 mL (1 tsp.) garlic, finely chopped
30 mL (2 tbsp.) olive oil
15 mL (1 tbsp.) sake or dry white wine
250 mL (1 cup) shellfish stock (see note)
250 mL (1 cup) whipping cream
About 10 mL (2 tsp.) commercial black bean sauce, to taste
Salt and pepper, to taste

Sauté the shallots and garlic in the oil until soft. Add the wine and boil until reduced by half. Add the stock and continue boiling until reduced by half. Add the cream and reduce until thick. Season to taste with black bean sauce and with salt and pepper.

Note: To make a shellfish stock, take shells of shrimp or prawns, cover with water, add a piece of onion, bayleaf, parsley and three or four peppercorns, and bring to a boil. Turn down the heat and simmer for about 20 minutes. Strain the liquid into a bowl. Discard the shells, etc. If there isn't 250 millilitres (1 cup) of liquid, add chicken stock.

GRILLED SWORDFISH WITH BASIL BUTTER

Swordfish can produce very large steaks. The meat is dense and rich.

Swordfish steaks, 250 g (½ lb.) per person
Black peppercorns, freshly cracked

Oil
60 mL (4 tbsp.) unsalted butter
15 mL (1 tbsp.) fresh lemon juice
30 mL (2 tbsp.) fresh basil leaves, finely chopped
15 mL (1 tbsp.) fresh chives, finely chopped
Dash of freshly ground pepper

Mix together the butter, lemon juice, herbs and pepper and form into a log. Chill until firm.

Bring the swordfish to room temperature. Press the cracked peppercorns into both sides of the meat. Let stand a few minutes before grilling. Brush the hot grill with oil. Place the swordfish on the grill and sear well on each side, about three minutes. Turn down the heat, or raise the grill and continue cooking for about four to five minutes on each side or until the flesh is firm to the touch. Another way of testing is to cut into the centre of the meat; it should be white and juicy looking.

Serve each swordfish steak with a thick slice of basil butter. (Freeze any leftover butter for future use; it is wonderful with snapper or sole.)

SWORDFISH BROCHETTES

The flavor of a marinade penetrates the flesh of the fish within 30 minutes. Use leftover sauce to brush on while grilling or for a dipping sauce.

Swordfish, 250 g (½ lb.) per person
Small onions
Cherry tomatoes
125 mL (½ cup) soy sauce
60 mL (4 tbsp.) sherry
15 mL (1 tbsp.) vegetable oil
1 clove garlic, minced
5 to 10 mL (1 to 2 tsp.) fresh ginger, minced
15 mL (1 tbsp.) sugar, optional

Cut the swordfish into 2.5-centimetre (1-in.) cubes. Thread on skewers, alternating with onions and tomatoes. Mix together the remaining ingredients and pour into a flat glass container that will hold the fish on the skewers. Marinate the fish for approximately 30 minutes, turning several times.

Broil over hot charcoal or in a preheated broiler, turning frequently and brushing with marinade until the meat is golden brown on all sides, about 10 to 12 minutes.

SHARK

Shark is used mainly in steaks and may be prepared like any other firm-fleshed fish. It is wonderful when grilled and served with a brown butter sauce. It is very good in skewer-type recipes because the meat does not break easily.

BROWN BUTTER

Put approximately 15 millilitres (1 tbsp.) butter per person in a small frypan and cook over high heat until it foams and begins to turn a rich golden brown. Immediately remove from the heat and pour over the cooked fish. Scatter on chopped parsley or green onions.

MARINATED SWORDFISH

Swordfish and shark take well to marinades. Try this tasty Mexican-influenced one. Grill the fish and baste with reserved marinade. Serve with lime wedges and additional cilantro.

Swordfish or shark steaks, 250 g (½ lb.) per person
Juice of 3 limes
125 mL (½ cup) olive oil (not strongly flavored extra virgin)
175 mL (¾ cup) fresh cilantro, finely chopped
60 mL (4 tbsp.) soft unsalted butter
Lime wedges and chopped cilantro for garnish

Mix together the lime juice, oil and chopped cilantro. Spread over the fish and marinate in a shallow glass bowl for at least 30 minutes, turning occasionally.

Grill the fish, basting with marinade until done.

Spread butter over the steaks and sprinkle with cilantro for garnish and decorate with lime wedges.

MONKFISH, CREOLE STYLE

Creole cooking is becoming popular, and monkfish lends itself very well to the spicy mixtures. It is often called poor man's lobster as it has the same texture. Try it grilled with brown butter for a wonderful treat, as well. It is very rich; a 2.5-centimetre-thick (1-in.) steak per person will be enough. The following batter will cover about six steaks.

125 mL (½ cup) masa harina (corn flour available at large grocery or specialty stores)
5 mL (1 tsp.) ground cumin
5 mL (1 tsp.) mild red chili powder
2 mL (½ tsp.) garlic salt
2 mL (½ tsp.) oregano
30 mL (2 tbsp.) parsley, minced
250 mL (1 cup) milk

Mix together in a shallow bowl the masa harina, cumin, chili, garlic, oregano and parsley. In another bowl, place the milk.

Dip the fish steaks into the milk and then into the spicy coating mixture. Place on a cake rack to dry.

Heat a mixture of butter and oil in a frypan and fry the steaks about four to five minutes on each side.

BLACKBERRY BUTTER SAUCE

We are indebted to Pia Carroll of Sooke Harbour House on Vancouver Island for this sauce, which goes well with steamed black cod, monkfish or swordfish.

Blackberry Vinegar:
500 mL (2 cups) blackberries (frozen can be used)
1 L (1 qt.) apple cider vinegar (Bezzola's is best)

In a non-metallic container, combine the blackberries and vinegar and stir well with a wooden spoon to bruise the fruit, but do not mash. Cover and let steep for two days. Bring to a boil and strain through cheesecloth into sterilized bottles.

Sauce
60 mL (¼ cup) fish stock
30 mL (2 tbsp.) white wine
30 mL (2 tbsp.) blackberry vinegar
45 mL (3 tbsp.) cold unsalted butter, cut into small cubes

In a small pan over high heat, bring the fish stock and white wine to a boil and reduce by half. Add the blackberry vinegar and reduce by half again. Off the heat, incorporate the cubes of butter slowly. Serve.

Note: If not used immediately, this butter sauce will hold together at room temperature. To reheat, gently stir over the lowest heat; do not boil.

SKATE

Akin to the ray, skate has triangular wings with fairly soft bones that are easily cut. The flesh is delicate and is similar to scallops. Allow about 250 grams (½ lb.) per person.

Poaching for 15 to 20 minutes and adding a creamed sauce is a popular way of serving.

Another delicious method is to deep fry small pieces of skate (no need for a batter) and serve with a tartar sauce. To eat, scrape bits of meat from the bones and dip in the sauce.

TARTAR SAUCE

There are many variations for this classic accompaniment to fish of all kinds. This is ours.

1 recipe homemade mayonnaise (see below) or 425 mL (1¾ cups) of a good commercial type
30 mL (2 tbsp.) capers, finely chopped
30 mL (2 tbsp.) parsley, finely chopped
45 mL (3 tbsp.) dill pickle, finely chopped
5 mL (1 tsp.) Dijon mustard
Freshly ground black pepper
Squeeze of fresh lemon juice to taste

Fold all the ingredients together and refrigerate for one to two hours for the flavors to blend.

HOMEMADE MAYONNAISE

This is best made in the food processor or blender as it requires the tediously slow addition of the oil while whisking by hand.

1 large egg
5 mL (1 tsp.) fresh lemon juice

5 mL (1 tsp.) red or white wine vinegar
5 mL (1 tsp.) Dijon mustard
Freshly ground white pepper
375 mL (1½ cups) oil, a mixture of
45 mL (3 tbsp.) olive oil and the rest vegetable oil

Place all the ingredients except the oils in a food processor, blender or small bowl. If mixing by hand, whisk briskly while very, very slowly dripping in the oils. Or, with the food processor or blender running, drizzle in the oil. As the mixture thickens, the oil can be added faster until it is all incorporated. Chill.

PLAICE WITH MUSTARD GLAZE

Cooked under the broiler and brushed with a tangy glaze, plaice is absolutely delicious. Serves four.

4 fillets of fish
90 mL (6 tbsp.) soft butter
60 mL (4 tbsp.) Dijon or other flavorful mustard
45 mL (3 tbsp.) fresh lemon juice
Dash of paprika
Salt and pepper to taste

Preheat the broiler and place the fish on a broiler rack.

Mix together the remaining ingredients to form a soft basting sauce, adding more lemon juice if necessary. Brush one side of the fish. Broil, about 7.5 centimetres (3 in.) from the heat, for about three to four minutes or until the mustard sauce is bubbling. Turn fish over carefully, remembering it is fragile, and brush the other side. Broil again until done. Serve with additional sauce. □

Chinese Sweets and Savories

Mildly sweet and often savory, these rather substantial pastries are considered more of a food than a confection by the Chinese, who eat them at any hour of the day, accompanied by a steaming bowl of tea.

If you can't find your way to a Chinese bakery, you can make these pastries at home with fine results. They are easy to prepare and require little in the way of equipment.

GOLDEN EGG PUFFS

375 mL (1½ cups) all-purpose white
   flour
15 mL (1 tbsp.) baking powder
250 mL (1 cup) water
30 mL (2 tbsp.) shortening
4 eggs
175 mL (¾ cup) fine granulated sugar

Combine the flour and baking powder. Bring the water and shortening to a boil and remove from the heat. Stir in the flour mixture to make a heavy paste. Beat in the eggs, one at a time, until smooth.

Drop the batter by tablespoons into hot oil (190°C/375°F), turning occasionally for about five minutes as the puffs expand and brown. Drain and roll in granulated sugar while warm. Serve warm or cold.

GOLDEN BUTTERFLIES

This is the Chinese version of what must be a universal pastry shape. The black sesame seeds are purely decorative and can be omitted, or replaced by white sesame seeds, poppy seeds or very finely chopped nuts.

375 mL (1½ cups) all-purpose white
   flour
75 mL (⅓ cup) sugar
60 mL (¼ cup) black sesame seeds
2 mL (½ tsp.) salt
1 mL (¼ tsp.) baking powder
2 large eggs
15 mL (1 tbsp.) oil

Combine the first five ingredients in a mixing bowl. Beat the eggs and oil, and stir into the dry ingredients. Knead until smooth. Set aside for 15 minutes.

Roll half of the dough very thin on a floured pastry cloth, lifting often to re-flour. Stretch the dough even thinner by hand. Cut into 2½ by 10-centimetre (1 by 4-in.) strips. Make a five-centimetre (2-in.) slit down the centre and pass one end through the slit to make a twist.

Deep fry the pastries a few at a time in medium-hot oil (160°C/325°F), just until their edges turn brown. Drain on paper towels, sprinkle with sesame seeds and store in an airtight container. Makes about eight dozen.

STEAMED PINE NUT SPONGE CAKE

This feathery-light cake doesn't need baking powder to rise high above the pan. The pine nuts add an interesting flavor, but can be omitted or replaced with walnuts, almonds or finely shredded candied fruit.

6 eggs, separated
250 mL (1 cup) sugar
375 mL (1½ cups) cake flour, sieved
60 mL (4 tbsp.) pine nuts

Prepare and preheat a utensil for steaming. (We use a wok with a close-fitting lid, with four wooden chopsticks crossed in the bottom to form a platform to keep the cake pan above the water.) Grease a 20-centimetre (8-in.) round or square pan and line the bottom with greased wax paper.

Beat the egg-whites until soft peaks form. Gradually beat in the sugar. Beat in the egg yolks until the batter is pale yellow. Fold in 60 millilitres (¼ cup) flour at a time. Pour the batter into the prepared pan; smooth the surface and sprinkle on the pine nuts.

Steam over medium-high heat for 25 minutes, without removing the lid. Test with a toothpick and continue steaming for five minutes if the toothpick does not come out clean. When done, cool for five minutes in the pan before inverting onto a cake rack. Remove wax paper and slice into diamonds or squares. Serve warm with tea.

CRISP COCONUT COOKIES

425 mL (1¾ cups) all-purpose white
   flour
2 mL (½ tsp.) baking soda
2 mL (½ tsp.) baking powder
150 mL (⅔ cup) sugar
250 mL (1 cup) shredded coconut
125 mL (½ cup) shortening
1 egg, beaten
1 egg yolk, beaten
8 red cherries

Combine the first five ingredients in a mixing bowl and cut in the shortening. Stir in the beaten egg. Form into a soft dough and shape the dough into a log. Cut into 24 pieces, roll each into a ball and flatten with the greased and floured base of a tumbler. Place on a greased cookie sheet. Press a third of a cherry into the centre of each one and brush with egg yolk. Bake for 15 to 20 minutes at 150°C (300°F), until golden. Cool on wire racks. Store in an airtight container.

GOLDEN SESAME DUMPLINGS

Filling
30 mL (2 tbsp.) oil
125 g (4 oz.) raw pork or chicken,
   diced
125 g (4 oz.) raw shrimp, diced
4 dried mushrooms, soaked
125 mL (½ cup) water chestnuts,
   diced
15 mL (1 tbsp.) soy sauce
5 mL (1 tsp.) sesame oil
2 mL (½ tsp.) sugar
2 mL (½ tsp.) five-spice powder
3 green onions, minced
15 mL (1 tbsp.) cornstarch
60 mL (¼ cup) water

Sauté the pork in oil until almost done. Add the shrimp and cook until done. Squeeze the mushrooms dry, remove the tough stems and chop. Stir in the minced mushrooms, water chestnuts, soy sauce, sesame oil, sugar, five-spice powder and green onions. Thicken with a solution of cornstarch and water. Set aside to cool.

Dough

550 mL (2¼ cups) glutinous rice flour
60 mL (4 tbsp.) sugar
250 mL (1 cup) hot water

Mix the flour and sugar together and stir in enough hot water to form a smooth, soft dough.

To make the dumplings, divide the dough into 20 equal pieces. Flatten into eight-centimetre (3-in.) rounds. Place 15 millilitres (1 tbsp.) of filling in the centre of each. Draw up edges to form round dumplings. Seal well and roll in sesame seeds to coat. Deep fry in medium-hot oil (180°C/350°F) until brown. Drain and serve warm.

BAKED BARBECUE PORK BUNS

These make wonderful picnic food and are a welcome change from sandwiches in a lunch box. You can vary the filling by using any meat or meat-and-vegetable combination you like.

Filling

30 mL (2 tbsp.) oil
1 onion, diced
250 g (8 oz.) barbecued pork, diced
15 mL (1 tbsp.) oyster or soy sauce
5 mL (1 tsp.) sesame oil
2 mL (½ tsp.) sugar
2 mL (½ tsp.) salt
1 mL (¼ tsp.) pepper
125 mL (½ cup) chicken stock or water
15 mL (1 tbsp.) cornstarch
60 mL (4 tbsp.) water

Sauté the onion in oil until fragrant. Stir in the pork, oyster sauce, sesame oil, sugar, salt, pepper and stock. Bring to a boil and cook down a little. Mix cornstarch and water and stir it in to thicken the meat mixture. Set aside to cool.

Yeast Dough

125 mL (½ cup) warm tap water
5 mL (1 tsp.) sugar
15 mL (1 tbsp.) dry yeast
625 mL (2½ cups) all-purpose white flour
75 mL (⅓ cup) sugar
2 mL (½ tsp.) salt
2 eggs (reserve 1 yolk)
60 mL (4 tbsp.) melted shortening

Stir the sugar and yeast into the water. Set aside until foamy. Combine the flour, sugar and salt in a mixing bowl. Stir in the yeast, one beaten egg, an egg-white and the shortening. Knead until smooth and elastic. Cover and let rise, until doubled in size.

Divide the risen dough into 16 equal pieces. Knead each piece briefly and flatten into 10-centimetre (4-in.) rounds. Place an equal amount of filling on each. Draw up the edges to form round buns. Seal well and place on two greased cookie sheets to rise until doubled in size. Brush with beaten egg yolk. Bake at 190°C (375°F) until golden, 10 to 15 minutes.

COCONUT COCKTAIL BUNS

In Chinese, these are actually called "cock tail" buns.

Filling

60 mL (4 tbsp.) butter
175 mL (¾ cup) sugar
5 mL (1 tsp.) salt
45 mL (3 tbsp.) milk
125 mL (½ cup) cornstarch
60 mL (4 tbsp.) flour
5 mL (1 tsp.) vanilla extract
175 mL (¾ cup) shredded coconut

Sugar Solution

15 mL (1 tbsp.) sugar
5 mL (1 tsp.) water
30 mL (2 tbsp.) sesame seeds

Prepare the yeast dough given for Baked Barbecue Pork Buns.

Cream the butter, sugar and salt until light. Stir in the milk, cornstarch, flour and vanilla. Knead in the coconut. Divide into 12 portions. Shape into 10-centimetre (4-in.) lengths and chill.

Divide the risen dough into 12 pieces. Flatten these into 13-centimetre (5-in.) ovals. Lay the filling in the centre of ovals and draw up the edges to form oval buns. Seal well. Place on two greased cookie sheets to rise until double. Brush with beaten egg yolk. With a clean razor blade, score a shallow Z at each end of the top of the buns. Bake at 190°C (375°F) until golden, 15 minutes.

Heat the sugar and water until sugar melts. Brush this mixture on the warm buns and sprinkle with sesame seeds.

SPICY CHINESE DOUGHNUTS

Fermented red bean curd is a condiment that can be found in most Chinese markets. Salty brown bean paste that comes in jars or cans is a good substitute and is widely available in the Oriental foods section of many supermarkets. You can use the remainder in your Chinese cooking.

1 or 2 cubes fermented red bean curd or 15 mL (1 tbsp.) bean paste
5 mL (1 tsp.) five-spice powder
2 mL (½ tsp.) salt

Prepare the yeast dough given for Baked Barbecue Pork Buns, increasing the sugar to 150 millilitres (⅔ cup) and using two whole eggs.

Roll the risen dough into a 25 by 30-centimetre (10 by 12-in.) rectangle. Mash the fermented bean curd; spread it, or the bean paste, over the dough. Sprinkle with the five-spice powder and salt. Roll up, starting with the shorter edge. Slice into 12 rounds. Flatten slightly, then place on an oiled cookie sheet to rise for 15 minutes. Deep fry in medium-hot oil (180°C/350°F) until brown. Drain on absorbent paper.

CANTONESE CUSTARD TARTS

3 eggs
125 mL (½ cup) sugar
375 mL (1½ cups) water or milk
Pastry for two 22-centimetre (9-in.) pies

Beat the eggs and sugar. Stir in the water, and pour through a strainer to remove the strings of egg.

Roll the pastry into two 24 by 32-centimetre (9½ by 12½-in.) rectangles. Let rest for 10 minutes. Cut out 24 eight-centimetre (3-in.) rounds. Place them in muffin or tart tins, and fill them two-thirds full of custard. Bake at 180°C (350°F) until custard is firm, 25 minutes. Cool on a wire rack and store in the refrigerator.

CURRIED TURNOVERS

15 mL (1 tbsp.) oil
1 small onion, diced
125 g (4 oz.) raw pork, diced
10 mL (2 tsp.) curry powder
2 mL (½ tsp.) sugar
1 mL (¼ tsp.) salt
1 mL (¼ tsp.) five-spice powder
30 mL (2 tbsp.) chicken stock or
    canned broth
Packaged pastry for 4 pie crusts
1 egg yolk, mixed with 5 mL
    (1 tsp.) water

Sauté the onion in the oil until fragrant. Add the pork and cook until done. Stir in the curry powder, sugar, salt, five-spice powder and chicken stock. Bring to a boil and cook until liquid is reduced. Set aside to cool.

Roll the pastry into two 24 by 32-centimetre (9½ by 12½-in.) rectangles. Cut out 12 10-centimetre (4-in.) rounds. Place an equal amount of filling on each. Fold in half, dampen edges with egg yolk and water and pinch together tightly. Crimp the edges for a decorative effect and brush the tops with egg and water mixture.

Bake at 180°C (350°F) until golden, following package directions. □

Tiny temptations: clockwise, from top left, golden sesame dumplings, steamed pine nut sponge cake and spicy doughnuts; golden butterflies with black sesame seeds, custard tarts, egg puffs and crisp coconut cookies; sesame dumplings, curried turnovers and barbecue pork bun.

Uptown Grill

Grilling is the hot new fad in many restaurants, and truly, it brings relief to diners who have had one too many beef cuts under pastry wrap and fish fillets swimming in hollandaise. Elegant cooking does not mean frillery, and the simplicity of food from the grill is the logical conclusion of the movement to eliminate fuss for fuss's sake.

What separates grilling from charcoal barbecueing is simply that you can grill indoors safely. The best way is to buy a cast-iron or coated grill pan that can sit directly on a stove element (we prefer the cast-iron version). A grill pan is about the size of a phone book, only a centimetre or two thick, and has a handle for easy manipulation. The raised parallel ridges are what produce the attractive grill marks on the food. It should be seasoned before first use, as you would season any cast-iron frypan. The element should be red-hot before the pan is set on it, to assure that all the meat juices will be sealed in. Some vegetables and fruits are excellent grilled. These require oiling beforehand, to prevent them from sticking. With meat, trim off excess fat to prevent spattering.

An alternative method, of course, is to use the broiler, but we've found the relatively inexpensive grill pan worth it, considering the visual appeal it lends the food and the flavors it seals in. When summer arrives, store the grill pan away and fire up the charcoal.

MENU *(Serves Four)*

- Prawns in Black Bean Sauce
- Grilled Lamb with Basil Cream Sauce
- Roasted Potatoes with Herbs and Garlic
- Grand Marnier Mocha Dacquoise

PRAWNS IN BLACK BEAN SAUCE

A wonderful blending of flavors learned from the chef of the Mount View Hotel in Calistoga, California. Allow six large prawns, shelled or unshelled, per person.

Prawns
30 mL (2 tbsp.) olive oil
10 mL (2 tsp.) shallots or green onion, finely chopped
5 mL (1 tsp.) garlic, finely chopped
15 mL (1 tbsp.) sake or dry white wine
250 mL (1 cup) crayfish or fish stock (see below)
250 mL (1 cup) whipping cream
Prepared black bean sauce to taste, about 10 mL (2 tsp.)
Salt and pepper to taste
Clarified butter

Sauté shallots and garlic in olive oil until soft. Add the sake and boil until reduced by half. Add the stock and continue boiling until reduced by half. Add the cream and reduce until thick. Season to taste with black bean sauce, salt and freshly ground pepper.

Sauté the prawns in clarified butter until cooked, about five minutes. Season with salt and pepper. Cover bottom of serving plate with sauce and arrange prawns over top. Garnish with green onion brushes, if desired, and serve with French bread.

To make a shellfish stock, take shells of shrimps or prawns, cover with water and add a piece of onion, bay leaf, parsley and three or four peppercorns. Bring to a boil. Turn down the heat and simmer about 20 minutes. Strain the liquid into a bowl. Discard the shells, onion, etc. If this makes less than 250 millilitres (1 cup) of liquid, add chicken stock.

Hot off the grill: plump prawns in the shell, French rib lamb chops basted with butter and Dijon, roasted potatoes with herbs and garlic, grilled papaya, and Grand Marnier dacquoise for dessert.

GRILLED LAMB WITH BASIL CREAM SAUCE

Ask your butcher to cut French rib chops from a rack of lamb. These are double chops with one bone left untrimmed (see photo). Allow one chop per person, unless you're cooking for heavy meat eaters.

4 French rib chops
Salt and freshly ground black pepper
60 mL (4 tbsp.) soft butter
30 mL (2 tbsp.) Dijon mustard
One clove garlic, mashed

Trim the chops of any heavy fat. Mix together a dash of salt and pepper with the butter, mustard and garlic. Spread thinly over both sides of the chops. Let stand for half an hour.

Grill for six to seven minutes on each side, or until golden and crusty on the outside and pink inside. If barbecueing, place about 15 centimetres (6 in.) over the coals. Serve with basil cream sauce.

Basil Cream Sauce
250 mL (1 cup) whipping cream
Salt
Freshly chopped basil

Whip the cream and lightly salt it. Fold in enough chopped basil to make a well-flavored sauce. Do not use dry basil – try fresh chervil or cilantro (coriander) instead.

ROASTED POTATOES WITH HERBS AND GARLIC

Best baked in the oven, you can also wrap these potatoes in individual foil packets and bake in charcoal on the barbecue.

10 to 12 small red potatoes, cut in half if large
75 mL (⅓) cup olive oil
Salt and pepper
6 to 8 whole cloves garlic
Fresh herbs such as rosemary, thyme, oregano, savory (dry herbs can be substituted, if necessary)
2 whole shallots or onion slices

Scrub the potatoes well and put them in a small baking pan. Coat with olive oil and tuck the herbs, garlic and shallots around them. Sprinkle generously with salt and pepper. Cover with foil and roast until tender, about 40 to 45 minutes at 200° C (400° F).

Serve whole, squeezing the soft garlic onto the roasted potatoes.

GRAND MARNIER MOCHA DACQUOISE

This rich dessert, easily made well ahead, is a nut meringue sandwiched together with flavored butter cream and decorated with whipped cream and nuts.

6 egg-whites at room temperature
Dash of salt
1 mL (¼ tsp.) cream of tartar
5 mL (1 tsp.) vanilla
250 mL (1 cup) white sugar
375 mL (1½ cups) hazelnuts, almonds or walnuts, ground and toasted
25 mL (4½ tsp.) cornstarch

Beat the egg-whites to soft peaks with the salt, cream of tartar and vanilla. Gradually add 125 millilitres (½ cup) of sugar, a spoonful at a time, until the mixture is stiff and glossy and all the sugar is dissolved.

In a small bowl, mix together the ground nuts, remaining sugar and cornstarch.

Fold in the nut mixture, one-third at a time. Spread onto a parchment-lined baking sheet about 25 by 30 centimetres (10 by 12 in.) in size. You may make this into rounds instead, if desired.

Bake at 120° C (250° F) for 1½ to two hours depending on thickness. It should be totally crisp. To ensure crispness, turn the oven off after two hours and leave the meringue in for a further hour. Cool. If the meringue sticks to the parchment it has not dried out enough. Bake a further 15 or 20 minutes.

When thoroughly cool, cut into thirds. Don't worry about any cracking that may occur. Spread two layers with buttercream and sandwich together with the best layer on top. Chill until buttercream is firm. May be frozen at this point.

Buttercream
This is a very quick and easy recipe, and it is as smooth and delicious as any of the more difficult cooked creams. A doubled recipe is required for the two layers of dacquoise.

3 egg yolks
45 mL (3 tbsp.) white sugar, or more to taste
5 mL (1 tsp.) vanilla
250 mL (1 cup) butter, cut into 2.5-cm (1-in.) cubes

Place eggs, sugar and vanilla in food processor. Blend for 10 seconds. With machine running, add soft butter gradually until it is absorbed into the yolks. Then add remaining butter to make a thick cream. Add flavoring. Add more sugar if needed.

Make one recipe adding 15 millilitres (1 tbsp.) Grand Marnier and a second recipe adding 30 millilitres (2 tbsp.) sifted, unsweetened cocoa plus five millilitres (1 tsp.) instant coffee powder.

Just before serving time, remove from the refrigerator to mellow at room temperature. If cake is frozen, remove three hours before serving time.

Garnish
Icing sugar
250 mL (1 cup) whipping cream, whipped
30 mL (2 tbsp.) icing sugar, or to taste
15 mL (1 tbsp.) Grand Marnier
Sliced toasted nuts

Sprinkle a little sifted icing sugar over the top meringue. Whip the cream with the icing sugar and Grand Marnier. Spread along the sides of the cake. Gently press the sliced nuts onto the whipped cream.

May be refrigerated for an hour or so at this point. Slice into serving pieces. Serve small slices – it is very rich. □

A Chinese Family Meal

For the Chinese, eating has always been a celebratory event. Getting together for the mid-day or evening meal represented an opportunity for socializing as well as for sustenance.

Food at such family gatherings was served all at once; only at parties or banquets do the Chinese serve one course following another, as we do in the West. The common element at family meals, of course, was rice – the workhorse of eastern cuisine, somewhat like potatoes in a western meal. Rice serves to absorb the piquancy of the other dishes, and adds bulk to the meal.

Kenneth Lo, author of *Chinese Cooking,* says that lunch and dinner are usually similar, and typically consist of four or five dishes with one or two soups. To accommodate extra people, more dishes are added, rather than increasing the quantities of each dish. This idea is taken to magnificent lengths when Chinese gather at large festive or formal occasions. "Traditionally," says Lo, "there should be 300 dishes served at a great Manchu-All-China Banquet...."

This menu, supplied and prepared by Edwin Lee and his sister Mae, is economical to prepare, and has the added advantage of requiring a trip to your local Chinatown, especially for such items as the winter melon and Chinese parsley (though some Chinese grocers outside of Chinatown may have these things, too).

Edwin and Mae, third-generation Canadians with family roots in Canton, are well-acquainted with Chinese cooking. While they were growing up, their father ran a Chinese restaurant in Vancouver, and at home, Edwin recalls, they helped prepare family meals from an early age.

In this meal, they suggest, the dishes should be served hot and all at once, though serving by courses is possible, too, if preferred.

Garnishes, such as the scallion brushes shown with the stuffed melon, add visual appeal, another characteristic of Chinese cooking. To make scallion or leek brushes, cut an eight-centimetre (3-in.) section from the stem (white) end, with tip removed. Sliver both ends, keeping the middle intact. Then, place the brush in icy water for about a day; this creates the curl.

MENU *(Serves Four)*

- Melon Soup (Ong Guah)
- Paper Wrapped Chicken (Gee Bow Guy)
- Hot Spinach and Beef
- Stuffed Hairy Melon (Dick Gwah)
- Steamed Whole Rock Cod

MELON SOUP (Ong Guah)

Ham or pork bones for soup stock
1 kg (2 lbs.) winter melon
2 dried duck gizzards
4 large scallops, diced
60 mL (4 tbsp.) ham, diced
125 mL (½ cup) fresh crab meat
60 mL (4 tbsp.) Chinese mushrooms, diced

Make a soup stock by placing bones into four litres (16 cups) of water and bring to a boil. Discard this fatty water, add four litres (16 cups) fresh cold water and return to boil.

Soak mushrooms in boiling water until soft. Drain, discarding liquid. Cut up melon into 1.2-centimetre (½-in.) cubes and add to the stock, along with the dried duck gizzards. Simmer until the melon becomes clear. Add the remaining ingredients.

This dish is best made one or two days before serving.

PAPER WRAPPED CHICKEN (Gee Bow Guy)

½ chicken (1 to 1½-kg fryer)

30 mL (2 tbsp.) soy sauce
30 mL (2 tbsp.) oyster sauce
Dash of Chinese cooking wine
Dash of hot chili oil or Tabasco
3 slices of fresh ginger
5 mL (1 tsp.) tapioca starch
1 clove garlic
15 mL (1 tbsp.) sugar
2 mL (½ tsp.) sesame oil
Peanut cooking oil
Foil or parchment paper

Bone chicken and pat dry. Cut into bite-sized pieces. Dice ginger into fine slices. Grind together the ginger, garlic, soy sauce, wine, sugar, chili, sesame oil and starch. Place chicken pieces into this mixture and marinate overnight.

Cut parchment into 13-centimetre (5-in.) squares. Divide the chicken pieces among the squares and wrap carefully. Hold the ends together with a toothpick.

Deep fry in small batches in peanut oil for five to seven minutes. (The oil is hot enough when it "shimmers.")

This dish may also be baked in the oven. Place on a baking sheet and bake at 190°C (375°F) for 20 minutes or until done.

HOT SPINACH AND BEEF

2 pkgs. fresh spinach, washed and dried
125 g (4 oz.) hamburger
5 mL (1 tsp.) soy sauce
5 mL (1 tsp.) salt
5 mL (1 tsp.) Chinese red chili sauce (available in Chinatown)
Cornstarch
5 mL (1 tsp.) dried chili pepper chips (optional – gives a hotter taste)

Sauté hamburger, adding salt and red chili sauce, for two minutes. Set aside. Sauté spinach in some peanut oil for two minutes. Add a few drops of water and cover to steam for two minutes.

Mix the soy sauce with a little cornstarch in a small dish. Add the hamburger mixture to the spinach and stir in the soy sauce. Cook for another two minutes and serve.

STUFFED HAIRY MELON
(Dick Gwah)

750 g (1½ lbs.) melon, peeled
250 g (½ lb.) minced pork
*3 or 4 Chinese mushrooms (soaked in
    hot water, then drained)*
6 fresh water chestnuts, peeled
2 mL (½ tsp.) salt
15 mL (1 tbsp.) soy sauce
5 mL (1 tsp.) tapioca starch
*1½ lengths Chinese sausage (lup
    cheong)*

Cut the melon in half lengthwise
and scoop out the seeds, leaving a
cavity for the stuffing. Dice the
Chinese sausage. Drain the
mushrooms and dice them along
with the water chestnuts. Mix
together with the salt, soy sauce
and tapioca starch. Add 45
millilitres (3 tbsp.) of cold water to
the mixture. Fill the melon cavity
and steam for 25 minutes or until
the melon is tender.

STEAMED WHOLE ROCK
COD

*1 to 1½ kg (2 to 3 lbs.) fresh whole
    rock cod*
125 g (¼ lb.) barbecued pork, slivered
3 sleeves Chinese parsley
*3 lengths green onion, cut into 5-cm
    (2-in.) lengths, then into slivers*
3 slices fresh ginger, diced
45 mL (3 tbsp.) soy sauce
5 mL (1 tsp.) sesame oil
45 mL (3 tbsp.) peanut oil

Wash and scale the fish. Slash fish
in two or three places across the
back to speed cooking and to
allow flavoring to penetrate.

 Place 125 millilitres (½ cup) of
water into a wok or steamer and
bring to a boil. Use a steamer tray
or chopsticks as support for the
platter of fish. Add ginger, soy
sauce and green onion to the fish.
Steam for 15 to 20 minutes.

 Mix the sesame oil with the
peanut oil and heat. Pour hot oil
over the fish. Garnish with the
barbecued pork and chopped
parsley. ☐

*Variety is the spice: clockwise, from
left top, paper-wrapped chicken,
melon soup, hairy melon stuffed with
pork and Chinese mushrooms, hot
spinach and beef, and steamed rock cod.*

California Bistro Meal

A bistro is a small bar or restaurant, sometimes called a bar and grill by North Americans. In California, especially in the Napa Valley and Berkeley, bistros have become synonymous with good, country-style food served in a jovial, crowded and noisy atmosphere. Tables are very close together, and, as there is no waiting area, people are pressed against the walls and the bar until they can have a turn at the food. There is a definite English pub feel to some of them.

When we tour California, we always start in the Napa Valley with some wine tours and a meal at one of the five-star restaurants that specialize in *nouvelle* dining. Then we move on to a bistro. Here is the same excellent food, served in informal surroundings at affordable prices.

The Napa Valley is a trend-setter in the California food scene. A fair number of the wineries have kitchens, and the staffs are constantly inventing new dishes to complement the wines that are produced. Most of the chefs are young, and just discovering country cooking. They insist on using only fresh ingredients, making most of their dishes from scratch. They realize that good food does not need to be rich or highly flavored.

In this meal the terrine (or pâté) is a classic and is meant to have a rather rough texture. Pâtés are on many California bistro menus. Pasta (no one says spaghetti any more) is everywhere, of course, and interesting variations appear regularly. Filled pastas are becoming very popular, and our rotolo is a typical example.

No-nonsense nouvelle: curly endive salad with walnut oil dressing; terrine of pork, veal, liver and pistachios; spinach, ham and cheese rotolo in tomato sauce; strawberry meringue.

- Classic Country Terrine
- Rotolo with Tomato Sauce
- Curly Endive Salad
- Strawberry Meringues

CLASSIC COUNTRY TERRINE

A pâté is simply a fresh meat loaf, usually baked in a hinged mould in a pastry crust and served unmoulded. A pâté cooked and served cold in its baking dish is called a terrine, and the dish bears the same name. Classic terrines are cooked in glazed earthenware. Today, the words pâté and terrine have become interchangeable. Pâté often refers to a blended mixture served from a small pot as a spread. Terrines are very easy to make and are best served the next day, when the flavors have had a chance to mellow. In the following recipe, don't hesitate to vary the meats to suit your tastes. The total weight, however, should remain the same.

250 g (½ lb.) sliced bacon
60 mL (4 tbsp.) brandy
125-g (4-oz.) piece of smoked ham, cut into 1-cm (½-in.) strips
1 medium onion, chopped
2 cloves garlic, chopped
30 mL (2 tbsp.) butter
500 g (1 lb.) ground pork
250 g (½ lb.) ground veal (or beef, if veal is unavailable)
125 g (¼ lb.) chicken livers, coarsely chopped
2 eggs
5 mL (1 tsp.) salt
2 mL (½ tsp.) dried thyme
2 mL (½ tsp.) dried savory
Pinch each of ground allspice, cloves and nutmeg
Freshly ground pepper
125 mL (½ cup) green pistachios, coarsely chopped
Fresh herbs for garnish

In a large frypan, cover the bacon with water and simmer for 10 minutes to remove some of the saltiness and excess fat. Drain and pat dry. Set aside. Marinate the ham strips in the brandy.

Sauté the onion and garlic in the butter until soft. Mix together all the remaining ingredients except the ham, pistachio nuts and herb garnish. Drain the ham and add the marinade to the meat mixture. Mix thoroughly.

Make a small, sample patty and fry until cooked through. Taste for seasonings in the cooked sample and then adjust the seasonings in the raw mixture.

Preheat the oven to 180°C (350°F). Arrange the bacon slices across the bottom and up the sides of a terrine mould or loaf pan. Spoon half the meat mixture into the pan. Sprinkle on half the pistachio nuts. Arrange the ham slices lengthwise over the nuts. Cover with remaining nuts, then spread on the balance of the meat, pressing lightly. Fold bacon over top. Decorate with fresh herbs.

Cover the pan with foil. Place in a large, deep baking pan and add enough boiling water to reach halfway up the sides of the terrine. Bake for 1½ to two hours or until juices run clear when pierced with a skewer – 70°C (160°F) on an instant meat thermometer.

Remove terrine from oven and place on a rack. Cool slightly. Remove from water bath and drain off some of the fat. Weight the terrine with heavy cans or a foil-covered brick. Refrigerate, weighted, for at least 24 hours before serving.

To serve, remove weight and foil. Carefully turn out on to a plate and then turn back, bottom side down, on to the serving platter. Slice to serve.

Pâtés and terrines are traditionally served with crusty bread and tiny sour pickles called cornichons (gherkins).

ROTOLO WITH TOMATO SAUCE

For this recipe, an entire sheet of pasta dough is rolled up with a spinach and ham stuffing, wrapped in cheesecloth and then poached. When it is cool, it is sliced, dotted with a little butter or tomato sauce and baked briefly in a hot oven. It can be made a day ahead and reheated at serving time. Different sauces, including béchamel and brown butter glaze, can be used to vary this recipe.

Pasta
3 eggs
15 mL (1 tbsp.) olive oil
500 mL (2 cups) all-purpose white flour

In a small bowl, beat the eggs with the olive oil. Place the flour in a pile on the tabletop and make a well in the centre. Add the eggs to the well. With a fork, whisk the eggs and gather in a bit of flour until the mixture begins to form a ball. Using your hands, draw in more flour as needed and knead until the ball is smooth and silky, about 10 minutes. All the flour may not be required. Form into a ball, place under a bowl and let rest for 10 minutes before rolling.

Food processor method: place eggs and oil in the work bowl of the food processor. Start the machine and add the flour slowly until the mixture forms a ball. Remove from work bowl and knead a few minutes longer. Dough should be smooth and silky. Let rest under a bowl for 10 minutes before rolling out.

Meanwhile, make the filling.

Filling
1 kg (2 lbs.) fresh spinach, washed and briefly cooked, or 2 300-g pkgs. frozen spinach, squeezed dry
1 small onion, chopped
30 mL (2 tbsp.) butter
3 eggs
2 mL (½ tsp.) nutmeg
2 mL (½ tsp.) freshly ground pepper
250 mL (1 cup) parmesan cheese
500 g (1 lb.) ricotta or creamed cottage cheese
10 to 12 thin slices of a good ham such as Black Forest
Cheesecloth and string

Sauté the onion in the butter until soft. Place the spinach in the work bowl of the food processor along with the onion, eggs, seasonings and cheeses. Process briefly, until the spinach is chopped and the ingredients well blended.

Or: chop the spinach finely by hand, and, in a medium bowl, mix the eggs, seasonings and cheeses. Add the spinach and onion.

Roll out the pasta dough on a lightly floured surface to a very thin, 50-centimetre (20-in.) square. Cut the dough in half.

On each half, spread the spinach filling, leaving a 2.5 centimetre (1-in.) border down the long sides and a 5-centimetre (2-in.) border top and bottom. Divide the ham slices between the halves, placing over the filling. Brush the uncovered edges with a little water.

Turn the long sides inward about 2.5 centimetres (1-in.) and roll up like a jelly roll from the narrow end. There will be two 20-centimetre (8-in.) rolls. Wrap each roll in cheesecloth and tie at the ends.

Put the rolls into boiling, salted water in a large roasting pan and cook, covered, for 20 minutes. Let stand in the cooking water for another 20 minutes. Remove carefully, as they may break in the centre while still hot. Cool to room temperature in the cheesecloth. Remove cheesecloth and allow rolls to dry on a rack. The dish may be prepared ahead to this point. When cool and dry, wrap in aluminum foil and store in the refrigerator or freezer until ready to serve.

While the rolls are cooking, prepare the tomato sauce.

Tomato Sauce
2 398-mL tins of Italian-style whole
  tomatoes, finely chopped
1 large onion, finely chopped
2 cloves garlic, chopped
7 mL (1½ tsp.) oregano
7 mL (1½ tsp.) basil or 3 or 4 large
  fresh leaves, chopped
Salt, pepper
60 mL (4 tbsp.) olive oil

Sauté the onions in the olive oil until soft. Add the garlic and cook about three minutes. Add the remaining ingredients. Cook over medium heat for about 15 minutes, stirring from time to time. Fast cooking will help to reduce the sauce and make it thick. This sauce freezes well.

When ready to serve, cut the rotolo into one centimetre (½ in.) thick slices and place in a well-greased baking dish, overlapping each slice. Dot with butter and bake at 200°C (400°F) until hot, about 15 minutes if the rolls are at room temperature, 25 minutes if they are chilled.

Heat up the tomato sauce and spoon into the centre of the warm serving plates. Place two or three of the rotolo slices on the plate so that they overlap. Serve with curly endive salad (recipe follows) on the side.

The tomato sauce can be spooned over the rotolo and baked in the oven if you want to serve this dish as a casserole.

Each roll should make 12 slices.

CURLY ENDIVE SALAD

The curly endive is of the chicory family of lettuces and should not be confused with the Belgian endive. It is sometimes called chicory or escarole. Radicchio, a red-leafed chicory, is popular for salads and could be substituted.

1 large head curly endive
Croutons toasted in butter and garlic
Walnut oil dressing (recipe follows)

Tear the endive into bite-sized pieces and place in a large bowl. Chill.

Melt some butter in a large frypan and lightly sauté one whole clove of garlic. Remove the garlic as it begins to brown. Add croutons and toss them in the butter until it is absorbed. Place in a bowl and set aside until serving time.

When ready to serve, toss the chilled endive with the dressing and place on individual, chilled salad plates. Top with croutons. Pass extra dressing separately.

WALNUT OIL DRESSING

Walnut oil is very popular in California. It is rather expensive to buy in Canada, but a little goes a long way. The following recipe makes 250 mL (1 cup).

60 mL (4 tbsp.) wine vinegar, red or
  white
15 mL (1 tbsp.) Dijon mustard
Salt and pepper to taste
125 mL (½ cup) vegetable oil
60 mL (4 tbsp.) walnut oil

Beat together the vinegar, mustard and salt and pepper in a bowl. Add the oils in a stream, beating the

dressing until it is well combined. Keep at room temperature.

STRAWBERRY MERINGUES

This recipe makes 10 to 12 eight-centimetre (3-in.) meringues.

4 large egg-whites (125 mL/½ cup)
250 g (8 oz./1½ cups) fine berry
  sugar
Pinch of salt

Beat egg-whites in a clean mixing bowl until frothy. Add the sugar, 30 millilitres (2 tbsp.) at a time, along with the pinch of salt until the mixture is stiff and looks like satin.

Line a large baking sheet with parchment paper. Form eight-centimetre (3-in.) circles of the meringue on the paper. If using a pastry tube, draw a circle on the parchment and, starting from the pencil line, form a spiral to the centre.

Bake in a cool 150°C (300°F) oven for 50 to 60 minutes or until very lightly colored and quite dry.

Remove to a wire cooling rack until cold. The meringues can be stored for several weeks in a tight tin or in the freezer.

Topping
170 g (6 oz.) semi-sweet chocolate
  (try Belgian or Swiss)
15 mL (1 tbsp.) brandy
250 mL (1 cup) whipping cream
5 mL (1 tsp.) vanilla
Fresh strawberries

Melt the chocolate with the brandy and set aside to cool. Whip the cream, adding sugar to taste. Fold in the vanilla.

Place a cooled meringue on individual dessert plates. Gently spread on a little melted chocolate. Mound on some whipped cream and top with sliced or whole fresh strawberries.

Refrigerate for up to two hours to allow the meringue to mellow slightly and become a little chewy. □

Food in the Fast Lane

The test of a good cook is not in preparing a formal dinner party with each course thoughtfully planned, color co-ordinated, seasoned with the trendiest herbs and served in pleasing deco designs on gigantic white plates. Heck, anyone with a fridge full of fresh produce, a good cookbook and a couple of days off work can do that.

The true test is arriving home at 7:30 p.m., harried and hungry, nothing in the fridge but a couple of eggs and last night's nail polish, and The Joneses due to descend for dinner at 8. So what will it be? Press the panic button? Call Gourmet-On-The-Go (again)? Make a last-minute reservation at L'Impulsif (again)? Or lock the doors, disconnect the phone and go underground for the evening?

Tut tut, you've failed the test. If it's any consolation, you are not alone. The last-minute meal is the ruination of many fine cooks – people with educated palates who can tell the difference between virgin and extra-virgin olive oil blindfolded but who can't for the life of them cope with the daily routine of cooking supper.

In our own survey, we discovered a good percentage of sworn gourmets who go home at night and surreptitiously open a can of tuna. We can only hope they find the time to reach for a jar of mayo. To them and to their fast-lane friends we dedicate this feature. We offer a selection of quick and easy alternatives for last-minute meals that can be thrown together by the average cook working with a poorly stocked fridge and a 20-minute deadline.

Of course, there are limits even to our corner-cutting ingenuity. To make a meal worth eating, you must have a few basics on hand. A freezer stocked with appropriately portioned, boneless cuts of meat, chicken or fish gives you an enormous head start. Soup and sauce stocks, either homemade or purchased from specialty shops, should also be frozen in single-meal sizes. The same goes for partially baked pizza crust, taco shells or pita bread – the foundation of several quick, tasty meals.

Microwaves are invaluable for cutting corners, as are programmable timers on conventional ovens. On the low-tech side, don't forget the good old crock pot for slow simmering stews or savory bean dishes that are always ready when you are. The bare essentials in your pantry: cream of mushroom soup, whole or crushed tomatoes, spaghetti sauce and canned fish. In your fridge: try to keep a week's supply of crisp, washed lettuce – mixed varieties for interest – to which you can quickly add other vegetables, cheese or deli favorites.

STIR FRY SALMON CHUNKS

With a nutty brown rice, this is a tasty meal for one, which can be multiplied for up to four (the cooking time will increase accordingly). Thin slivers of beef can be substituted.

30 mL (2 tbsp.) peanut or vegetable oil
1 medium salmon steak, cut into 2.5-cm (1-in.) cubes
1 green onion, sliced on the diagonal
A few slices of red onion
15 mL (1 tbsp.) soy sauce
3 to 4 snow pea pods, slivered
Slivers of fresh oyster mushroom, optional
Salt and pepper, to taste

Heat the oil in a wok or medium frypan over medium heat. Add the salmon cubes and sear on all sides. Add the green and red onion along with the soy sauce and toss gently.

Cover and cook for two minutes. Add the pea pods and mushrooms. Cover and cook for one minute. Taste for seasoning, adding salt and pepper if desired. Serve immediately.

SALMON SOUFFLE IN TOMATO CUPS

Beautiful canned B.C. sockeye is the fish for this quickie. Any leftover cooked salmon, of course, could be used as well. Serve on a lettuce leaf with lots of bread and butter. This dish can be baked in individual ramekins or in one soufflé dish.

1 213-g can sockeye salmon
1 egg, separated
1 egg-white
15 mL (1 tbsp.) Dijon mustard
5 mL (1 tsp.) lemon juice
60 mL (4 tbsp.) mayonnaise
60 mL (4 tbsp.) celery, chopped
30 mL (2 tbsp.) pickle relish
Pinch of cayenne
Salt and pepper, to taste
8 medium tomatoes

Preheat oven to 200°C (400°F).

Drain the salmon and flake it into a medium bowl. Add the egg yolk. In another bowl, beat the two egg-whites until stiff. Stir the remaining ingredients, except the tomatoes, into the salmon mixture. Fold in the beaten egg-whites.

Slice off a small amount of skin on the bottom of the tomatoes to make them stand perfectly straight. Slice off the top cap and scoop out the pulp. Turn upside-down to drain.

Spoon the salmon mixture into the tomato cups. Do not overfill. Bake until puffed and golden, about 20 minutes. A large soufflé will bake in an hour.

GRILLED FILLET WITH CRAB

You can substitute chicken for

Prize dinner in a pinch: a total cooking time of under five minutes for this delightful stir-fry salmon dish.

fish, but the cooking will take a few minutes longer. Remove the tenderloin and save for another dish. Oven-proof your frypan by wrapping the handle in several layers of foil. Serves two.

30 mL (2 tbsp.) yellow pepper, diced
30 mL (2 tbsp.) red pepper, diced
30 mL (2 tbsp.) zucchini, diced
60 g (2 oz.) crab meat (or imitation crab)
15 mL (1 tbsp.) breadcrumbs
10 mL (2 tsp.) fresh dill, parsley or chive, chopped
10 mL (2 tsp.) Dijon mustard, or more
Salt and pepper, to taste
2 medium fillets of red snapper or 2 chicken breast halves, boned, skinned, tenderloin removed
15 mL (1 tbsp.) each butter and oil

Mix together all the ingredients except the fish and the butter and oil, moistening with enough mustard to lightly bind the mixture together. Divide between the fillets and press onto the top of each.

Heat the butter and oil in a frypan. Cook the fish, plain side down for four to five minutes over medium heat. Place the frypan under a preheated grill and cook 8 centimetres (3 in.) away from the heat for another four to five minutes or until the crab mixture is golden and the fish is cooked through.

Place on a serving plate and brush with any butter left in the pan.

BROILED LAMB CHOPS WITH STIR FRIED SPINACH

A quick and delicious dish using New Zealand spring lamb loin chops, which you can have on hand in your freezer. Allow two or three per person.

8 lamb loin chops, thawed if previously frozen
5 mL (1 tsp.) lemon zest
60 mL (4 tbsp.) fresh lemon juice
Salt and pepper, to taste
15 mL (1 tbsp.) oil
1 clove garlic, minced
300 g (10 oz.) fresh spinach, washed and dried
Juice of ½ lemon

Trim any fat from the chops and divide the lemon zest over all, pressing well into the meat. Place on a broiler rack and drizzle lemon juice over all. Let stand while the broiler is heating.

When it is hot, place the chops about 10 centimetres (4 in.) from the heat and broil about four minutes. Turn and broil on the other side for three to four minutes or until done to your liking (slash into the meat to check). Season with salt and pepper.

While the meat is cooking, heat the oil in a wok or large frypan, swirling the oil to coat the pan. Add spinach, garlic and lemon juice. Stir fry over medium heat until the spinach is just wilted and flavored, about two to three minutes. Season with salt and pepper.

Divide the spinach among the serving plates and place chops on it. Serve immediately.

GRILLED KEBABS OF LAMB WITH CUMIN AND GINGER

Wonderful middle-eastern aromas are created by this dish, which cooks in about seven minutes. While the meat is standing at room temperature, make a Greek salad and start some rice. Serves six to eight.

Small lamb roast, boned
60 mL (4 tbsp.) oil
30 mL (2 tbsp.) fresh ginger, peeled and finely chopped
1 or 2 cloves garlic, crushed
10 mL (2 tsp.) ground cumin
10 mL (2 tsp.) ground coriander
Pinch of salt and cayenne

Start the barbecue or broiler.

Trim the lamb and cut into four-centimetre (1½-in.) cubes. Set aside. In a small bowl mix together the remaining ingredients until well blended. Add the lamb and stir well. Let stand while you set the table, make the salad and start the rice.

Thread the lamb on skewers, leaving a small space between each piece. Place on a greased grill about 10 centimetres (4 in.) from the heat. Barbecue or grill about three minutes on each side, or until done to your liking. Serve immediately.

VEGETABLE OMELETTE

This recipe serves one person. Omelettes are best made in individual sizes; they cook quickly and can be kept warm while you whip up a second, or third, or fourth. Cook them in an omelette pan that is never washed, only wiped clean. Many ingredients can be added before cooking, or they can be cooked separately and spread on before folding.

Pre-cooked leftover vegetables, including some onion mixed with a spoonful or two of tomato ketchup
Parsley, chive or basil, dried or fresh
Ham or cheese, or both
2 eggs
15 mL (1 tbsp.) water
Salt and pepper, if desired
15 mL (1 tbsp.) butter

Prepare the vegetables. Julienne or dice the ham and grate the cheese. Chop the fresh herbs. Beat together the eggs, water and seasonings. Add the vegetables, ham, cheese and herbs, or set them aside for spreading on just before folding.

Heat the omelette pan over medium-high heat. Add the butter, which should immediately sizzle and melt. Pour on the egg mixture. Cook until almost set but still very slightly runny on top. If filling has not been added, spread on now. Slip the omelette onto a warmed serving platter, folding the top half over the bottom as it slides out of the pan.

If you prefer a puffy omelette, separate the eggs. Beat the yolks with the water and fold in stiffly beaten whites.

EGGS MEDITERRANEAN

Savory scrambled eggs stuffed in a pita pocket make a quick supper or lunch. Serves two.

½ small onion, finely chopped
30 mL (2 tbsp.) butter
2 medium tomatoes, peeled, seeded and coarsely chopped
A few slices of ham, diced
4 large eggs
Salt and pepper, to taste
Parsley, chive or basil, dried or fresh
Pita bread

Over medium heat, sauté the onion in the butter until soft, add the tomatoes and ham and cook for another two to three minutes. Stir in the lightly beaten eggs and season to taste with salt, pepper and a herb of your choice. Continue cooking, stirring occasionally, until the eggs are just set, about two minutes more.

Cut the pita bread into halves and stuff the egg mixture into the pockets. Serve at once.

BARBECUED SAUSAGES

The spicy basting sauce adds tang to an oven-baked dish. Serves three.

500 g (1 lb.) sausages (pork, beef, lamb, turkey or chicken)
30 mL (2 tbsp.) olive oil
30 mL (2 tbsp.) tomato sauce or chili sauce
10 mL (2 tsp.) Dijon or other flavorful mustard
Dash of Worcestershire sauce
Drop of Tabasco
Salt and pepper, if desired

Pierce the skin of the sausages with a fork. Place on a rack on a baking sheet. Mix together the remaining ingredients and spread over all.

Bake at 200°C (400°F) for 20 minutes, basting occasionally, until the sausages are well browned.

Serve hot with mashed potatoes and some colorful vegetables.

TACO PORK WITH LEMON

Pork tenderloin, simmered in a lemony sauce, is wonderful served in a taco shell. We had this dish rolled in a flour tortilla at a colorful market in Guanajuato, Mexico. Serves four.

500 g (1 lb.) pork tenderloin
15 mL (1 tbsp.) oil
1 clove garlic, crushed
3 slices of lemon
2 mL (½ tsp.) cumin
2 mL (½ tsp.) coriander
Salt and pepper, to taste
125 mL (½ cup) dry white wine
Taco shells
Sour cream
Grated cheese

Cut the tenderloin into 1.2-centimetre (½-in.) rounds and quarter each one. Heat the oil and sauté the meat. Add the garlic and cook for a few seconds. Stir in the remaining ingredients and bring to a boil. Boil three minutes and remove the meat. Continue boiling until the liquid is reduced and slightly thickened.

Place the meat on the bottom of the taco shell, spoon on a little sauce, add shredded lettuce and grated cheese and a dollop of sour cream. Heat briefly at 180°C (350°F) and serve immediately. Or roll the same ingredients in a flour tortilla, wrap in foil and heat in the oven.

QUICK AND EASY PIZZA

Using a frozen pizza crust, you can bake a pizza in less time than it takes to have one delivered. Bake at 230°C (450°F), directly on the oven rack or on a preheated baking sheet, for approximately 15 minutes or until the cheese is bubbling. Spread spaghetti sauce, pizza sauce or homemade salsa over the crust, add shredded mozzarella cheese and then pick your toppings:

Chopped tomatoes
Sliced olives
Crumbled bacon or ham
Cooked, crumbled ground beef
Sliced artichokes
Sliced onion or peppers
Drained tuna or salmon
Sliced hot dogs or sausage
More cheese – Cheddar or parmesan
Herbs
Spicy peppers

PERFECT PASTA

While the water is boiling for the pasta, any number of wonderful sauces can be made using the method set out in the following recipe for Fettuccine alla Carbonara. After tossing the pasta with egg-and-cream sauce or with thickened cream, add any of the following ingredients: your favorite caviar, sun-dried tomatoes, pitted black olives, green onions, tiny shrimp, clams, mussels, smoked salmon, canned fish, cooked chicken, cooked vegetables or fresh herbs. Top with parmesan and serve.

FETTUCCINE ALLA CARBONARA

If this sauce is too rich, eliminate the eggs, increase the cream to 500 millilitres (2 cups) and boil for a few minutes to thicken slightly. Serves six.

500 g (1 lb.) fettuccine or linguine
4 eggs
60 mL (4 tbsp.) whipping cream
250 g (8 oz.) bacon or ham, cooked and cut up
125 g (4 oz.) parmesan cheese, freshly grated
Freshly ground pepper
Snipped parsley

Bring a large amount of water to the boil. Add the fettuccine. If freshly made, cook for only one to two minutes; if freshly made but dried or frozen, cook for only four to five minutes; if packaged, cook about 15 to 20 minutes. Sample a piece; it should be tender but slightly firm. Drain.

Meanwhile, beat together the eggs and cream until well blended. If not using eggs, boil the cream to thicken slightly. Turn the pasta out onto a heated serving platter. Toss with the uncooked egg mixture or the hot cream until well coated. Add bacon, cheese, pepper and parsley. Toss and serve.

PASTA WITH PRAWNS

Serves one.

Bring 175 millilitres (¾ cup) cream to a boil and let cook until slightly thickened. Add six or eight cooked tiger prawns. Toss cream and prawns with the cooked pasta. Garnish with parmesan cheese and parsley. □

SUMMER

A fresh approach: artistic presentation of the fluffy pimientos and scallop mousse, roasted duck and orange salad, and halibut fillet in tomato and basil aspic.

Summer Coolers

When we asked Claude Téton and Olivier Chaleil to create cold summer entrées for us, the two chefs were busy revising the menus at Vancouver's Hotel Meridien. Téton, who is the executive chef of this elegant hotel, explains that the main dining room opened with what was considered a safe menu. Now, after a great deal of experimenting, he says he has a better feel for local tastes, and local tastes aren't quite as conservative as he'd been led to believe.

Nevertheless, since coming here from Nuits-St. Georges, Chaleil has found that French food preferences are sometimes not accepted. "In France," he says, "people expect to eat fish with the bone in; a fillet of trout in France is impossible to find. We had trout served here whole. People said, 'I can't eat it because I don't know how to handle the bones.'"

The halibut recipe he has created for us begins with poached fish "cooked green" – or slightly underdone. "If you overcook by one minute," he warns, "it becomes soft and dry to taste."

Téton and Chaleil considered a dozen cold entrées, rejecting some that might be too difficult to prepare in a home kitchen and finally selecting five that are varied and relatively simple to prepare.

Much of the appeal of our cold entrées (each of which serves four people) lies in the presentation that Chaleil created for our photograph. His finishing touches – tying a long strand of chive around a slice of red onion, for instance – delight the eye and will tempt summer-weary appetites.

AVOCADO AND PRAWN GAZPACHO

3 large ripe avocados
1 small onion, chopped
2 mL (½ tsp.) curry powder
500 to 625 mL (2 to 2½ cups) half-and-half cream
Salt and white pepper powder to taste
Juice of half a lemon
¼ red pepper
¼ green pepper
8 large prawns

Remove the pulp of two avocados, chop coarsely and place in a blender with the onion, curry powder, cream, salt, pepper and lemon juice. Purée. Strain through a fine sieve. (If too thick, add a little water.) Chill well.

Cut the remaining avocado into small dice. Cut the peppers into small dice and plunge them into boiling water for two to three minutes. Drain and cool under running cold water. Cook the prawns in boiling water until bright pink (two to three minutes). Run them under cold water, peel, split in half and hold in the refrigerator.

To serve, place the gazpacho in chilled individual cups or a large bowl and sprinkle the pieces of pepper and avocado and the prawns on top. Serve well chilled.

This gazpacho can be prepared several hours before serving, but if it is held for a long time, it will blacken. Serves four.

ROASTED DUCK AND ORANGE SALAD

The meat in this salad is not chilled (unless, of course, you plan to hold it for several hours).

1 large duck (over 2 kg), fresh, if
* possible*
4 oranges
2 red onions
1 carrot
1 head butter lettuce
1 head red leaf lettuce
250 mL (1 cup) walnut oil
45 mL (3 tbsp.) red wine vinegar
75 mL (⅓ cup) fresh orange juice
30 mL (2 tbsp.) sugar
Salt and pepper to taste

Cut one orange in half and rub the halves all over the duck. Place the orange halves in the breast cavity,

season the duck inside and out with salt and pepper and prick its skin to allow fat to escape. Place the duck on its side in a roasting pan and surround it with chopped carrot and a quartered onion. Roast at 200°C (400°F) for 45 minutes to one hour (or until the juices run clear), basting with the accumulating fat and turning the duck twice – once onto its opposite side and then breast up to finish.

When the roasted duck has cooled somewhat, carefully remove the breasts, each in one piece so that they can be sliced later. Remove and bone the legs. Return all the bones to the roasting pan and roast for 15 minutes more. Remove all fat, add 500 millilitres (2 cups) water to the roasting pan and bring to a boil on top of the stove. Reduce the stock to about 45 millilitres (3 tbsp.). Strain.

In a small saucepan over medium heat melt the sugar and cook without stirring until light brown. (Watch carefully; once the sugar begins to brown, it will darken quickly.) Add the vinegar, orange juice and stock. Reduce by half to about 75 millilitres (5 tbsp.). Let cool and then whisk in the walnut oil. Season to taste.

Zest one orange (cut the peel into thin strips, avoiding the white pith) and blanch the zest in boiling water for three minutes. Drain. Peel the three oranges and divide them into segments.

Slice the onions thinly. Shred the legs of the duck. Thinly slice the breast meat. Wash and trim the lettuces. Toss together the lettuces, onion slices, half the orange segments and half the zest with half the dressing. Place on a serving dish. Add some shredded leg meat. Arrange the thinly sliced breast attractively over the leg meat and decorate with the remaining orange segments, zest and a couple of onion rings. Top with the rest of the dressing and serve. Serves four.

FLUFFY MOUSSE OF PIMIENTOS AND SCALLOPS

4 sweet red peppers, seeded
250 mL (1 cup) whipping cream
1 envelope unflavored gelatin
4 heads butter lettuce
Juice of half a lemon
12 large, fresh scallops
White wine
Salt and white pepper powder to taste
Dash of Tabasco

Cut the peppers into processor-sized pieces and plunge them in a small amount of boiling water for three minutes. Drain and cool under running cold water. Place on a double layer of paper towel and pat dry. Purée the pepper in a food processor and strain through a fine sieve.

Soak the gelatin in 60 millilitres (4 tbsp.) cold water. Place the scallops in a small saucepan with a little white wine and water. Bring to a simmer over medium heat and cook for two to three minutes. Do not let boil. Remove and reserve the scallops and reduce the stock to about 45 millilitres (3 tbsp.). Dissolve the softened gelatin in the hot scallop stock.

Whip the cream to a firm peak and fold in the pepper purée. Season with salt, pepper, lemon juice and Tabasco. Then incorporate the melted gelatin, folding quickly so as not to form lumps of gelatin.

Slice the scallops and line the bottom of four custard cups or ramekins, using half the slices. Pour in half the cream mixture. Add the remaining scallop slices and top with the rest of the mousse. Chill well.

At serving time wash the whole lettuce heads, remove any unattractive outer leaves and pinch out the centre heart to make enough space for the mousse. Unmould each mousse by dipping it in hot water for a few seconds, and then turn it out into a lettuce cup.

Serve on a cold plate with Chantilly sauce. Serves four.

Chantilly Sauce

125 mL (½ cup) mayonnaise, homemade if possible
125 mL (½ cup) whipping cream
Juice of half a lemon
Dash of Tabasco

Whip the cream softly and mix all the ingredients together.

MUSSELS ON THE HALF SHELL IN VINAIGRETTE

1.5 kg (3 lbs.) mussels
3 shallots, finely chopped
250 mL (1 cup) white wine
Few grindings of pepper
45 mL (3 tbsp.) cider vinegar
250 mL (1 cup) olive oil
15 mL (1 tbsp.) fresh coriander, coarsely chopped
15 mL (1 tbsp.) chives, coarsely chopped
15 mL (1 tbsp.) parsley, coarsely chopped

Wash and scrub the mussels clean; remove the beards, if any. In a saucepan, bring the white wine, the shallots and a few grindings of pepper to a boil. Add the mussels and cook covered, shaking the pan from time to time until the shells have opened, about five minutes. Drain in a colander, reserving the stock. Let cool.

Remove one of the shells, leaving the meat on the other, and place on a serving dish.

Prepare the vinaigrette by whisking together the cider vinegar, olive oil, 30 millilitres (2 tbsp.) of the cooking stock and the herbs. Season to taste and pour over the mussels. Serves four.

HALIBUT FILLET IN TOMATO AND BASIL ASPIC

800 g (1¾ lbs.) halibut fillet, boneless and skinless
250 mL (1 cup) white wine
250 mL (1 cup) water
1 small carrot, chopped
1 branch celery, chopped
1 medium onion, chopped
1 bay leaf
4 fresh tomatoes (2 chopped for the stock, 2 reserved for garnish)
Parchment paper
1 small bunch basil leaf (reserve nice leaves for garnish)
125 mL (½ cup) tomato paste
4 egg-whites
2 envelopes unflavored gelatin
Salt and pepper to taste
Lettuce and spring vegetables for garnish

Prepare a stock by bringing to boil the white wine, water, carrots, celery, onion, bay leaf, two tomatoes, basil and salt and pepper. Simmer for 10 minutes.

Place the fish on the vegetables in the hot stock. Cover with parchment paper (or wax paper) and simmer until the flesh is opaque but still shiny and firm to the touch. Remove from the stock, let cool and then refrigerate. Strain the stock.

Add the tomato paste to the lukewarm stock. Lightly whisk the egg-whites until they form very soft peaks and stir them into the stock. Bring to the simmering point (do not let boil) for 10 minutes until the broth appears clear.

Meanwhile soak the gelatin in 120 millilitres (8 tbsp.) cold water. Strain the stock through a fine sieve and reserve 500 millilitres (2 cups). Dissolve the softened gelatin in the stock, heating if necessary, and then refrigerate until it comes to a syrupy consistency, about 30 minutes.

As the aspic thickens, peel and seed the remaining tomatoes and cut them into julienne strips. Decorate the chilled fish with the tomato strips and with a few basil leaves. Now, begin to build up a 6-millimetre (¼-in.) layer of aspic on the fish, applying several coatings and letting each set in the refrigerator for about five minutes. Keep the aspic at room temperature as you work.

Serve on lettuce leaves with boiled spring vegetables as garnish. Accompany with a mayonnaise thinned with a few spoonfuls of cream or sour cream and flavored with finely chopped basil. Serves four. □

Brunchtime

Brunch is technically described as the first point between sunrise and noon when champagne can in all good conscience be served.

Between 10 and 11, some sort of compromise between breakfast instincts (largely conservative) and lunch instincts (more venturesome) must be reached. Eggs, comfortingly familiar yet open to experimentation, usually figure, as they do in our brunch menu.

Our egg dish is an Italian high omelette, a frittata. The traditional method of cooking a frittata is with two pans over fire. The beaten eggs are poured into the first pan along with whatever other ingredients are being added. The mixture is allowed to set over heat. While the top of the frittata is still the consistency of wet scrambled eggs, a second pan is placed over the first, and the two are flipped, landing the frittata in the second pan, wet side down. The frittata is cooked for just a minute or two longer and then served.

Our method requires only one pan, placed over heat and then under it, and it produces a fluffy frittata that must go straight from broiler to table, where it promptly begins to settle. To the egg mixture we add large prawns, green onions and a scattering of intensely flavorful sun-dried tomatoes. The result is wonderful.

Homemade cream cheese, which is not difficult to make but takes time, has a noticeably pure flavor, while homemade jams and conserves — such as the strawberry-rhubarb conserve and lime-raspberry jam presented here — emphasize the fruit by reducing the sugar.

Sweet and savory: nectarines with homemade cream cheese in a raspberry sauce, prawn frittata with sun-dried tomatoes and warm munk cakes served with a selection of conserves.

- Fresh Nectarines with Homemade Cream Cheese in a Raspberry Sauce
- Prawn Frittata with Sun-Dried tomatoes
- Munk Cakes
- Strawberry-Rhubarb Conserve
- Blueberry-Lime Jam
- Gooseberry Jam

FRESH NECTARINES WITH HOMEMADE CREAM CHEESE IN A RASPBERRY SAUCE

4 perfect medium nectarines
Homemade cream cheese (recipe follows)
500 mL (2 cups) fresh raspberries
Raspberry liqueur (or liqueur of your choice)

Wash and dry the nectarines. (If you are using peaches instead, drop them in boiling water for 30 seconds; the skin will slip off easily.) Slice the fruit in half and remove the pit. Form some of the cream cheese into a ball a little larger than the pit and place in one half of the fruit. Brush the fruit with some lemon juice if you are not serving the dish immediately.

Purée the raspberries and press through a strainer to remove some of the seeds. Stir in a little liqueur and taste for sweetness. Some icing sugar can be added if necessary.

At serving time, spoon some of the purée onto the centre of a dessert plate. Place the half of the fruit with the cream cheese on the plate and the other half slightly overlapped on top. An alternative is to slice the fruit and fan the slices out, placing some of the cheese to one side.

Homemade Cream Cheese
Simple and wonderfully flavorful, this cheese is good for sweet or savory dishes and can be flavored with herbs, peppers or onions and rolled in chopped parsley or cracked peppercorns for variety.

If available, use cream and milk from a small, local dairy; these products are often sold in health food stores or gourmet food stores. Rennet tablets are found in most grocery stores.

1 L (1 qt.) whole milk
250 mL (1 cup) whipping cream
60 mL (4 tbsp.) very fresh buttermilk
1 Junket rennet tablet
15 mL (1 tbsp.) water
Dash of salt
5 mL (1 tsp.) sugar for a slightly sweeter cheese, if desired

Combine the milk, cream and buttermilk in a stainless steel or enamelled saucepan. Warm the mixture over low heat, stirring, until it reaches 38°C (100°F) on a thermometer (a few drops on your wrist will feel neither warm nor cool). Remove from heat.

Dissolve the rennet tablet in the water. Add to the milk and stir for one minute.

Cover the pot. Leave it, absolutely undisturbed, at room temperature for 16 to 24 hours, or until a firm curd has formed. The clear liquid surrounding the curd is, of course, the whey.

Line a fine-mesh sieve with two layers of dampened cheesecloth. Set the sieve over a medium bowl and ladle the curd into it. Discard the whey. Let the mixture drain until only an occasional drop of whey falls into the bowl. The curd will still be quite soft. Continue draining for four to five hours. If your kitchen is very hot, do the draining process in the refrigerator.

Turn the curd out into a medium bowl. Stir in a little salt and sugar. Herbs, peppers, etc., can be added at this point if you are making a savory cheese. Rinse out the cheesecloth and replace it in the sieve. Add the seasoned curd. Fold the cheesecloth over top. Weight it down with a bowl or small plate and a 500-gram (1-lb.) can. Refrigerate. Discard the final whey as it accumulates. Remove the can after two hours. For a firmer consistency, double the weight for a couple more hours.

Remove the cheese from the cloth and taste for seasonings. It is possible to work in a little more salt if needed at this point. Dampen your hands and form the cheese into the shape desired. It can also be put into a small wicker basket or a *coeur à la crème* mould that has been lined with cheesecloth.

Drain the cheese overnight in the refrigerator.

The next day, put the cheese in plastic wrap and chill to mellow the flavors. The cheese will be at its best for about three days, although it does keep longer.

PRAWN FRITTATA WITH SUN DRIED TOMATOES

30 mL (2 tbsp.) olive oil
30 mL (2 tbsp.) butter
500 g (1 lb.) raw, peeled prawns or shrimp
3 or 4 green onions, diagonally sliced
6 large eggs, well-beaten
A few sun-dried tomatoes, whole or in large chunks (see note)
Salt and freshly ground pepper to taste

Turn on the oven to broil.

Heat the oil and butter in an 20-centimetre (8-in.) heavy, ovenproof frypan. (If you do not have a pan that will go into the oven, a regular pan handle can be protected by several layers of aluminum foil.) Add the prawns and cook until just barely pink. Add the green onions and cook briefly over medium heat.

Pour the beaten eggs over everything and cook until the egg mixture begins to look done around the edges. The mixture can be lifted gently from time to time at the edges to allow some of the egg mixture on top to flow underneath. This will help speed up the cooking time.

As the mixture begins to firm slightly, add the sun-dried tomatoes, pushing them a little under the surface of the liquid.

Place the pan under the broiler until the top turns a golden brown and puffs at the edges.

Remove from the oven and slip onto a serving platter. Sprinkle on a little salt and pepper. Cut into wedges to serve.

Sun-Dried Tomatoes
Dried tomatoes have a tart, intense flavor and a meaty, chewy texture. Imported jars are costly, but with a little time you can make your own.

Start with small pear-shaped tomatoes such as the roma variety. Cut open the washed and dried tomatoes lengthwise, or cut

6-millimetre (¼-in.) slices. Place on a screen or rack and sprinkle with salt.

The tomatoes can be dried in the sun, oven or dehydrator.

To dry in the dehydrator: place tomatoes, cut side up, about 2.5 centimetres (1 in.) apart on dehydrator rack. Put in a 55°C (125°F) dehydrator until individual tomatoes shrivel to flattish, small ovals and feel dry to touch – flexible, not brittle. Drying time will vary according to the thickness of the pieces, the ripeness of the vegetable and the outside humidity. On average, it will be from 12 to 14 hours. Turn or rotate the racks once during this process.

To dry in the oven: set the tomatoes, cut side up, on wire racks placed in shallow baking pans. Bake at 95°C (200°F) until the tomatoes look and feel as described above. This usually takes seven to nine hours.

Dried tomatoes in flavored oil
1.5 kg (3 lbs.) pear-shaped tomatoes
Salt
Rosemary, bay leaves, chives, oregano, savory, peppercorns or garlic, in any combination
Olive oil

Pack the dried tomatoes loosely in jars with the herbs of your choice. Pour in a good olive oil; cover the tomatoes entirely, as they may mould if exposed to air.

The tomatoes are good to eat right away, but will develop more flavor if left standing for 45 days or so. Store airtight at room temperature. They will keep as long as the olive oil stays fresh.

Dried tomatoes are good in salads, pizzas, antipasto and pasta sauces.

MUNK CAKES

This recipe makes lots of little cakes which will freeze well. It can be cut in half, if desired. The batter is cooked in a special pan called a munk or *ableskiver* pan (see photo), which is available at most kitchen supply shops.

750 mL (3 cups) milk
60 mL (4 tbsp.) butter

750 mL (3 cups) all-purpose white flour
4 large eggs
15 mL (1 tbsp.) dry yeast
15 mL (1 tbsp.) sugar
60 mL (4 tbsp.) milk, warmed
Pinch of salt
Raspberry or other jam

Heat the milk and butter until the butter is melted. Place the flour in a large bowl and beat in the milk/butter mixture. Beat in the eggs. Dissolve the yeast and sugar in 60 millilitres (4 tbsp.) of additional milk. Add to the flour/milk mixture along with the pinch of salt. Stir well. Cover and let stand for about half an hour.

Heat the munk pan on a medium to hot burner (about as hot as you'd use for pancakes), put a little butter in each hole, and when the butter is melted, drop 15 millilitres (1 tbsp.) of batter in each hole. Add a drop of jam and cover with a bit more batter. Cook until the top looks firm around the edges, but is still slightly soft in the centre. Turn with two forks and cook until lightly brown.

Best served warm.

STRAWBERRY RHUBARB CONSERVE

A conserve is a jam-like mixture in which fruit is left whole or roughly chopped. It is not as solidly set as jam. A liqueur can be added for variety. This recipe makes 625 millilitres (2½ cups).

250 mL (1 cup) rhubarb, cut into 2.5-cm (1-in.) pieces
375 mL (1½ cups) white sugar
500 mL (2 cups) strawberries, sliced in half

Place the rhubarb in a medium bowl and cover with the sugar. Let stand for 12 hours. Transfer to a medium or large saucepan and, over high heat, melt the sugar and bring to a boil. Add the sliced strawberries. Turn down the heat and boil gently, stirring frequently, for one hour or until slightly thickened. The longer the cooking, the thicker the mixture.

Spoon into sterilized jars. It will firm up a bit more upon standing. Refrigerate after 24 hours.

For variety, just before spooning into the jars, stir in 60 millilitres (4 tbsp.) Grand Marnier or brandy.

BLUEBERRY LIME JAM

This jam does not contain pectin. The lime juice, combined with the natural sugars of the fruit, along with the cooking, thickens the mixture.

1.5 L (6 cups) blueberries
Grated rind of two limes
80 to 125 mL (⅓ to ½ cup) fresh lime juice
1.125 L (4½ cups) white sugar

Crush or purée the berries, place in a large, heavy pot and add lime peel and juice. Simmer over medium heat until berry pieces are tender. Add sugar, stirring constantly. Cook over low heat 20 to 35 minutes, until a small amount of jam, when dropped on a plate, remains firm. Spoon jam into sterilized jars and seal with hot paraffin.

GOOSEBERRY JAM

Gooseberries can be hard to find, but if your local produce market carries them, or if you have a plant (they're easy to grow), here's an excellent use for them. There are many varieties, in colors of white, yellow, red and green. The small green ones are the best. To prepare the berries, rinse, discard those that are blemished and cut off tops and bottoms with a sharp knife.

1 L (1 qt.) gooseberries, stems and blossoms removed
125 mL (½ cup) water
750 mL to 1 L (3 to 4 cups) white sugar

Place the gooseberries in a large, heavy saucepan. Add the water and bring to a boil, stirring constantly. Add the sugar. Return to a boil, then turn down the heat and simmer, stirring, until the berries are clear and the mixture thickens. This takes about 15 minutes.

For added flavor, stir in 60 millilitres (4 tbsp.) brandy.

Spoon into sterilized jars and cover with hot paraffin, or store in the refrigerator. □

Sea Fare

Anyone who has eaten seafood within moments of its capture knows the significance of freshness. On beach or boat, the experience of eating just-caught salmon or just-dug clams is sublime. The sea air, and the fact that you caught your dinner (or witnessed the catch), have something to do with your enthusiasm, but the importance of minimizing the seawater-to-potwater time cannot be too strongly stressed.

For those who *buy* their seafood, knowing the signs of freshness is very important.

The first thing to look for in a fish is brightness. Check for bright colors and clarity in the eyes. As deterioration begins, scales start to fall off and the fish goes soft. A fresh salmon, when it comes in, or a fresh ling cod, is stiff as a board. But the older it gets, the softer it gets. In prawns, the heads go black not long after being caught, another sign of less than optimum freshness. About 90 per cent of all prawns are frozen on the boats today, a practice that allows fishermen to remain at sea until their holds are full, without worrying about deterioration. Prawns or fish that have been frozen (and, if necessary, dressed) at sea are often superior to so-called fresh products that have languished too long in a boat hold or in a fishmonger's cooler.

The final indication of freshness is, of course, odor. Any fish whose flesh (as opposed to its outer slime, which can be washed off) has an unpleasant odor should be discarded. If seafood has been properly frozen and kept stored at a stable temperature, it will last for months or years. Temperature changes – which occur in a home freezer if the door is frequently opened – will dry seafood out, and freezer burn may result. It's unlikely that buyers of Pacific seafood will find anything for sale that has been frozen too long, since demand for seafood exceeds supply.

Regarding clams: frozen are almost as good as fresh, but they should be dropped into the steamer or pot directly from the freezer. They can lose some of the flavor of fresh clams if they thaw out before cooking. When buying fresh clams, make sure they're alive.

MENU *(Serves Six)*

- Steamed Clams
- Grilled Salmon with Mayonnaise
- Spinach Chiffonade with Mustard Vinaigrette
- Nanaimo Bars

STEAMED CLAMS

The most common commercially sold Pacific clams are the butter and littleneck varieties. Manila and razor clams are also popular with diggers, and may be found for sale. Geoducks (pronounced gooey-ducks), which have been more and more exploited recently, are so large that they are cut into steaks. Geoduck and other clam meat is often sold frozen, but for this recipe, buy small clams in the shell, either frozen or alive. Scrub fresh clams well and rinse one by one under cold running water or put in a large pot and cover with fresh, cold sea water and let stand for several hours, then rinse in cool water. (Frozen clams are sold pre-washed, and go directly from freezer to cooking pot.) Discard any clams that are open. Cornmeal added to the soaking water will help get rid of sand that may be inside the shells.

Allow 18 to 24 clams per person, depending on size and appetites. If you have a special

Now that's fresh: grilled salmon, steamed clams, buttered new potatoes, plenty of fresh fruit plus nanaimo bars for a surprise ending.

steamer, put the clams in the top with five centimetres (2 in.) of salted cold water in the bottom. Otherwise, put the same amount of salted cold water in a large pot or kettle with a secure lid and add the clams. Cover.

For a more flavorful broth in which to steam the clams, use wine, or half wine and water, along with diced onions and celery. When the liquid comes to a rolling boil, steam just until the clams open, three to five minutes.

Cook carefully – overcooked clams are rubbery and tough. Discard any that remain closed. Drain off the broth, strain if desired, and serve in bowls. Each diner should also have a bowl of melted butter.

To eat, dip each clam morsel first in broth, then in the melted butter. The clam broth is an excellent finishing touch to this course. Drink it from a mug or from the bowl.

Note: West Coast clamdiggers should always obtain the Schedule 1 guide to unsafe digging areas from a Department of Fisheries and Oceans office.

GRILLED SALMON

Allow about 250 grams of salmon (½ lb.) per person. Fillet each fish by cutting away the head and tail and snipping off the fins. Run a sharp filleting knife down the back bone. Using short strokes, slice the meat from the top layer of bones, trying to keep the fillet in one piece and fairly smooth. Turn the fish over and cut the meat from the other side of the bones. Keep the skin intact. Place the whole fillets side by side on an oiled rack. The ideal rack is one that is hinged, similar to the old-fashioned toast rack.

Place over the hot coals, skin side up, with 28 grams (1 oz.) of butter on each fillet at the thickest part. When the butter starts to melt, brush over the skin and either turn the whole hinged grill over or (carefully, with large spatulas) turn the fish over. Place another pat of butter on the grilled flesh and, as it melts, brush over the meat. The fish will be done by the time the butter is completely

melted and the meat flakes easily. The total cooking time will be not more than half an hour.

(You can also bake the salmon in an oven by placing the fillets on oiled foil, on a baking sheet, skin side down. Preheat the oven to 230°C (450°F) and bake, brushing with butter, for 20 minutes or until meat flakes easily.)

Serve from the grill, lifting the meat from the skin.

Flavorful mayonnaise is a nice accompaniment. Begin with homemade mayonnaise and add flavorings as described below.

Serve salmon with tiny new potatoes which have been boiled and tossed in butter and chopped parsley.

Mayonnaise

1 large egg
5 mL (1 tsp.) fresh lemon juice
5 mL (1 tsp.) red or white wine
  vinegar
5 mL (1 tsp.) Dijon mustard
375 mL (1½ cups) oil (a mixture of
  45 mL or 3 tbsp. olive oil and the
  rest vegetable oil)

In blender or food processor, whirl together the egg, lemon juice, vinegar and mustard. With machine running, very slowly pour in the oil until mixture becomes thick and shiny. Makes about 375 mL (1½ cups).

Curry Mayonnaise

1 small, finely chopped onion
1 clove garlic, mashed
30 mL (2 tbsp.) butter
15 mL (1 tbsp.) curry powder or 15
  mL (1 tbsp.) curry paste
5 mL (1 tsp.) tomato paste
125 mL (½ cup) chicken stock or
  canned broth, divided
30 mL (2 tbsp.) orange marmalade
375 mL (1½ cups) mayonnaise

Cook onion and garlic in butter until tender. Add curry powder or paste and cook a few minutes longer. Stir in the tomato paste and 60 millilitres (4 tbsp.) of the chicken stock and cook for three to four minutes. Add marmalade and mix well. Cook and strain. Add the curry liquid to the mayonnaise and additional chicken stock, if necessary, to thin out the sauce,

which should be the consistency of sour cream. Adjust seasonings to taste.

Other Tasty Mayonnaises

All these variations will keep several days in the refrigerator.

Green: Finely chop 125 millilitres (½ cup) very dry spinach to a purée. Add to 375 millilitres (1½ cups) mayonnaise with 15 millilitres (1 tbsp.) fresh chopped tarragon and 30 mL (2 tbsp.) chopped fresh parsley.

Seafood (Remoulade) Sauce: Fold into 375 millilitres (1½ cups) mayonnaise a finely chopped hard boiled egg, 30 millilitres (2 tbsp.) finely chopped capers, six finely chopped parsley sprigs, a squeeze of lemon juice and salt and pepper to taste. Fresh dill adds a nice touch.

Tomato: Peel two medium tomatoes, seed and chop finely. Add to 375 millilitres (1½ cups) mayonnaise with 25 millilitres (1½ cups) finely chopped basil or five (1 tsp.) dried basil. Blend and add salt and pepper.

SPINACH CHIFFONADE WITH MUSTARD VINAIGRETTE

This salad is very easy to make ahead and keeps well.

1 bunch of fresh spinach, washed and
  dried
3 slices of good ham
3 slices of Swiss cheese
5 mL (1 tsp.) Dijon mustard
25 mL (1½ tbsp.) red or white wine
  vinegar
90 mL (6 tbsp.) olive oil

Roll spinach leaves into cigar shapes and slice at half-centimetre (¼-in.) intervals. This is a chiffonade. Place in plastic bag and chill until serving time. This will keep several days.

When ready to serve, sliver the ham and cheese slices. Whisk together the mustard and vinegar and slowly whisk in the oil. Add more mustard or season to taste.

Toss the chiffonade with the mustard vinaigrette and garnish with the slivered ham and cheese.

NANAIMO BARS

125 mL (½ cup) butter
60 mL (4 tbsp.) white sugar
75 mL (5 tbsp.) cocoa
1 egg, beaten
5 mL (1 tsp.) vanilla
500 mL (2 cups) crushed graham
 wafers or graham wafer crumbs
250 mL (1 cup) fine coconut
125 mL (½ cup) finely chopped
 walnuts
60 mL (4 tbsp.) butter
45 mL (3 tbsp.) milk
30 mL (2 tbsp.) Bird's vanilla custard
 powder
500 mL (2 cups) icing sugar
125 g (4 oz.) semi-sweet chocolate
15 mL (1 tbsp.) butter

Melt the butter in a medium saucepan and add the sugar, cocoa and beaten egg. Cook, stirring, until mixture resembles a custard. Stir in the vanilla. Add the graham wafer crumbs, coconut and walnuts. Mix well. Lightly grease a 20-centimetre (8-in.) square pan and dust with icing sugar. Press the cocoa mixture firmly into the pan and let stand until cool.

Cream the 60 millilitres (4 tbsp.) of butter until soft. Mix the milk and the custard powder together and add to the butter. Blend in the icing sugar until the mixture is a soft icing. Spread over the cooled base with a small spatula. Dip the spatula in water to help with the spreading. Let stand 15 minutes.

Melt the chocolate and butter in a small pot and then spread over the custard icing. Let set in the refrigerator. Cut into 25 bars. □

Breaking Bannock

Food is perhaps the most enduring characteristic of a culture. We may change the way we dress, forget our mother tongue and those curious customs of our grandparents, but we will still crave the foods of our people. The Indians of B.C. are no different. Even though their lives have changed dramatically, their food customs and preferences persist.

Sharing food has been a hallmark of Indian culture. In some tribes, the first fish of the season is shared with everyone, even if each person gets only a sliver. One tribe in the interior has built a huge iron pot to make a soup that will serve 150 people at communal dinners. The soup requires a side of beef and is stirred with carved wooden paddles.

Janice Silver, who helped us with our recipes, married into the Stalo tribe and lives with her husband, Raphael, on the reserve in the Sumas River valley. She reports that a month before her husband and the other men go deer hunting in the fall, a dinner is planned at which there will be five sittings of 100 people. Everyone brings food, but the main offering is a stew made from the deer the men have caught.

Every spring, Janice and Raphael spend a week on the Fraser River between Chilliwack and Abbotsford netting oolichans. These small fish are so oily that a dried one will burn like a candle if it is lit at one end. Before white settlers brought sugar, the Indians used oolichan oil as a condiment, even dipping fruits and berries in it. Janice hasn't seen oolichan oil used, but it is on the menu at the Quilicum, a native Indian restaurant in Vancouver, where its medicinal properties are extolled. It has been given to a visiting opera singer who had a sore throat, and is regularly quaffed by a patron who insists it will prevent hangovers.

B.C. Indians still consume much salmon, duck and moose. Janice's husband goes north once a year to hunt for moose, and every fall he hunts duck in the Sumas valley. Janice says the moose is shared with family and friends (she freezes some and uses some for jerky), and she freezes the ducks for soup because they are too tough and lean for anything else. Her soup recipe includes the wonderful Indian bread known as bannock. She often serves it as dumplings but sometimes "bakes" it in an inch of lard in a frypan.

The Stalo people catch their salmon on the Fraser near Hope. While the men net the fish, the women gut, fillet and slice them for wind drying. Wind-dried salmon is hard to get, Janice says. Only the elders know the technique and the small quantity they prepare is bought quickly by other Indians.

In other times, B.C. Indians ate more roots and tubers. What they called wild rice was actually the tiny bulblets of the chocolate lily plant, and their wild potatoes were the corms of the Mariposa lily. The Stalo children today still know how to find outdoor snacks. They like to eat what they call "saskies" – salmonberry shoots that they peel and dip in sugar. Janice says the children, who won't eat spinach, love to eat the cooked leaves of stinging nettles. We've included a recipe for this treat. If you intend to try it, take a tip from the Stalo children. Go armed with a large box and a pair of scissors and carefully snip the leaves off, letting them drop, untouched, into the box.

Our dessert is a fine treat, once you get used to its slight bitter tang. Indian ice cream is made from soapberries (or soopolallie, if you prefer). The crushed berries or their juice whip up like soap. Indian cooks used to use their hands to do the job, just as kids will whip soapy water to a foam. We expect that, like contemporary Indians, you'll find it easier to use a beater or a blender.

Tasty traditions: a feast in the west coast Indian style, featuring watercress salad with bacon and egg, wholewheat bannock, barbecued steelhead trout and wild rice.

MENU (Serves Six)

- Duck Soup with Bannock Dumplings
- Wholewheat Bannock
- Watercress Salad
- Steamed Nettles
- Wild Rice
- Barbecued Steelhead Trout
- Indian Ice Cream
- Juniper Tea
- Jerky

DUCK SOUP WITH BANNOCK DUMPLINGS

This is a favorite dish in the Silver household; Janice makes it in large batches.

1 duck, approximately 1.5 kg (2½ to 3 lbs.)
Water to cover, approximately 2 L (2 qts.)
4 medium potatoes, peeled and washed
6 stalks of celery, cut into large dice
6 carrots, peeled and sliced
Salt and pepper to taste
Bannock (recipe follows)

With a cleaver or scissors, chop or cut the duck into small chunks. Heat a frypan to medium heat and brown the meat, bones and giblets. Place them in a large stock pot or stove-top casserole. Cover with water and bring to a boil. Turn down the heat and simmer for about 1½ hours.

Add the vegetables and seasonings and simmer for about 30 minutes or until the vegetables are tender.

Drop bannock dough by the tablespoonful onto the simmering soup and, as soon as the dumplings float to the surface, cover the pot. The dumplings will cook in about 10 to 15 minutes; test with a toothpick to see if they are done.

Serve each guest a large shallow bowl filled with meat, vegetables, soup juices and a dumpling.

JANICE'S BANNOCK FOR DUMPLINGS

The secret of making light dumplings is to keep them steaming on top of simmering liquid. Never crowd the pan.

750 mL (3 cups) all-purpose white flour
30 mL (2 tbsp.) baking powder
5 mL (1 tsp.) salt, optional
375 mL (1½ cups) water, more or less

Mix together the flour, baking powder and salt. Make a well in the centre and pour in the water. Stir to mix, adding more water if necessary for a sticky dough. Drop onto simmering liquid as described above.

This basic dough can be used in many ways. For hotcakes, add more water to make a batter-type mixture and fry as you would any hotcake or pancake. For deep-frying, the dough should be sticky but firm enough to form into loose balls, which can be dropped into hot oil or lard and fried a few minutes on each side. For baked bread, the dough should be a little drier so that it can be dropped in biscuit shapes onto a greased cookie sheet. Bake at 180°C (350°F) for 20 minutes or until golden brown. (You could stir in fresh berries for a sweet touch.) For a sourdough tang, let the batter stand overnight at room temperature before using in any of the above ways.

WHOLEWHEAT BANNOCK

There are as many bannock recipes as there are cooks. This one makes one tasty loaf.

375 ml (1½ cups) wholewheat flour
375 mL (1½ cups) all-purpose white flour
12 mL (2½ tsp.) baking powder
2 mL (½ tsp.) baking soda
Pinch of salt
1 large egg
30 mL (2 tbsp.) honey
30 mL (2 tbsp.) molasses
30 mL (2 tbsp.) vegetable oil
325 mL (1⅓ cups) milk

Stir together the flours, baking powder, baking soda and salt. In another bowl, mix together the egg, honey, molasses, oil and milk. Make a well in the dry ingredients and rapidly pour in the liquids. Stir quickly and mix thoroughly.

Pour the mixture into a greased loaf pan, approximately 12 by 19 centimetres (4½ by 7½ in.). Bake at 180°C (350°F) for one hour and 15 minutes or until a toothpick inserted in the centre comes out clean. Turn out onto a rack to cool. The bread is best served warm.

WATERCRESS SALAD

Watercress is found growing wild by the banks of free-running streams. It has small leaves and a peppery taste.

Enough watercress for 6 salads
Pinch of sugar
Pinch of salt
Freshly ground pepper
½ strip of bacon per person
Vinegar
Yolk of 1 hard-cooked egg, crumbled

Rinse the watercress and pat dry. Place on individual serving plates. Sprinkle on a little sugar, salt and pepper.

Fry the bacon until crisp and set aside. To the bacon fat, add twice as much vinegar as fat. Bring to a boil and then pour over the watercress and toss lightly.

Garnish with egg yolk and crumbled bacon bits.

STEAMED NETTLES

Carefully pick the leaves of the stinging nettle. Rinse off and cook briefly over high heat as you would spinach.

WILD RICE

Wild rice is really a seed from a grass that grows in rivers and lakes; it is expensive because it is difficult to harvest. Wild rice triples in volume when it is cooked.

250 mL (1 cup) wild rice
1 L (1 qt.) water
Pinch of salt

Rinse the rice and place in a large saucepan. Add water and salt, cover and bring to a boil. Turn down the heat and simmer, without stirring, for 40 minutes or until tender. Drain off the water.

BARBECUED STEELHEAD TROUT

Simply grilled over coals and basted with a butter sauce, trout steaks or fillets are fabulous. A touch of onion and tarragon add to the delicate flavor.

60 mL (4 tbsp.) olive oil
30 mL (2 tbsp.) lemon juice
30 mL (2 tbsp.) onion, finely chopped
  (optional)
30 mL (2 tbsp.) tarragon, finely
  chopped (optional)
Salt and pepper to taste
Steelhead trout or salmon to serve 6,
  cut into steaks or fillets
60 mL (4 tbsp.) butter, melted

Mix together the oil, juice and seasonings, and rub onto the fish. Let stand at room temperature for one hour for the flavors to permeate the meat.

Place the fish on a greased grill 10 centimetres (4 in.) from coals that are hot to medium hot. Cook about six to seven minutes on each side, basting often with the melted butter. The cooking time will vary according to the heat of the coals and the thickness of the meat.

This recipe works equally well for grilling under the broiler. Place the fish on a rack on a baking sheet to prevent spatters in the oven.

INDIAN ICE CREAM

Berries are a favorite dessert and there are many, many kinds available. The soapberries we are using for the ice cream whip up into a cloud that resembles soap and has a faintly tart taste. Packages of dried soapberries are available, but you may have to search for them.

1 pkg. dried soapberry mix
250 mL (1 cup) water
Sugar to taste

Add water and sugar to the dried mix and whip until soft peaks form. Serve immediately.

To make a single serving from fresh berries:

45 mL (3 tbsp.) soapberries
90 mL (6 tbsp.) water
45 mL (3 tbsp.) sugar

Mash the berries with the water and sugar. Beat and whip until the mixture is thick and white and soft peaks form.

Soapberry juice is sometimes available at the Quilicum restaurant in Vancouver (604-681-7044). Their recipe serves four people.

30 mL (2 tbsp.) soapberry juice
60 mL (4 tbsp.) water
Sugar to taste

Place the ingredients in a blender and blend until white and foamy.

JUNIPER TEA

Aromatic and flavorful, this tea is worth trying.

1.5 L (6 cups) water
6 to 8 dried juniper berries (available
  at most specialty shops)

Pour boiling water over juniper berries and allow to stand for about five minutes until flavor develops.

JERKY

The Stalo Indians soak their wild meat in a brine overnight. They then smoke the meat, which has been cut into thin strips, for about eight to 10 hours. The following recipes have been taken from a cookbook prepared by the Department of Indian Affairs and Northern Development.

SUN DRIED JERKY

Cut fresh meat into long thin strips, 2.5 centimetres (1 in.) wide. Rub the strips with garlic or salt, if desired. Dry in the sun as quickly as possible by hanging over a line. Do not let the strips touch. Store in a dry place in clean jars or sacks.

COLD BRINED JERKY

Cut muscle meat lengthwise into strips 2.5 centimetres (1 in.) thick, four centimetres (1½ in.) wide and as long as you can make them. Put the strips into a wooden barrel or non-metallic container and cover with a sweet pickling or corning solution for three days. Hang the meat over a cord or string to drip for 24 hours and continue to hang it in a dry place. Keep the strips from touching each other and protect them from dirt and insects with a light cloth covering if necessary. The jerky will continue to dry as long as it is exposed to air; it should be taken down and put away in an airtight container as soon as it is dried to your liking. A light smoke will add to the flavor and help preserve the meat.

HOT BRINED JERKY

Hot-brined jerky is made in much the same way, except that the meat is cut into finer strips (like shoe-string potatoes) and salted in a hot brine. The hot solution is made by adding salt to boiling water until no more can be dissolved. Dip strips into the hot brine until they turn white, which takes about five minutes, and then string them up to dry, handling them the same way as cold-brined jerky. □

Garden
Harvest

Fresh garden vegetables are so good and so briefly around that they deserve a meal unto themselves. Ours features a soup that brings out the unique sweetness of fresh corn. We follow with a sweet and sour salad of melon, English cucumber, herbs and cashews in a vinaigrette, and then a "lasagna" of eggplant, provolone, tomatoes and fresh herbs. The bread, too, made from wheat berries and wholewheat flour, is delicious and filling, while the dessert, a mélange of fresh fruit and cream, plays richness and smooth texture against the tartness of fresh blackberries. Nor is the meal nutritionally lacking. The nuts, whole grains and cheese provide complementary proteins (essential in a vegetarian meal), and the grains and corn add fibre and carbohydrates. The fruits and vegetables, of course, deliver vitamins. Good eating; good health.

MENU *(Serves Six)*

- Fresh Corn Soup
- Melon-Tomato Salad
- Baked Eggplant and Provolone
- Sprouted Wheat Bread
- Blackberry Mousse
- Spiced Iced Tea

FRESH CORN SOUP

Corn is at its best in mid-August. One average-sized cob will yield about 125 millilitres (½ cup) of kernels.

Vegetarian plus: a colorful salad of melons and tomatoes garnished with cashews and mint; baked eggplant and provolone in a piquant sauce; tangy blackberry mousse for dessert.

60 mL (4 tbsp.) butter
2 medium onions, finely chopped
1 green pepper, finely chopped
500 mL (2 cups) milk
30 mL (2 tbsp.) parsley, chopped
30 mL (2 tbsp.) fresh savory,
    chopped, or 5 mL (1 tsp.) dried
    savory, crumbled
Dash of salt
Freshly ground pepper to taste
500 mL (2 cups) freshly scraped corn
    kernels
250 mL (1 cup) whipping cream
60 mL (4 tbsp.) corn kernels for
    garnish

Melt the butter and add the
chopped onions and pepper. Sauté
gently until butter is absorbed and
the vegetables are tender. Add the
milk, parsley, savory, salt, pepper
and corn. Bring to a boil. Reduce
the heat and simmer about 10
minutes.

Cool the soup slightly, then
purée in a blender (remember that
hot liquids tend to pop the blender
lid). Return the puréed mixture to
the saucepan and reheat to simmer.
Add the cream and adjust the
seasonings. Note: the cream
produces a smoother soup but is
not essential. You can reduce the
calories by using a Swiss-style
plain yoghurt. Or don't add
anything at all.

Serve hot, garnished with a
spoonful of the reserved whole
corn kernels.

MELON TOMATO SALAD

Prepare this salad well ahead and
chill for a refreshing treat on a hot
day.

1 honeydew melon, peeled, seeded and
    cut into chunks
500 g (1 lb.) thin-skinned tomatoes,
    seeded, drained, roughly cut
1 English cucumber, cut into chunks
    (peel and seed if desired)
Toasted cashews (see recipe below)
Butter lettuce leaves
Vinaigrette (see recipe below)

Taste the cucumber; if it seems
watery or a little bitter, place the
chunks on a large platter and
sprinkle with salt. Let stand about
half an hour, then rinse off the salt
and pat dry.
Place the melon, tomatoes and

cucumber in an attractive serving
bowl. Add the vinaigrette and mix
salad well. Cover and chill for at
least one hour. Stir before serving.

To serve, place a leaf of butter
lettuce on a chilled salad plate and
spoon on the melon mixture.
Sprinkle with toasted cashews.
Garnish with a sprig of mint and
serve with hot bread.

Vinaigrette
90 mL (6 tbsp.) light vegetable oil
30 mL (2 tbsp.) white wine vinegar
Dash of salt
Freshly ground pepper to taste
Pinch of dry mustard
Mixed herbs

Chop herbs such as parsley, mint,
chives and thyme. Mix remaining
ingredients and pour over the
herbs. Let the vinaigrette stand for
flavors to blend.

Toasted Cashews
To toast the cashews, place on a
baking sheet and bake at 180°C
(350°F) for approximately eight to
10 minutes or until golden and
toasted. Watch carefully, as nuts
burn easily.

BAKED EGGPLANT AND PROVOLONE

60 mL (4 tbsp.) good olive oil
1 large onion, finely chopped
2 cloves garlic, chopped or crushed
1 kg (2 lbs.) tomatoes, skinned, seeded
    and chopped
10 mL (2 tsp.) oregano
3 or 4 large leaves of fresh basil,
    chopped, or 10 mL (2 tsp.) dried
    basil
Salt and pepper to taste
1 medium to large eggplant
Olive oil
1 large sweet onion, in slices
Italian provolone cheese, sliced

Make the sauce first. In a large,
heavy frypan, heat the olive oil.
Add the finely chopped onion and
sauté until soft. Add the garlic and
cook briefly. Add the tomatoes,
oregano, basil and a bit of salt and
pepper. Cook over high heat until
the sauce is reduced, stirring
occasionally, about 15 minutes.
Taste for seasonings. Set aside.

Slice the eggplant into fairly thin

slices. Don't worry about the
seeds. Heat the olive oil in a large
frypan and quickly sauté the
eggplant rounds. Drain on paper
towelling. Add more olive oil as
needed, as the eggplant absorbs a
great deal of it.

Add more oil to the pan and
sauté the onion slices until very
soft. Place in the bottom of an au
gratin or ovenproof serving dish.

Spoon on half the tomato sauce.
Cut the eggplant and cheese
rounds in half and layer, on an
angle, as shown in the photograph.
Spoon a little of the tomato sauce
between the layers, if desired.
Spoon the remaining sauce around
the edge of the dish. Make ahead
to this point. No need to
refrigerate.

Bake at 200°C (400°F) until the
cheese is melted and the vegetables
are heated through. Serve hot.
This reheats well.

SPROUTED WHEAT BREAD

This recipe makes one loaf of
bread, but it doubles well. As the
wheat berries need time to sprout,
begin at least three days before the
bread is to be cooked. This bread
is made from a sponge, and
requires three risings instead of
two.

60 mL (4 tbsp.) wheat berries
2 mL (½ tsp.) sugar
300 mL (1¼ cup) warm water,
    divided
15 mL (1 tbsp.) dry yeast
250 mL (1 cup) all-purpose white
    flour
500 to 750 mL (2 to 3 cups)
    wholewheat or triticale flour
5 mL (1 tsp.) salt
30 mL (2 tbsp.) honey
15 mL (1 tbsp.) oil

Place the wheat berries in a large,
wide-mouthed jar. Fill the jar one-
third with water. Cover the top of
the jar with a piece of cheesecloth
and secure with a rubber band.
Leave the berries to soak
overnight. The next day,
completely drain the berries. Place
the jar on its side in a dark place,
leaving the cloth in place. Rinse
with fresh water twice a day to
moisten the berries. Once the

berries have sprouted (after two or three days), place the jar in a brightly lit area for an additional day. Once sprouted, the berries can be refrigerated for a few days.

To make the bread: dissolve the sugar in 125 millilitres (½ cup) of the warm water in a small bowl. Sprinkle on the yeast and let stand until bubbly.

Place the white flour, 175 millilitres (¾ cup) of the wholewheat or triticale flour and salt in a medium bowl. Stir in the honey, oil and remaining water. Add the yeast mixture. Beat until smooth. Cover with plastic wrap and let the mixture rise for one hour, or until light and frothy. This is the sponge.

Chop the sprouted wheat coarsely. Beat the risen mixture down to its original size. Stir in the chopped wheat and enough of the remaining wholewheat to yield a soft dough.

Turn out onto a lightly floured board and knead, working in white flour or wholewheat (this will make the outside crunchier) until the dough is smooth and will retain its shape when placed on the board. Place in a well-greased bowl, grease the top of the dough and let it rise in a warm place until it doubles in size — about one to 1½ hours.

When doubled, punch the dough down and shape into a free-form loaf or place it in a greased loaf pan. The dough will divide into four loaves for mini pans also. Let it rise until doubled or the top of the dough *in the centre* is 2.5 centimetres (1 in.) above the edges of the pan. Brush with a little egg yolk that has been mixed with a drop of water, and bake for 40 minutes at 190°C (375°F) or until the loaf sounds hollow when tapped on the bottom. This will take longer if your pans are of shiny metal. Be sure to bake thoroughly, as the dough tends to be a little wet.

BLACKBERRY MOUSSE

500 g (1 lb.) fresh blackberries
(raspberries can be substituted)
1 pkg. unflavored gelatine
45 mL (3 tbsp.) cold water
Grated zest of 1 orange

Juice of 1 orange
2 eggs
125 mL (½ cup) white sugar
30 mL (2 tbsp.) black currant liqueur
500 mL (2 cups) whipping cream
A few perfect blackberries for garnish

Mash or purée the blackberries, reserving a few for garnish. Strain to remove as many seeds as possible. Set aside.

Dissolve the gelatine in the cold water. Add the zest and juice of the orange and heat until just melted. Cool slightly. Stir in the blackberry purée.

Beat the eggs and sugar together until thick and lemon-colored.

Place the egg mixture in a medium saucepan. Cook and stir over low heat until the mixture is slightly thick and the sugar has melted. This does not take very long, about three to five minutes. Cool.

Mix together the blackberry purée and the egg mixture and stir until well blended. Stir in the liqueur.

Beat the whipping cream until soft peaks form. Fold one-quarter of the whipped cream into the blackberry mixture and stir to lighten the mixture. Gently fold in the remaining whipped cream.

Divide among serving dishes or place in a clear glass bowl. Chill until ready to serve. Garnish with the reserved blackberries and tiny leaves.

SPICED ICED TEA

For an unclouded, refreshing cup of iced tea, this is a simple recipe. Start with high-quality tea leaves.

30 mL (2 tbsp.) tea leaves
Spices or herbs of choice (see below)
1 L (1 qt.) cold water

Combine the tea, spices and water in a large jar. Cap the jar and shake it, or stir the leaves with a spoon for a minute or two. Leave the jar in the refrigerator for at least 12 hours. Strain and sweeten (with honey or sugar syrup) to taste.

An alternative, of course, is to use boiling water, steeping the tea as you regularly would. Allow it to cool, then refrigerate.

Boiling water brings out the flavor of some spices and herbs. You can either heat the spices in a small amount of water or tea and add them to the jar, or add the spices directly to the tea leaves and pour boiling water over all.

Among the spices and herbs that lend flavor to iced tea are cinnamon, cloves, dried citrus peel, peppermint, spearmint, lemon verbina and lemon balm. Be sparing when adding spices, however, as they can overpower the tea and yield a cloying drink.
□

Perfect Picnicking

The first picnics I remember were never elegant. They were often nothing more than a packed lunch eaten by the side of the road on our drive north to a rented summer cottage. We always packed a lunch for these trips: egg-salad sandwiches wrapped in wax paper, carrot and celery sticks in ice water, cookies with pink, blue, white and yellow sprinkles on top and a couple of plastic containers of Freshie, one grape, one lime.

Every summer, however, there were big picnics – the church affair, where you lined up with all the other eight-year-olds for hot dogs and chocolate-covered ice-cream bars, or the annual family reunions, one for each parent. The food at these two family picnics was indistinguishable, both clans being devoted to plain fare: cole slaw, macaroni salads, the inevitable and awful tomato aspic, pickled beets and watermelon rind, platters of ham (but never salami), berry pies and white cakes with orange peel in the icing. Several determined aunts would have outwitted the perishing heat and managed to transport multi-colored Jello salads containing grated carrots and miniature marshmallows. I remember once tasting three different potato salads, ignoring my mother's concern about mayonnaise left in the sun, although she was more likely to pronounce this warning when the food had been prepared by strangers.

When I had a family of my own, we worked hard to avoid doing what everyone else was doing, and so we had our picnics out of season. We would go to a deserted park in mid-winter, and

Romance on the rocks: baguette stuffed with spinach, carrots and cheese; marinated baby vegetables; cold lemon chicken; giant cookies and an assortment of fresh fruit coolers.

we'd light the coals in the barbecue and keep the ice cream cold by burying it in the snow that surrounded the table at which we sat in delicious isolation.

Sometimes we'd come across a place perfect for a picnic, and we'd go away and plan the perfect picnic for the place. Once it was a shoreline of undulating rock that rose gently to a west-facing perch high above the ocean. We saw ourselves there at sunset with some cooked lobster, sourdough bread, green grapes and a Chardonnay, which we would lower on ropes to chill in a tidepool below, and we did do that with friends one summer evening, except that we spared the wine its perilous descent.

This month's summer picnic requires such a place, a place secluded and with a view, where six good friends can enjoy an elegant meal alfresco. The cooking is all done ahead, and so there's no need to worry about barbecue coals and equipment. You have only to pack a hamper with attractive tableware and linens and to fill a pre-chilled cooler with cold food, beverages and frozen brick coolers to keep it all well chilled.

— *Audrey Grescoe*

MENU *(Serves Six)*

• Stuffed Baguette
• Lemon Chicken
• Baby Vegetables Marinated in Vinaigrette
• Oatmeal Pecan Cookies
• Double Chocolate Cookies
• Fruit Syrups

STUFFED BAGUETTE

Delicious hot or cold, sliced into small appetizer snacks or cut into hearty portions and served with a spicy mustard, this makes a tasty addition to any picnic.

Baguette dough, raised once (recipe follows)
2 300-g (10-oz.) pkgs. frozen chopped spinach, thawed and squeezed dry
1 medium onion, finely chopped
30 mL (2 tbsp.) butter
5 mL (1 tsp.) salt

5 mL (1 tsp.) pepper
Dash nutmeg
30 mL (2 tbsp.) fresh herbs, chopped
4 carrots, peeled, whole or cut in half lengthwise, cooked until tender
375 mL (1½ cups) shredded Cheddar cheese

Make the bread dough and set to rise. Sauté the spinach and the onion in the butter in a frypan. Season with salt, pepper, a little nutmeg and chopped fresh herbs.

When the dough has risen, divide into four balls and set aside for 10 minutes. Roll out two of the balls into rectangles about 15 by 25 centimetres (6 by 10 in.). Divide the spinach into four portions and spread one portion on each rectangle, leaving a one-centimetre (½-in.) border. Divide the carrots between the portions and sprinkle on the cheese. Add the remaining spinach. Roll out the two remaining balls of dough and place over top of the filled bases, stretching as necessary to fit. Crimp the edges as you would a pie crust.

Grease a double baguette pan or large cookie sheet. Using a spatula, carefully pick up the loaves and place them in or on the pan. Brush with a little egg yolk and cut a few slashes on top for the steam to escape.

Bake without further rising at 190°C (375°F) for 35 minutes or until the top is dark golden brown. Cool well. Serve with a spicy mustard.

Baguette Dough
300 mL (1¼ cups) warm water
15 mL (1 tbsp.) sugar
10 mL (2 tsp.) salt
10 mL (2 tsp.) yeast
625 to 750 mL (2½ to 3 cups) all-purpose white flour

Place the warm water in a warm bowl and stir in the sugar and salt. Sprinkle the yeast over top and let stand until dissolved and bubbly, about 10 minutes. Add flour, one cup at a time, until the dough forms a ball. Knead in as much flour as necessary to make the dough smooth and silky.

Grease the top of the dough and place it in a greased bowl. Let rise

until double, punch down and divide as required.

LEMON CHICKEN

Marinated in a fragrant mixture of lemon, garlic and good olive oil, this chicken is irresistible. Weighting down the meat during cooking keeps in the moisture. Chill well before packing for the picnic.

8 fresh lemons
4 cloves garlic, finely minced
60 mL (4 tbsp.) good virgin olive oil
Freshly ground pepper
6 or 8 chicken breast halves (or a half chicken per person) with skin and bones

Squeeze the juice from four of the lemons and mix together with the garlic, olive oil and a few twists of pepper. Rub into both sides of the chicken. Place chicken in a shallow glass pan and let marinate for one hour at room temperature. If leaving longer, refrigerate and bring to room temperature about half an hour before cooking.

Remove the chicken to a plate and strain out the garlic from the marinade. Heat the marinade in a large frypan, adding a little more oil if needed. Use two pans, if one will not hold all the chicken, or fry in two stages. Teflon-coated pans help keep the skin from sticking.

Place chicken skin-side down and brown lightly over medium-high heat. Turn down the heat to medium low and place a lid or small pan directly onto the chicken and weight it down with heavy cans or a foil-wrapped brick. Let the chicken cook slowly and turn a deep golden brown (about 10 minutes for the breasts, 25 for a half chicken).

Remove weights and turn the chicken skin-side up. Slice some lemons thinly and place rounds on the browned skin. Baste with some of the cooking juices and replace weights. Cook another 10 minutes for breasts and 25 minutes for half chicken over medium-low heat.

Remove chicken to a platter and squeeze on a little more lemon juice. Cool thoroughly. Wrap carefully, placing a fresh slice of lemon over each piece.

BABY VEGETABLES MARINATED IN VINAIGRETTE

Baby or miniature vegetables are fully mature, just tiny. Ask your supermarket produce manager to get them in for you.

Various baby vegetables, as available
Radicchio
Mâche or lamb's lettuce
Vinaigrette with a good virgin olive oil

Rinse off the vegetables, bring water to a boil and cook them briefly until barely tender-crisp. Run under cold water to stop the cooking and place them in a bowl of vinaigrette, stirring to coat. Chill. Remove from marinade and place in containers to transport to picnic site, taking along the vinaigrette in a separate container.

Serve with radicchio or mâche as the base, arranging vegetables on top and sprinkling on a little of the reserved vinaigrette.

Vinaigrette

Taste the virgin olive oil before adding to this recipe. If it is very strong, mix with a little vegetable oil to get the right flavor.

The classic proportion is three or four parts oil to one part lemon juice, lime juice or vinegar. Add salt and pepper to taste, and various other condiments (herbs, garlic, Worcestershire sauce, chili sauce or chutney) according to your whim.

Place in a jar and shake.

OATMEAL PECAN COOKIES

Coarsely chopped semi-sweet chocolate (170g/6 oz.) can be added to this basic recipe.

250 mL (1 cup) butter
250 mL (1 cup) white sugar
250 mL (1 cup) brown sugar, lightly packed
1 large egg
15 mL (1 tbsp.) molasses
5 mL (1 tsp.) vanilla
375 mL (1½ cups) all-purpose white flour
5 mL (1 tsp.) baking soda
5 mL (1 tsp.) baking powder

7 mL (1½ tsp.) cinnamon
5 mL (1 tsp.) nutmeg
5 mL (1 tsp.) allspice
250 mL (1 cup) coconut
250 mL (1 cup) rolled oats, any type
250 mL (1 cup) pecans, coarsely chopped

Cream together the butter, sugars, egg, molasses and vanilla. Stir together the flour, soda, baking powder and spices. Stir into the creamed mixture. Add the coconut, rolled oats and pecans. Mix well. Form into 2.5 or five-centimetre (1 or 2-in.) balls and freeze on a cookie sheet. Store in freezer bags and bake as needed. Bake frozen at 180°C (350°F) for 12 to 15 minutes or thawed for 10 to 12 minutes. Taken from the oven while puffy, the cookies flatten down and are chewy in the centre. (Parchment paper on the baking sheet will prevent burned bottoms.)

DOUBLE CHOCOLATE COOKIES

This is a cookie that is best freshly baked. Make the whole recipe into large or small balls and store in the freezer, taking out as many as you want to bake.

425 mL (1¾ cups) all-purpose white flour
5 mL (1 tsp.) baking soda
3 mL (¾ tsp.) salt
300 g (10 oz.) semi-sweet chocolate, cut into 2.5-cm (1-in.) cubes
250 mL (1 cup) unsalted butter at room temperature
125 mL (½ cup) white sugar
250 mL (1 cup) light brown sugar, firmly packed
2 large eggs
15 mL (1 tbsp.) vanilla
125 g (4 oz.) white chocolate, coarsely chopped

Stir together the flour, baking soda and salt and set aside. Melt the semi-sweet chocolate over low heat and cool. Beat together the butter and sugars until light and fluffy. Add the eggs and vanilla and mix well. Stir in the melted chocolate. Add the flour mixture and stir until blended. Stir in the white chocolate, reserving some pieces for a final garnish. Chill for

easier handling.

To prepare the dough for the freezer, form into five-centimetre (2-in.) or 2.5-centimetre (1-in.) balls and place close together on a sheet of wax paper on a large cookie sheet. Place in the freezer until frozen. Remove from wax paper and store in a freezer bag. Bake frozen at 180°C (350°F) for 12 to 15 minutes, or thawed for eight minutes for a chewy cookie, nine minutes for a crispy one. Be sure to leave space between each one, as they melt down to form quite a flat shape. Add a piece of reserved white chocolate to the centre of each cookie as soon as they are flat.

FRUIT SYRUPS

Sugar syrup infused with the essence of fruits makes a wonderful concentrate to which you can add soda water, mineral water or wine. This recipe makes 1 L (1 qt.) of each concentrate.

Lemon Concentrate
500 mL (2 cups) sugar
250 mL (1 cup) water
Rind of 2 lemons
Juice of 6 lemons or 375 mL (1½ cups) lemon juice

Use a potato peeler to take the rind from the lemons, avoiding the bitter, white pith. Over medium heat, bring the sugar, rind and water to a slow boil to dissolve the sugar. Turn up the heat and boil rapidly for five minutes. Let stand to cool. Remove the rinds, reserving the partly candied strips for garnish if desired. Stir in the lemon juice. Refrigerate in a covered jar.

For a refreshing drink, fill a tall glass with ice cubes. Add six ounces of soda water and two ounces of lemon concentrate. Stir and garnish with lemon strip or mint.

Orange Concentrate
300 mL (1¼ cups) sugar
300 mL (1¼ cups) water
Rind of 2 oranges
Juice of 7 oranges or 500 mL (2 cups) orange juice

Follow instructions for lemon concentrate. □

Newest New Mex

The cuisine of New Mexico is a cultural stew. The base is Mexican but there are Indian, Spanish and Anglo-American flavors in the pot.

New Mexico has remained more faithful to the cuisine of Mexico than have the other states of the American southwest. Its cooking is not like Tex-Mex or California-Mex, those other Mexican descendants that have gone their own way. New Mexican cookery has retained more authentic dishes and old-time methods and it is more Indian-influenced.

It was the Indians, for instance, who taught the New Mexicans to use blue cornmeal to make tortillas, which are the base for so many dishes. Today, blue-corn tortillas are the variation that makes an enchilada dish authentically New Mexican. The Indians also taught the New Mexicans to treat fresh corn with lime to make hominy. The New Mexican dish known as *posole* is a simple stew of hominy, flavored with pork (the quantity of meat depending on the importance of the occasion) and herbs and chilies. New Mexicans are so used to the taste of lime-treated corn that they give up much of their fresh corn to make hominy.

The state can claim *sopaipillas* as its own. These "soft pillows" of deep-fried dough are held under hot fat briefly, until they puff up, and then they are cut open and stuffed with beans, meat or chili con carne. They even appear at dessert with honey and butter drizzled inside.

New Mexicans use chilies more than the other states in the southwest. Green chilies appear in

Crossover classics: clockwise from left, tostada with avocado salsa and crab; blue cornbread with chilies and cheese; and posole salad in lettuce cups.

everything from hamburgers to potato soup, and ground red chilies are the foundation upon which New Mexicans build their version of what we call chili. *Carne con chile colorado* starts with a red pepper sauce – *chile colorado*. Cooked shredded meat and beans, but never tomatoes, are added to this fiery paste, which is always served with extinguishers – bread or soft tortillas, accompanied by a little honey because sweetness seems to help put out the fire, too.

Even though its traditional Indian-Spanish-Mexican cuisine still flourishes, the state is not immune to what's going on gastronomically in the rest of the country. In New Mexico today they speak of a crossover cuisine. It combines the state's multicultural food tradition with the look of nouvelle cuisine. For instance, restaurateurs in Santa Fe serve a *timbale*, which is essentially French, with a sauce made of ancho chilies, or they present one tortilla stuffed with *carne adovada* on a plate with tiny vegetables.

Our New Mexican meal is an admirable combination of old and new. It will give you a chance to try blue cornmeal – in a bread rather than in the time-consuming traditional tortillas. And it presents *posole* in a delectable salad rather than as a filling stew. By stacking and filling tortillas, we have created a manageable version of *tostadas*, the filling of which is usually a production-line chore.

Inevitably, New Mexican cooking is labor intensive. Many dishes depend upon breads that must be rolled, shaped and fried before they are filled and covered with a sauce. Or there are breads that must be made and served at the last minute. Our meal is not simple, but it can be done in several stages.

Many days before the party, you can make and freeze the *chile con queso* and the chicken strips, and you can prepare and store the salsa. The day before, make the *posole* salad, *carne con chile*, orange sherbet and the cookies. You could also make the cornbread and the *sopaipillas*. On the day of the party, fry the tortillas for the crab *tostada*, mix the crab ingredients

and make the avocado salsa (but do not add the avocado). Prepare and roll out the fry-bread.

When your guests have arrived, gently heat the *chile con queso*, fry and serve the chicken strips, bake the *carne con chile* and the cornbread (or reheat the cornbread if you have made it ahead), fry the Navajo bread and serve it with the salad, build the avocado *tostada* and heat it, fry the *sopaipillas* and serve them with sherbet and cookies.

If shopping is a problem, try Que Pasa Mexican Foods at 530 West 17th Avenue, Vancouver V5Z 1T4. They will also take mail orders.

MENU *(Serves Ten)*

- Margueritas
- Mexican Coffee
- Mexican Chocolate
- Chile con Questo
- Crisp Spicy Chicken Strips
- Daryl's Hot Salsa
- Posole Salad
- Navajo Fry Bread
- Carne con Chile
- Blue Cornbread
- Tostada with Avocado Salsa and Crab
- Orange Sherbet
- Sopaipillas

MARGUERITAS

Wonderfully refreshing with Mexican food, this mixture can be frozen and served as a slush. Freeze the glasses ahead of time and roll their rims in a little salt at serving time.

1 part lime juice, freshly squeezed
1 part Triple Sec or orange liqueur
3 parts Tequila, preferably 80-proof natural
1 egg-white
Ice cubes

Mix in a blender. Add one eggwhite and blend. Add four or five ice cubes and blend again until frothy and the ice cubes are broken up.

MEXICAN COFFEE

Coffee and chocolate are the most popular drinks. Here are interesting versions of each.

3 7.5-cm (3-in.) cinnamon sticks
1 vanilla bean

175 mL (¾ cup) ground dark-roasted or espresso coffee beans
2.5 L (10 cups) cold water
125 mL (½ cup) whipping cream
Dark brown sugar

Brew the coffee by your normal method, placing the cinnamon sticks and vanilla bean in with the ground coffee. Whip the cream, adding brown sugar to taste, until stiff. Pour coffee into cups and top with a dollop of cream.

MEXICAN CHOCOLATE

This thick, exotic brew should be served frothy. If necessary, whisk it up again before serving. For a special treat, mix it half and half with hot coffee.

60 g (2 oz.) semi-sweet chocolate, coarsely chopped
500 mL (2 cups) milk
250 mL (1 cup) whipping cream
45 mL (3 tbsp.) white sugar
5 mL (1 tsp.) cinnamon
Pinch of cloves, optional
Pinch of salt
1 egg
5 mL (1 tsp.) vanilla

In a medium saucepan, melt the chocolate in the milk and cream. Add the sugar, spices and salt. Whisk the mixture over medium heat until it comes to a boil, and then lower the heat and cook for five minutes, whisking constantly. (You'll be glad you did!)

In a small bowl, beat the egg and vanilla together until frothy. Slowly add a little of the hot chocolate to the egg to warm it up, before whisking the egg mixture into the hot chocolate mixture. Whisk for another three minutes and serve.

CHILE CON QUESO

The Southwest's most popular hot fondue-like dip is traditionally served with *tostadas*. Try El Torito taco strips, which seem to hold the sauce best of all. This dip freezes well for up to four months.

75 mL (⅓ cup) vegetable oil
125 mL (½ cup) finely chopped onion, or 3 green onions with tops
1 clove garlic, minced

*15 mL (1 tbsp.) all-purpose white
  flour*
175 mL (¾ cup) evaporated milk
1 red bell pepper, chopped
*500 g (1 lb.) processed cheese, such as
  Velveeta, cut into 2.5-cm (1-in.)
  cubes*
*60 mL (4 tbsp.) sharp Cheddar
  cheese, grated*
*60 mL (4 tbsp.) Monterey Jack
  cheese, grated*
*45 mL (3 tbsp.) finely minced
  jalapeño chilies and juice, to taste*

In a heavy skillet, heat the oil and add the onion, then sauté until soft. Add the garlic and cook another minute or so. Stir in the flour. Gradually add the evaporated milk and cook until the mixture thickens slightly. Add the bell pepper, cheeses, *jalapeños* and juice. Cook and stir until thick and smooth, about five minutes. Keep warm in a chafing dish.

CRISP SPICY CHICKEN STRIPS

For a succulent interior, fry the chicken strips while still frozen. A great variation is to use them in a taco: place a little shredded lettuce in a crisp taco, add a couple of fried chicken strips, a little salsa, a bit of shredded cheese and pop into the oven until the cheese melts. Top with some sour cream or more salsa. This recipe makes hors-d'oeuvres for 10 and can be doubled successfully. Masa harina is a cornmeal flour available from large grocery chains.

125 mL (½ cup) masa harina
5 mL (1 tsp.) ground cumin
5 mL (1 tsp.) mild red chili powder
2 mL (½ tsp.) garlic salt
2 mL (½ tsp.) oregano
30 mL (2 tbsp.) parsley, minced
250 mL (1 cup) milk
*750 g (1½ lbs.) boneless chicken
  breasts*

Mix together in a shallow bowl the masa harina, cumin, chili, garlic salt, oregano and parsley. In another small bowl, place the milk.

Trim the chicken breasts and remove the skin. Cut into strips about 7.6 centimetres (3 in.) long and 1.2 centimetres (½ in.) wide.

Dip the chicken strips into the milk and then into the spicy coating mixture. Place on a waxed-paper-lined baking sheet and freeze at least 40 minutes, or overnight.

In a deep-fat fryer or frypan with sides, heat about 5 centimetres (2 in.) of oil to 180°C (350°F). Remove the chicken strips from the freezer and fry, a few at a time, until dark golden brown. Drain on paper towels. Serve immediately with a hot salsa for dipping.

The chicken may be frozen, uncooked, for up to three months.

DARYL'S HOT SALSA

A terrific recipe developed by the company that produces El Torito taco and tortilla chips and salsa, this salsa may be purchased in jars in supermarkets. For the sake of accuracy, we have reproduced the Imperial measurements we were given, even though canned products available to the home cook aren't sold in these quantities. To make up the 100 ounces of tomatoes, use three 796-millilitre cans and one 398-millilitre can. For the crushed tomatoes, substitute a 398-millimetre can. Ortega makes good canned green chilies, available in a 735-gram can. The other ingredients are easily reproduced. The recipe makes four litres (4 qts.) and can be halved.

*3 L (100 oz.) canned tomatoes,
  drained*
500 mL (16 oz.) crushed tomatoes
687 mL (22 oz.) green chilies, diced
750 g (1½ lbs.) fresh onions, diced
125 mL (4 oz.) vinegar
*30 g (1 oz.) garlic, chopped (10 to 12
  cloves)*
*30 g (1 oz.) fresh cilantro, chopped
  (about 2 bunches, or to taste)*
Salt to taste
*114 mL can jalapeño peppers, stems
  and seeds removed, diced*

Place all the ingredients except cilantro in a large pot and heat just to boiling. Immediately remove from the heat, cool and add the cilantro. Place in quart jars and store, if using within a month. Otherwise process in a hot-water

bath according to your canner's instructions.

As well as being a topping for tacos or a dip, salsa can be stirred into cooked rice, added to cooked beef, poured over enchiladas and baked, stirred into crab or shrimp dishes and used as a relish.

POSOLE SALAD

Often called hominy, *posole* is dried corn that has been treated with lime. When ground it becomes grits. Que Pasa Mexican Foods in Vancouver is importing this starchy vegetable, but any cooked bean, such as garbanzo or pinto, could be substituted for a similar look, if quite different flavor. Do not use canned hominy as it has a tinny taste in this dish.

500 mL (2 cups) dried posole
*125 mL (½ cup) pitted black olives,
  sliced*
2 to 3 green onions, sliced
*125 mL (½ cup) celery, finely
  chopped*
*60 mL (4 tbsp.) fresh cilantro,
  chopped*
2 to 5 mL (½ to 1 tsp.) salt
A few grinds of pepper
45 mL (3 tbsp.) sugar
60 mL (4 tbsp.) white-wine vinegar
175 mL (¾ cup) vegetable oil
10 leaves butter lettuce

Place the dried *posole* in a large pot and add water, to cover by at least five centimetres (2 in.). Bring to a boil and then simmer until tender, about two hours. Drain and chill. The day before, or at least three or four hours before serving, add the olives, onion, celery and cilantro.

In a small jar, mix together the salt, pepper, sugar, vinegar and oil. Cover and shake until the sugar is dissolved. Pour over the *posole* mixture and stir well. Cover and chill until serving time.

At serving time, place a leaf of lettuce on 10 chilled salad plates. Spoon on some *posole* and serve.

NAVAJO FRY BREAD

This traditional recipe will make 16 discs of this most popular Indian bread. The Navajos sometimes use cornmeal instead of wheat flour and add wild berries, seeds or nuts for variety. Lard is traditionally used for frying, but it does tend to flare up easily. We usually use Crisco oil and fry in an electric pan set up outside on the picnic table. This bread is best eaten right after it is made.

500 mL (2 cups) all-purpose white
 flour
20 mL (4 tsp.) baking powder
5 mL (1 tsp.) salt
About 150 mL (⅔ cup) warm water
Cornmeal
Oil

Combine the flour, baking powder and salt in a medium bowl. Stir in 125 millilitres (½ cup) of the water and continue adding more until a soft dough is formed. Knead until smooth.

Cut the dough into 16 pieces and form each into a smooth ball. Lightly dust a board with cornmeal and roll the pieces out into a circle six millimetres (¼ in.) thick. Prick lightly or punch a hole in the centre of each piece. The hole is a traditional characteristic of fry-bread and comes from the Navajo custom of sticking a branch into the bread and lowering it into the hot oil.

Put oil in a deep fryer to a depth of five to seven centimetres (2 to 3 in.) and heat to 200°C (400°F). Fry one disc at a time, turning each as it becomes golden. Drain on paper towels and serve immediately. Nice with honey or icing sugar.

This dough will hold, rolled into circles, for about an hour and could be prepared to this stage in advance. Fry as needed just before serving.

CARNE CON CHILE

This specialty from the north part of the state gave rise to the American chili con carne, of which there are as many variations as there are cooks. This recipe has been developed as a base for various combinations. You might add cooked kidney beans, chopped fresh tomatoes, green bell peppers or other vegetables. You might cube the meat or use ground beef instead. Chili powders sold in

specialty stores come in varying strengths; add them cautiously, tasting as you go. Be sure to read the label; you do not want the commercial spice products that contain oregano, cumin and preservatives.

This stew is best made the day before and reheated from room temperature. Serve with blue cornbread or flour tortillas to sop up the juices.

1.5 kg (3 lbs.) round steak
45 to 90 mL (3 to 6 tbsp.) oil
1 large onion, chopped
3 cloves garlic, chopped
About 30 mL (2 tbsp.) hot chili
 powder
About 60 mL (4 tbsp.) mild or
 Mexican chili powder
15 mL (1 tbsp.) cumin
5 mL (1 tsp.) freshly ground pepper
796-mL can tomatoes or 500 mL (2
 cups) beef stock or canned broth (for
 the Texan style)
Garnishes: small bowls of chopped
 green onion, green chilies, chopped
 cilantro, a mixture of Cheddar and
 Monterey Jack cheeses, sour cream,
 lime wedges

Cut the beef into 1.2-centimetre (½-in.) dice. Heat the oil in a large frypan and brown the meat in small batches to prevent steaming, adding oil as needed. Remove to a large Dutch oven or stove-top casserole. In the same frypan, adding more oil if necessary, cook the onion gently until soft. Add the garlic and cook a few more minutes. Be careful not to burn the garlic.

As chili powder burns easily, remove the frypan from the heat before stirring in the two powders, the cumin and the pepper. Stir well. Return to the heat and add the tomatoes or beef broth. Bring to a boil and pour over the meat in the casserole. Stir it all together. Place over medium heat and simmer, covered, stirring occasionally for one hour. Uncover and simmer one hour more or until thick and meat is tender. Add additional liquid (water is fine) if needed. Taste and add more seasonings if desired.

Cool, degrease if necessary and chill. The next day bring back to room temperature and reheat

gently at 190°C (375°F) for one hour. Serve with small bowls of garnish.

This is a good meat sauce for enchilada fillings.

BLUE CORNBREAD

Blue cornmeal is rare outside New Mexico, but Que Pasa in Vancouver is planning to import it. Yellow cornmeal can be substituted, although the flavor of blue cornmeal is fuller, richer and nutlike. This tasty cornbread is extra hearty, moist and delicious.

250 mL (1 cup) blue or yellow
 cornmeal
50 mL (1 tbsp.) baking powder
5 mL (1 tsp.) salt
2 eggs
125 mL (½ cup) butter, melted
250 mL (1 cup) sour cream
350-g bag frozen corn niblets, thawed,
 or 500 mL (2 cups) fresh kernels
100 g (3½ oz.) Monterey Jack
 cheese, sliced 3 mm (⅛ in.) thick
4 large whole canned chilies

Grease a 22-centimetre (9-in.) cast-iron frypan or baking pan. Preheat oven to 190°C (375°F). In a medium bowl, mix the dry ingredients together and make a well in the centre. Add the eggs, butter and sour cream and blend thoroughly. Fold in the corn kernels.

Pour one-third of the batter into the prepared pan. Cover with cheese slices and whole chilies. Pour remaining batter over top.

Bake for 40 minutes or until lightly browned and a toothpick inserted in the centre comes out clean. May be made the day before and reheated in foil, 20 minutes at 190°C (375°F), although it is best freshly baked.

TOSTADA WITH AVOCADO SALSA AND CRAB

Tostadas are usually a lightly fried flour tortilla with a filling spread on top, heated briefly in the oven and served as finger food. In this recipe, we fill layers of fried tortillas with an avocado salsa, crab, cheese and olives and cut the stack into wedges. In New Mexico the meat would be cooked, shredded chicken or beef.

3 25-cm (10-in.) flour tortillas
Oil
250 g (8 oz.) fresh crab meat
4 green onions, finely chopped
125 mL (½ cup) pimiento stuffed olives, chopped
125 mL (½ cup) sour cream
Avocado Salsa, recipe follows
250 g (8 oz.) Monterey Jack cheese, grated

In a large frypan heat about 1.2 centimetres (½ in.) oil. Fry the tortillas to a light golden brown, about 25 seconds on each side. Drain on paper towels and reserve at room temperature.

Keep some crab for garnish and mix the rest with the onions, olives and sour cream. Chill until serving time.

Make the salsa and reserve at room temperature. Grate the cheese. Shred the romaine for garnish.

At serving time place one tortilla on an oven-proof platter. Spread one-third of the salsa over top. Add one-half of the crab mixture. Sprinkle on one-third of the cheese. Place a second tortilla over all. Spread on the next third of the salsa, the remaining crab and another third of the cheese. Top with the last tortilla. Spread over the remaining salsa and sprinkle on the last of the cheese. Garnish with reserved crab. Heat at 190°C (375°F) for five or eight minutes or until the cheese melts. Encircle with the shredded romaine and serve immediately. This will cut into about 15 small wedges.

Avocado Salsa
A wonderful creamy sauce that would make an interesting addition to poached fish, grilled meats or vegetables. Do not add avocado until serving time.

30 mL (2 tbsp.) butter
15 mL (1 tbsp.) onion, chopped
30 mL (2 tbsp.) flour
Pinch of salt
250 mL (1 cup) chicken stock or canned broth
1 whole canned green chili, chopped
Pinch of cumin
125 mL (½ cup) sour cream

15 mL (1 tbsp.) fresh lemon or lime juice
2 ripe avocados, mashed

In a small saucepan, melt the butter and add the onion. Sauté until tender. Whisk in the flour and salt and cook a few minutes. Whisk in the chicken broth and bring to a boil. Cook until smooth. Stir in the chilies and cumin. Cool.

Stir in the sour cream, lemon juice and mashed avocado. Store at room temperature if using within two hours.

ORANGE SHERBET
Coolly refreshing after a fiery meal.

8 fresh naval oranges
250 mL (1 cup) sugar syrup, recipe follows
125 mL (½ cup) whipping or light cream
15 mL (1 tbsp.) Triple Sec or orange liqueur

Squeeze the juice from the oranges. Add the sugar syrup, cream and liqueur. Freeze according to your ice-cream maker's instructions, or place in a metal pan in your freezer. Just before it becomes solid, scrape out of the pan, whip and freeze again. Continue until the mixture is smooth. Store in a plastic container.

Sugar Syrup
250 mL (1 cup) water
250 mL (1 cup) sugar

Place the sugar and water in a medium saucepan and bring to a boil, stirring until sugar melts. Simmer, not stirring, for five minutes. Cool.

SOPAIPILLAS
These hollow "soft pillows" originated in Old Town, Albuquerque, about 300 years ago. Again, like the Navajo fry-bread, they are best eaten as they are made. We found that refrigerating the dough for a day before rolling it out worked very well.

60 mL (4 tbsp.) warm water
15 mL (1 tbsp.) dry yeast
300 mL (1¼ cups) lukewarm milk
5 mL (1 tsp.) baking powder
5 mL (1 tsp.) salt
About 1 L (4 cups) all-purpose white flour
Oil

Place the warm water in a small bowl and sprinkle on the yeast. Let stand until dissolved. Place the milk in a medium bowl and add the dissolved yeast. Mix together 250 millilitres (1 cup) of the flour with the baking powder and salt and beat into the liquid. Add flour, 125 millilitres (½ cup) at a time, until a firm dough is reached. Knead until smooth. Let stand for about 15 to 20 minutes or refrigerate in plastic wrap for up to a day.

Heat the oil in a deep fryer to 200° to 220°C (400° to 425°F).

Roll out one-quarter of the dough to a six-millimetre (¼-in.) thickness. Cut into five-centimetre (2-in.) squares or triangles. To assure puffing, slightly stretch each piece of dough before lowering into the hot fat. Hold each piece under the fat until it puffs. The dough should puff up and become hollow within seconds. Cook until a very light tan color, a few seconds on each side. They should be soft when cool.

Drain on paper towelling and serve as bread. Delicious served with honey or rolled in cinnamon and sugar.

Like pita bread, sopaipillas can be filled with refried beans or *carne con chile* and served as a light lunch. They can be frozen. To serve, heat in foil at 180°C (350°F) for about 15 minutes. Just before serving open the foil so that they can dry out a little. □

Buen Apetito!

It is the fast-food chains of America that have shaped much of the world's perceptions about Mexican food. The narrowness of their interpretation, based as much on marketing and efficiency requirements as anything else, is not surprising, but it is unfortunate. From the fast-food perspective, a tortilla is basically a two-dimensional hamburger bun, a very handy device to be rolled or wrapped around ground meat, shredded lettuce, refried beans and salsa, and then — in a leap of the imagination — smothered in cheese. Some restaurants do this well, others poorly, but with a few exceptions, most show little vision when it comes to the imaginative preparation of Mexican food. The so-called Californian-Mexican restaurants are little more than American restaurants with an excess of greenery and theme. This is not to suggest that the staples of such restaurants — tacos, enchiladas, quesadillas and tostadas — are American inventions; they are authentically Mexican. But they represent, according to Richard Condon, novelist and author of a somewhat eccentric Mexican cookbook, only the first step in Mexican cooking. It is as if Americans had discovered the joy of hors-d'oeuvres and said to hell with the rest of dinner.

The taco-house interpretation of Mexican food leads the diner to conclusions about a tendency towards gloppiness and monotony in the cuisine. Unfair! From the chocolate-flavored *mole* that is the country's national dish to the simply grilled meats of Mexico City, subtlety and variety in approach characterize the full range of Mexican foods. Consider, for example, the delicious sauce on the *pollo pipian*, the central dish in our meal. This delicacy contains cinnamon, cloves, sesame seeds and pumpkin seeds, with nary a refried bean in sight. Tortilla soup, which opens our meal, is a classic dish, but not often served north of Mexico. Watermelon ice, the finishing touch, is frequently sold on the streets of Mexican towns (where tourists dare not sample it), and, along with *agua tropical* and *agua sandia*, is a superb refresher.

As to allegations about excessive spiciness, well, the number and kind of chilies used can be regulated by the cook, as they certainly are in Mexico, where dozens of varieties are favored for their different characteristics. Inexpensive chili powder, which often contains things other than ground chilies, is to be disdained in the same way one would disdain a bottle labelled simply "spice." If there is a Mexican or Latin American specialty shop in your area, scour its shelves and coolers for authentic chilies, cheeses and other ingredients. Used even in small quantities, they can be surprisingly important in developing the taste of a dish.

The recipes in this authentic Mexican home meal were supplied by Julie Garcia, formerly of Mexico, now a resident of Vancouver.

MENU *(Serves Four)*

- Sopa de Tortilla
- Salsa Ranchera
- Pollo Pipian
- Arroz Fiesta
- Ensalada de Nopal
- Corn Tortillas

Jalapeño heaven: clockwise, aqua tropical, watermelon ice, sopa de tortilla, ensalada de nopal (combining cactus leaves with garden vegetables and goat cheese), and pollo pipian served with a saucy blend of seeds, spices and chicken broth.

SOPA DE TORTILLA

10 stale tortillas
750 mL (3 cups) salsa (see recipe
   below)
Chicken stock or canned broth
150 mL (⅔ cup) mozzarella cheese,
   shredded
1 avocado, peeled and cut into strips
Oregano, fresh, crushed

The authentic cheese for this dish
is a cow's milk cheese called
Chihuahua (named after the city,
not the dog). Mozzarella is a good
substitute.

Cut the tortillas into one-
centimetre (½-in.) strips. Sauté in
oil until crisp, and set aside. Dilute
the salsa with an equal amount of
chicken broth. Season to taste with
salt. Place in a medium saucepan
and heat to just boiling.

Just before serving, divide the
tortilla strips among the bowls,
spoon in the heated salsa, sprinkle
generously with cheese and
oregano and garnish with a strip of
avocado.

BASIC SALSA RANCHERA

This will make one litre (4 cups) of
salsa, enough for both the rice dish
and the tortilla soup.

1 large can tomatoes (or equivalent of
   fresh)
1 medium onion, chopped
3 garlic cloves, chopped
2 fresh jalapeño chilies, seeded and
   chopped
Oregano, crushed
Chicken consommé cube, crumbled

Fill blender two-thirds full with
tomatoes, onion, garlic, chiles,
oregano and consommé cube. Add
water to just cover ingredients.
Blend well. Pour into a saucepan,
bring to a boil and simmer until
thick.

POLLO PIPIAN

45 mL (3 tbsp.) sesame seeds
125 mL (½ cup) pumpkin seeds,
   shelled
1 clove garlic
30 mL (2 tbsp.) oil
2 mL (½ tsp.) cinnamon
1 mL (¼ tsp.) ground cloves
5 mL (1 tsp.) ground jalapeño seeded
   chilies

250 to 500 mL (1 to 2 cups) chicken
   stock or canned broth
Salt
25 mL (1½ tbsp.) lime juice
2 whole boned chicken breasts or 4 legs
   with thighs
Butter
Shredded lettuce, chopped green onion,
   radishes, lime wedges for garnish

Combine seeds, garlic and oil in
frypan. Stir over medium heat
until seeds turn pale golden
brown. Remove and stir in
cinnamon, cloves and ground
chilies. Remove to blender and
whirl until smooth. Add 250
millilitres (1 cup) broth and salt to
taste.

Return to pan. Heat, stirring
until thick and bubbly. Add
chicken broth until desired
thickness is achieved; return to
blender and whirl until smooth.

In a separate pan, sauté chicken
breasts or legs in butter until just
done.

To serve, very gently heat sauce
with lime juice, stirring constantly
until just hot. Spoon over chicken
on a platter and garnish with
shredded lettuce, green onions,
radishes and lime wedges.

ARROZ FIESTA

The addition of salsa to this dish of
rice and chorizo sausage makes it
an attractive pink.

250 mL (1 cup) rice
250 g (½ lb.) Mexican or Spanish
   chorizo sausage
250 mL (1 cup) salsa (see recipe
   above)
250 to 375 mL (1 to 1½ cups)
   chicken stock or canned broth
60 mL (4 tbsp.) frozen peas
Avocado wedges
Tomato wedges
Cilantro (fresh coriander)

In a frypan, fry the chorizo in the
oil until crumbly. Drain off most
of the fat, add rice and fry until
translucent. Add the salsa, chicken
broth and peas. Season to taste.
Bring to a boil, cover and simmer
15 to 20 minutes. Decorate with
avocado, tomato and cilantro.

ENSALADA DE NOPALE

Nopales are the new leaves taken
from the bushy broad-leafed cactus
plant, and are available in jars in
Mexican specialty stores.

1 jar nopales
1 medium onion
1 large tomato
1 avocado
Bunch of cilantro
Juice of 1 lime
A dry, salty goat cheese to garnish

Drain and rinse the nopales
thoroughly. Chop the onion,
tomato and avocado into small
chunks. Coarsely chop the
cilantro. Mix them all together.
Sprinkle the lime juice over all.
Crumble on plenty of cheese.
Chill. Serve as a side salad with
tortillas.

CORN TORTILLAS

This recipe makes about 20
tortillas.

500 mL (2 cups) masa harina (corn
   flour)
60 mL (4 tbsp.) all-purpose white
   flour
Warm water

Blend the masa harina and flour.
Add enough water until dough is
the same consistency as pie dough.
Knead a few minutes. Roll into
balls approximately the size of a
ping-pong ball.

Flatten dough in a tortilla press
between layers of a plastic bag, or
roll out with a rolling pin into a
15-centimetre (6-in.) circle.

Heat a cast-iron or electric
frypan to the temperature you
would use for pancakes. Cook the
tortillas 30 seconds on each side,
and then press with a paper napkin
while still in the pan to remove
any air pockets. Remove from pan
and keep warm in a clean cloth. □

Paella by the Pool

The Spanish word *Paella* comes from the Latin word for the pan in which Spain's most famous dish is cooked.

Since paella is a traditional peasant dish, it will always vary from place to place, depending on the tastes of the locals and the ingredients available. Some say seafood and meat should never be mixed in a paella; others place emphasis on many vegetables. In Valencia, the true home of this dish, the original paella recipe calls for green vegetables, land snails and eels.

There is more agreement concerning the cooking method. Paella must be made in a wide, shallow, flat-bottomed dish (a *paellera*), and the rice must be cooked uncovered so that it will not be steamed. The rice is removed from stove or oven before it is thoroughly done, so that it can finish cooking away from direct heat. This prevents it from bursting and turning mushy.

The paella presented here is an authentic variation, which looks terrific. The perfume of real saffron is the irresistible, unifying agent that ties the dish together. And since much of the work can be done in advance, it's a good dish for a summer day, when you don't want to dwell too long in the kitchen.

Many Spanish soups are as hearty as paella and as suitable for the main course of a meal, but there are a few exceptions, the most notable and appropriate for hot weather being gazpacho, from Andalusia. Its fame as a hot-weather palliative has spread all over the western world. It is a delicious and healthy convenience food that can be stored for days in the refrigerator (indeed, storage improves its flavor).

The heavy use of egg yolks is common in Spanish sweets. One explanation is that yolk-rich recipes were developed because so many egg-whites were used to clarify Spanish wines. Our dessert is a simple flan made of cream and eggs, which must be gently cooked in a bain-marie (water bath) to yield a perfect, smooth consistency. Again, it can and should be made well before serving time — a period in the refrigerator improves flavor and texture.

MENU *(Serves Eight)*

- Sangria
- Gazpacho
- Paella a la Valenciana
- Crema Catalana

SANGRIA

125 mL (½ cup) sugar
250 mL (1 cup) water
250 mL (1 cup) brandy or cognac
1 bottle dry red wine
1 orange, sliced
1 lemon, sliced

In a medium saucepan, bring sugar and water to a boil. Cook until sugar is dissolved. Cool. Add brandy and wine. Stir to mix. Place in a large jug and add the fruit. Marinate overnight.

At serving time, place ice cubes in tall glasses, fill half full with marinade, then top up with soda and garnish each with a slice of fruit.

GAZPACHO

5 medium tomatoes, peeled and seeded
1 large green pepper, seeded
1 clove garlic, crushed
1 Spanish or milk onion, peeled and thinly sliced
1 English cucumber, peeled and seeded
125 mL (½ cup) or more fresh mixed herbs such as chives, parsley, basil, chervil and tarragon
125 mL (½ cup) good-quality olive oil
45 mL (3 tbsp.) lemon juice
1 290-mL bottle chili sauce
250 mL (1 cup) water

Place the tomatoes, pepper, garlic, onion and cucumber in a blender or food processor, and blend until finely chopped. Transfer to a large bowl.

Mix together the herbs, olive oil, lemon juice and chili sauce. Add to the chopped vegetables. Chill for four hours or more. If the soup becomes too thick, add up to 250 millilitres (1 cup) of water. Garnish with parsley or lemon slices.

PAELLA A LA VALENCIANA

Saffron, which consists of the stigmas of the purple crocus, is the world's most expensive spice, but it is indispensable for paella. Buy the Spanish variety, which comes in strands, and store it in your vault. Only small amounts are required; too much saffron is overpowering.

1 to 1½ kg (2 to 3 lbs.) rabbit or chicken, cut up into serving pieces
125 mL (½ cup) olive oil
500 g (1 lb.) spare-ribs or pork chops, cut into serving pieces
250 g (½ lb.) spicy sausage, cut in 1-cm (½-in.) slices
1 medium onion, chopped
4 green onions, chopped
750 mL (3 cups) uncooked short grain rice
2 cloves garlic, chopped
90 mL (6 tbsp.) chopped parsley
1 bay leaf, crumbled
1½ L (6 cups) very strong chicken stock, preferably homemade, or canned broth
2 mL (½ tsp.) saffron
125 mL (½ cup) dry white wine
15 mL (1 tbsp.) lemon juice
175 mL (¾ cup) diced pimientos
500 mL (2 cups) fresh or frozen tiny peas
Salt and pepper to taste
500 g (1 lb.) medium raw shrimp, shelled
24 small mussels, scrubbed

Heat the oil in a paella pan with a 40-centimetre (15-in.) base (or in a large casserole). Add the rabbit or

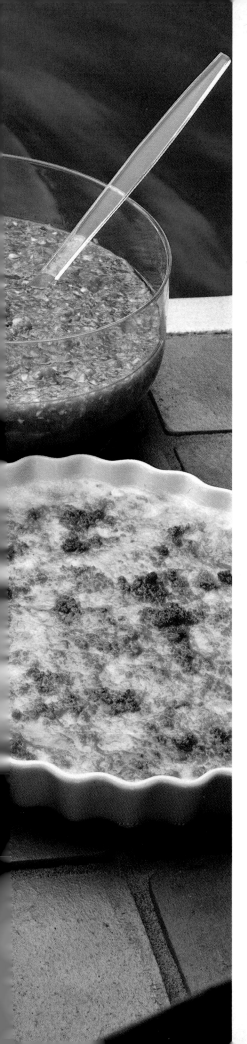

chicken pieces and fry until golden. Remove to a warm platter. Add the ribs and fry over high heat until crusty and brown. Remove to a warm platter. Add the sausage, onion and green onions and sauté about five minutes over medium heat until the onion is wilted. Remove to a warm platter. Add the rice to the pan and stir to coat it well with the oil and drippings. Sprinkle in the garlic, parsley and bay leaf. Stir in the stock, saffron and wine. This can be done ahead of time.

Begin final assembly about 45 minutes before serving. Bring the rice to a boil and cook uncovered, stirring occasionally, over medium-high heat for about 10 minutes. Add the lemon juice, pimientos, precooked rabbit or chicken, spare-ribs, sausage, onions and peas. Season to taste.

Bury the shrimp and mussels in the rice, turning each mussel so that the edge that will open is facing up. Decorate the top with additional whole shrimp, pushing them into the rice.

Bake uncovered at 180°C (350°F) for 20 to 25 minutes. Remove from the oven and let sit on top of the stove, lightly covered with foil, for about 10 minutes. Serve directly from the paella pan.

CREMA CATALANA

750 mL (3 cups) whipping cream
1 vanilla bean or 15 mL (1 tbsp.)
  vanilla extract (see note below)
5 large egg yolks
60 mL (4 tbsp.) white sugar
Light brown sugar

Put eight custard cups, ramekins or small ceramic bowls in a large pan. Pour hot water into pan until it reaches halfway up the sides of the dishes. A 25-centimetre (10-in.) quiche dish can also be used. Set aside.

Place the cream and the vanilla bean in a saucepan and heat to

scalding (tiny bubbles will form around the edges). Remove from heat. Remove the vanilla bean.

Meanwhile, beat the egg yolks and white sugar until very thick and the sugar dissolves.

Add the hot cream in a slow, steady stream to the egg mixture, beating constantly. If using vanilla extract, add it at this point. Pour carefully into baking dishes.

Butter pieces of parchment or wax paper to fit the tops of the baking dishes and place over the custard (but not touching it). This will prevent a skin from forming. Bake at 160°C (325°F) for 40 to 60 minutes, or until a knife inserted in the centre comes out clean. Remove from oven and from the bain-marie.

Refrigerate until very cold. Remove the parchment lids.

Place the custards on a baking sheet. Sprinkle the tops with light brown sugar to make a thin layer. Broil until the sugar is melted and medium brown. Watch carefully – this only takes a few minutes.

Chill again and serve cold. A bowl of lightly sugared fruit is a pleasant contrast to this rich dessert.

Note: while a vanilla bean may seem expensive, it can be used several times. The fresh bean is best when split down the centre. After using, pat dry and replace in its tube. When it has been used two or three times, place it in with some sugar to make vanilla sugar for your cereal or coffee. □

Mellow yellow: paella, enhanced by aromatic saffron, enriched by shrimp, mussels and tangy sausage; a classic gazpacho; sangria over ice; crema Catalana for the last course.

Meals On Ice

It's been one of those lazy, hazy, crazy days. The dinner hour looms, but the very last thing you feel like doing is slaving over a hot stove. Deep down (deep, deep down) you'd really like to serve tuna sandwiches tonight. But you haven't the courage, have you? The neighbors might see. The kids might tell their friends and it would get around. You'd be expelled from the dinner club—or worse, the family might love those tuna sandwiches and never let you cook *nouvelle* again.

Relax. We have a ready solution to your dinner dilemma—some refreshingly different and delightfully undemanding recipes that you can cook up without losing your cool. If visions of tepid tomato aspic and sweating ham loaf are floating through your head, give it a good shake. You're in the wrong decade. These summer dishes are fresh and distinctive, combining unusual ingredients in ways that will surprise and delight your family and dinner guests.

Texture and temperature are important in summer cooking. Most of these recipes should be served cold, even frozen. And the few that are hot should be kept crisp and fresh to ensure that your meal will be as light as an August breeze. No deep frying, and no heavy sauces. Even the normally weighty classic potato salad is lightened up here with the cool addition of cucumber. Our shrimp dish crunches with celery, waterchestnuts and cress; our Sichuan chicken salad is tossed over shredded iceberg lettuce.

For the last course, keep it smooth, cool and fruity: try our whippy peach *crème,* moulded raspberry dessert or the unusual purée of lime and avocado.

Cold comforts: a new-age gazpacho with chilled chilies; creamy avocado soup with a spray of chive flowers; and a shrimp salad that crunches thanks to alfalfa sprouts and chow mein noodles.

AVOCADO SOUP

This delicious cool green soup can be made in 10 minutes flat. Buy the avocados a few days in advance so that they can ripen. If you have any left over, see our recipe for Lime Avocado Cream. Makes one litre (1 qt.)

2 soft, ripe avocados, peeled and pitted
Juice of half a lemon
250 mL (1 cup) whipping cream
500 to 625 mL (2 to 2½ cups)
  chicken stock
Salt and pepper, to taste
Chopped chive, and chive flowers for
  garnish

Purée the avocado and lemon. Add the remaining ingredients, using as much chicken stock as you need to get the thickness you like. Serve immediately. If you let the soup sit, the top will darken. Just stir it to restore its attractive color, but don't try to keep it more than a few hours.

CREAMED PEA AND PARSLEY SOUP WITH CLAMS

Make this brightly colored, flavorful soup the day before. Serve hot or cold. Makes two litres (2 qts.).

3 slices bacon, chopped
1 small onion, chopped
1 small carrot, chopped
625 mL (2½ cups) chicken stock
Pinch of salt
2 mL (½ tsp.) pepper
15 mL (1 tbsp.) fresh thyme or 2 mL
  (½ tsp.) dried thyme
350-g pkg. frozen baby peas, thawed
  or 625 mL (2½ cups) fresh peas
125 mL (½ cup) fresh parsley,
  chopped
3 142-g cans baby clams, with juice

Sauté the bacon in a soup pot until the fat is rendered. Remove the bacon bits with a slotted spoon and save them for another use. Reduce the heat to low. Add the onion and carrot and cook over low heat for five minutes, or until soft. Do not let them brown. Add chicken stock, salt, pepper and thyme. Cover and bring to a boil. Reduce the heat and simmer for 10 minutes to mellow the flavors. Remove from the heat and add the peas and parsley. If using fresh

peas, cook for five minutes or until tender. Cool.

Purée in a blender. Place in a large storage container and add clams. Chill. Serve cold. If serving warm, reheat carefully, stirring.

GAZPACHO SORBET

An updated version of the wonderful soup of Spain. Freeze it or serve it well chilled. This soup keeps. Makes two litres (2 qts.).

5 medium tomatoes, peeled, seeded and
  coarsely chopped
1 large green pepper, seeded and sliced
1 clove garlic, crushed
1 medium Spanish or mild onion,
  peeled and thinly sliced
1 English cucumber, peeled, seeded and
  chopped
125 mL (½ cup) or more, mixed fresh
  herbs such as chive, parsley,
  chervil, tarragon
125 mL (½ cup) good-quality olive
  oil
45 mL (3 tsp.) lemon juice
285-g bottle chili sauce
250 mL (1 cup) chicken stock, more or
  less

Place the tomatoes, pepper, garlic, onion and cucumber in a blender or food processor and blend until finely chopped. Transfer to a large bowl.

Mix together the herbs, oil, juice and chili sauce. Add chicken stock, to taste. Pour over the chopped vegetables using more stock if the soup is too thick. Chill and serve. Or freeze in a metal pan with sides, stirring with a metal fork or spoon every hour until set. Store in a plastic container. To serve, let stand 10 to 20 minutes to soften slightly.

THREE VEGETABLE MARINADE

This salad is best made in the morning and allowed to marinate at room temperature until mealtime. Serves four to five.

3 to 4 medium new potatoes
Oil and Vinegar Dressing (recipe
  follows)
3 to 4 medium carrots
½ medium English cucumber

½ small red onion
2 mL (½ tsp.) salt
60 mL (4 tbsp.) water
45 mL (3 tbsp.) white wine vinegar
Pinch of sugar
Freshly ground black pepper, to taste

Boil the potatoes in water until tender. Drain. Peel if necessary and cut into thin slices. Place in a medium bowl and sprinkle with 60 millilitres (4 tbsp.) vinaigrette. Set aside.

Peel and dice the carrots. Boil in water to cover until tender. Drain, place in a medium bowl and stir in 45 millilitres (3 tbsp.) vinaigrette.

Thinly slice the cucumber and onion and place in a medium bowl. Add the salt, water, vinegar, sugar and pepper. Stir to mix. Set aside. Drain before serving.

Cover all the bowls and let stand at room temperature until serving time. For a pretty presentation, arrange the vegetables in separate groupings on a large serving platter.

OIL AND VINEGAR DRESSING

Blend together:

125 mL (½ cup) olive oil
75 mL (5 tbsp.) white wine vinegar
15 mL (1 tbsp.) Dijon mustard, or to
  taste
Salt and pepper, to taste

VEGETABLE FRITTERS

While fritters are generally deep-fried, these cook just as well in a frypan. They are wonderful with a steak. Grill the meat while you cook the vegetables, and they should be done at the same time. Serves three to four.

2 eggs
250 mL (1 cup) vegetables: finely
  grated carrot, zucchini and onion,
  julienned snow peas and red pepper,
  and corn kernels
160-g (medium) potato, grated
30 mL (2 tbsp.) flour
Salt and freshly ground pepper
30 mL (2 tbsp.) butter
15 mL (1 tbsp.) oil

Beat the eggs. Place the grated

carrot, zucchini and onion in a strainer over a bowl and press out the excess juices (or whirl in a lettuce spinner or place in a tea towel and wring out the moisture). Mix together with the rest of the vegetables and stir in the eggs. Mix in the flour, salt and pepper.

In a medium frypan, melt the butter and oil together. Divide the vegetable mixture into three or four servings and spoon into the pan, forming into pancakes. Fry over medium heat until crisp and golden, about three minutes. Turn and fry on the other side.

Can be kept warm for about five to 10 minutes in a low oven, but are best served immediately.

ALISON'S SHRIMP SALAD

A pretty dish for a luncheon. Serve with crispy crackers and the beautiful Raspberry Charlotte for dessert. Serves four.

450 g fresh hand-peeled shrimp
125 mL (½ cup) celery, chopped
A half to a whole 227-mL can water chestnuts, sliced
125 mL (½ cup) green onion, sliced on the diagonal
Salt and pepper, if desired
Bunch fresh watercress
250 g (8 oz.) fresh bean or alfalfa sprouts
1 small pkg. fine chow mein noodles, optional
Ginger Mayonnaise, recipe follows

Mix together the shrimp, celery, water chestnuts and green onion. Season to taste.

On each serving plate, place a few sprigs of watercress, some sprouts and chow mein noodles, if used. Add shrimp mixture and top with a generous spoonful of Ginger Mayonnaise. Pass extra mayonnaise.

GINGER MAYONNAISE

125 mL (½ cup) good mayonnaise, homemade if possible
125 mL (½ cup) sour cream
2 mL (½ tsp.) fresh lemon peel, finely chopped
5 mL (1 tsp.) ginger root, finely chopped

15 mL (1 tbsp.) fresh lemon juice

Mix together and chill thoroughly.

SICHUAN CHICKEN SALAD

This dish, which I learned at a cooking class in Santa Barbara, is easy to make and tastes wonderful. If you don't have cooked chicken on hand, poach some in the cool of the day. The peppercorns and hoisin sauce can be found in Chinese grocery stores.

1 very small head iceberg lettuce
2 whole (4 halves) cooked chicken breasts
1 slice ginger root
4 green onions, chopped
15 mL (1 tbsp.) Sichuan peppercorns, crushed with a rolling-pin
Pinch of red pepper flakes or cayenne pepper
60 mL (4 tbsp.) oil
3 cloves garlic
15 mL (1 tbsp.) soy sauce
15 mL (1 tbsp.) hoisin sauce
15 mL (1 tbsp.) dark corn syrup

Finely slice or shred the lettuce and set aside. Slice the cooked chicken thinly. Place in a medium bowl.

Drop the ginger into a running food processor to mince. Add the green onions and chop with on/off bursts. Add peppercorns, pepper flakes and oil. Process briefly. Pour into a small pan and heat to boiling. Remove from the heat.

Drop the garlic into a running food processor to mince. Add soy sauce, hoisin sauce and corn syrup and process briefly. Add to the ginger mixture and return to the heat. Bring almost to the boil and immediately pour over the chicken. Toss the mixture well. Arrange lettuce on each serving plate. Top with some chicken mixture. Serve with crusty bread.

PEACHES 'N' CREAM

Wait for fresh peaches before you try this attractive dessert; canned just won't do. Serves four.

750 g (4 medium) peaches, well ripened, peeled, pitted and quartered
175 mL (¾ cup) water
75 mL (5 tbsp.) sugar

25 mL (1½ tbsp.) dark rum
1 pkg. unflavored gelatin
125 mL (½ cup) whipping cream

Poach the peaches in the water with half the sugar until very soft, about 20 minutes. Purée the peaches and liquid, adding the rum. Pour into a medium saucepan. Sprinkle on the gelatin and let stand one minute. Heat to very low, stirring, until the gelatin is dissolved. Cool to room temperature, pour into a medium bowl, and refrigerate until the mixture mounds when dropped from a spoon, about 40 minutes.

Whip the cream, beating in the remaining sugar, until soft peaks form. Fold in 75 millilitres (5 tbsp.) of the peach mixture.

Alternate layers of the peach purée and the whipped cream into individual clear glass bowls or glasses. Refrigerate until firm, about four hours.

LIME AVOCADO CREAM

A South American recipe that will leave your guests guessing as to its ingredients. Serves six to eight.

1 soft, ripe avocado, peeled and pitted
Juice of two limes
60 mL (4 tbsp.) light rum
125 mL (½ cup) icing sugar
250 mL (1 cup) whipping cream
Julienned lime zest for garnish

Cut the lime zest into julienne (the strips will hold for several hours in cold water). Purée the avocado with the lime juice. Add the rum and half the icing sugar. Whip the cream until soft peaks form, adding the remaining sugar. Fold into the avocado mixture. Spoon into a pretty glass serving dish and chill. At serving time, garnish with the lime zest. This dish will hold for 24 hours before changing color.

INDEX

A

Alison's Shrimp Salad, 195
APPETIZERS
    Appetizer Crêpes, 72
    Caviar Crowned Mousse, 66
    Classic Country Terrine, 150
    Crispy Spicy Chicken
      Strips, 183
    Fluffy Mousse of Pimientos and
      Scallops, 159
    Liptauer Cheese, 14
    Mushroom Pâté in Brioche
      Cases, 59
    Mushrooms in Parchment, 58
    Mussels on the Half Shell in
      Vinaigrette, 159
    Periwinkles, 135
    Prawns in Black Bean
      Sauce, 143
    Punjabi Vegetarian
      Samosas, 112
    Salmon-Sole Mousse, 62
    Savory Pumpkin Pie, 36
    Stuffed Baguette, 178
    Tomato Gervais, 72
    Tostada with Avocado Salsa and
      Crab, 184

Apple Butter, 101
Apple Pots, 11
Apricot Cream, 91
Apricot Pineapple Conserve, 101
Avocado and Prawn Gazpacho, 158
Avocado Soup, 194

B

Bannock, 170
Bannock Dumplings, 170
Barley Pilaf, 32
Basil Cream, 144
BEEF
    Beef Pie with Beer, 28
    Brochettes, 128
    Broiled Marinated Flank
      Steak, 62
    Carne con Chile, 184
    Fillet of Beef with Crab
      Stuffing, 73
    Hot Spinach and Beef, 145
    Kefta, 128
    Tagine of Brochettes or
      Kefta, 128

BEVERAGES
    Champagne Framboise, 100

Juniper Tea, 171
Lemon Fruit Syrup, 179
Margueritas, 182
Masala Chai, 115
Mexicana Chocolate, 93, 182
Mexican Coffee, 182
Orange Fruit Syrup, 179
Sangria, 189
Spiced Iced Tea, 175

Black Bean Sauce, 136
Blackberry Mousse, 175
Brandy Butter, 70
Brazil Nut Genoise with
    Cranberry Raspberry Glaze, 84

BREADS
    Baguette, 178
    Baked Barbecue Pork Buns, 139
    Bannock Dumplings, 170
    Blue Corn, 184
    Brioche Dough, 59
    Bruschetta Romana, 50
    Calzone, 50
    Chive Rolls, 80
    Coconut Cocktail Buns, 139
    Corn Tortillas, 188
    Cream Scones, 121
    Crispy Flatbread, 106
    Crumpets, 121
    Homemade Crackers, 16
    English Muffins, 123
    Moroccan, 129
    Munk Cakes, 163
    Navajo Fry Bread, 183
    Paratha, 115
    Pizza, Quick and Easy, 155
    Quick Croissants, 101
    Rye, 66
    Sopaipillas, 185
    Sourdough, 107
    Spicy Chinese Doughnuts, 139
    Sprouted Wheat, 174
    Sticky Pumpkin Buns, 37
    Stuffed Baguette, 178
    Walnut, 76
    Welsh Cakes, 123
    Wholewheat Bannock, 170
    Wild Rice, 20
    Yeast Scones, 121

Bread Pudding with Meringue and
    Lemon Sauce, 41
Brie en Croute, 132
Broccoli Bisque, 62
Brochettes, 128
Bruschetta Romana, 50

Buffalo Tenderloin Fillet, 20
Buttercream, 144

C

Cabbage, Warm Red, 31
CAKES (see also DESSERTS)
    Basic Genoise, 32
    Brazil Nut Genoise with
      Cranberry Raspberry
      Glaze, 84
    Cherry Almond, 124
    Eccles, 124
    Grand Marnier Mocha
      Dacquoise, 144
    Madeleines, 133
    Meringue Cake with Apricot
      Cream, 91
    New York Cheesecake, 93
    Pear Shortcake, 32
    Poppy Seed, 124
    Steamed Pine Nut Sponge, 137
    Torta Terremoto (Earthquake
      Cake), 54
    Walnut Soufflé Torte, 17

Calzone, 50
Cantonese Custard Cups, 139
Carne con Chile, 184
Carrot Salad in Lettuce Cups, 31
Cauliflower and Broccoli Bhaji, 114
Caviar Crowned Mousse, 66
Cherry Almond Cake, 124
Cheshire Cat's Cheese Puffs, 45
Chicken (see POULTRY)
Chili con Queso, 182
Chinese Doughnuts, Spicy, 139
Chive Rolls, 80
Chocolate Sauce, 21
Chocolate Truffles, 77
Chocolate Walnut Fudge, 77
Chutney, Cucumber, 25
Chutney, Mint, 113
Chutney, Onion, 25
Coconut Cocktail Buns, 139
Coniglio alla Padella, 54
COOKIES AND BARS
    Brown Sugar Shortbread with
      Cherries and Almonds, 125
    Crisp Coconut, 138
    Double Chocolate, 179
    Madeleines, 133
    Nanaimo Bars, 167
    Oatmeal Pecan, 179
    Pumpkin Bars with Cream
      Cheese Frosting, 37
    Shortbread, 124

Cornbread, Blue, 184
Corn Consommé with Herb
Pastry, 11
Corn Soup, Fresh, 173
Corn Tortillas, 188
Cornish Pasties, 92
Cream Cheese, Homemade, 162
Cream of Oyster and Artichoke
Soup, 40
Creamy Carrot Soup, 92
Crema Catalana, 191
Crème Fraîche, 125
CREPES
Appetizer, 72
Basic Batter, 72
Hazelnut with Chocolate
Sauce, 21

Crumpets, 121
Cucumber Chutney, Fresh, 25
Cumberland Sauce, 67
Curried Nut Soup, 80
Curried Turnovers, 140
Curry Chicken, 24
Curry Mayonnaise, 132, 166
Curry Pork and Banana, 24
Curry Powder, 24
Curry Sauce, 24
Curry Shrimp, 24
Custard Tarts, Cantonese, 139

D

Dahi Raita, 113
Daryl's Hot Salsa, 183
Deluxe Travellers' Mix, 92
DESSERTS (see also CAKES)
Bread Pudding with Meringue
and Lemon Sauce, 41
Crema Catalana, 191
Fresh Nectarines with
Homemade Cream Cheese in
Raspberry Sauce, 162
Frittura Mista di Frutta, 54
Gajjar Halva, (Carrot
Pudding), 115
Grand Marnier Mocha
Dacquoise, 144
Hazelnut Filled Crêpes with
Chocolate Sauce, 21
Khanom Talai (Coconut and
Rice Flour Pudding), 49
Lime Avocado Cream, 195
Meringue Cake with Apricot
Cream, 91
Peaches 'n' Cream, 195
Pear Shortcake, 32
Pumpkin-Hazelnut Mousse with
Autumn Leaves, 13
Rice Pudding with Orange
Sauce, 29
Steamed Christmas Pudding, 70
Strawberry Meringues, 151

Strawberry Pinwheel with
Raspberry Sauce, 76
Strawberry Shortcake with
Devon Style Cream, 120

Dom Yam Gung (Hot and Sour
Prawn Soup), 48
Double Mushroom Soup, 55
Duck (see POULTRY, SOUPS)

E

Easy Omelette with Salsa, 44
Eccles Cakes, 124
Eggplant and Provolone,
Baked, 174
Eggs Mediterranean, 154
English Muffins, 123
Ensalada de Nopale, 188

F

FISH (see also SHELLFISH)
BBQ Steelhead Trout, 171
Grilled Fillet with Crab, 152
Halibut Fillet in Tomato and
Basil Aspic, 159
Monkfish, Creole Style, 137
Plaice with Mustard Glaze, 137
Quenelles of Pike Mousseline
with Red Pepper Purée, 118
Salmon Chunks, Stir Fry, 152
Salmon, Grilled, 166
Salmon Sole Mousse, 62
Salmon Soufflé in Tomato
Cups, 152
Shark, 136
Skate, 137
Sole on a Purée of
Watercress, 106
Steamed Whole Rock Cod, 146
Swordfish Brochettes, 136
Swordfish, Grilled with Basil
Butter, 136
Swordfish, Marinated, 136
Trout with Roasted Pecans and
Creole Meunière Sauce, 40

French Toast, Nouvelle, 45
French Toast Sandwich, 45
Frittata, Prawn with Sun-Dried
Tomatoes, 162
Frittata, Vegetable, 51
Fritters, Vegetable, 194
Frittura Mista Di Frutta, 54
FRUIT
Blackberry Mousse, 175
Fresh Nectarines with
Homemade Cream Cheese in
Raspberry Sauce, 162
Frittura Mista di Frutta, 54
Fruit Syrups, 179
Marinated Fruit, 25
Peaches 'n' Cream, 195

Seasonal Fruit with
Rosewater, 129

Fudge, Chocolate Walnut, 177

G

Gai Hor Bai Toey (Chicken in
Screwpine Leaves), 49
Gajjar Halva, 115
Gazpacho, 189
Gazpacho Sorbet, 194
Genoise Sponge Cake, 32
Ginger Beets, 70
Golden Butterflies, 138
Golden Egg Puffs, 138
Golden Sesame Dumplings, 138
Goose (see POULTRY)
Grand Marnier Mocha
Dacquoise, 144
Granola, 44
Green Beans Amandine, 76

H

Hairy Melon, Stuffed, 146
Halibut Fillet in Tomato Basil
Aspic, 159
Hazelnut Filled Crepes with
Chocolate Sauce, 21
Homemade Croutons, 120
Hors D'oeuvres (see
APPETIZERS)
Horseradish Mayonnaise, 11

I

ICE CREAM AND ICES
Blueberry Sorbet, 63
Champagne Sorbet, 90
Indian Ice Cream, 171
Kiwifruit Ice, 133
Orange Sherbet, 185
Pumpkin Ice Cream, 37
Raspberry Sorbet, 63

Il Minestrone di Roma, 108
Insalata di Finocchi, 51

J

Jam, Blueberry Lime, 163
Jam, Gooseberry, 163
Jerky, Cold Brined, 171
Jerky, Hot Brined, 171
Jerky, Sun Dried, 171
Judy's Rhubarb Marmalade, 101

K

Kefta, 128
Khanom Talai (Coconut and Rice
Flour Pudding), 49

Kholrabi with Remoulade
   Sauce, 16
Kiwifruit Ice, 133

L

LAMB
   Brochettes, 128
   Broiled Lamb Chops with Stir-
      Fried Spinach, 154
   Grilled Kebabs of lamb with
      Cumin and Ginger, 154
   Grilled Lamb with Basil
      Cream, 144

Lemon Chicken, 178
Liptauer Cheese, 14
Lobster, Caviar and Endive
   Salad, 86

M

Madeleines, 133
Make-Ahead Muffins, 44
Makhani Murgh, 113
Marinated Fruit, 25
Masala Chai, 115
Mayonnaise (see VINEGARS and
   MAYONNAISE)
Meat (see BEEF, LAMB, PORK,
   POULTRY)
Melon Soup, 145
Melon Tomato Salad, 174
Meringue Cake with Apricot
   Cream, 91
Meringues, Strawberry, 151
Mexican Chocolate, 93, 182
Mincemeat, 70
Mincemeat, Cranberry and
   Pumpkin Tartlettes, 70
Mint Chutney, 113
Monkfish, Creole Style, 136
MOUSSE
   Blackberry, 175
   Caviar Crowned, 66
   Ham, 11
   Pimientos and Scallops,
      Fluffy, 159
   Pumpkin-Hazelnut, 13
   Salmon-Sole, 62
   Shrimp, 80

Mung Dhal, 114
Munk Cakes, 163
Mushrooms (see VEGETABLES,
   SALADS, SOUPS)
Mussels (see SHELLFISH)

N

Nanaimo Bars, 167
Navajo Fry Bread, 183
New York Style Cheesecake, 93

Nouvelle Potato Salad, 98

O

Oatmeal Pecan Cookies, 179
Onion Chutney, 25
Onion Relish, 70
Onions, Quick Glazed, 73

P

Paella a la Valenciana, 189
Pancakes, Diane's Puff, 44
Pancakes, Sour Cream, 45
Papaya and Pepper Salad, 105
Paratha, 115
PASTA
   Fettuccine alla Carbonara, 155
   Pasta Salad, 98
   Pasta with Prawns, 155
   Poppy Seed Noodles, 17
   Ravioli alla Piemontese, 51
   Rotolo with Tomato Sauce, 150

Pâté, Vegetable, 83
Pear Shortcake, 32
Pheasant with Rice and Fruit
   Stuffing, 81
PIES/PASTRY
   Banbury Tarts, 125
   Cantonese Custard Tarts, 139
   Coconut Cocktail Buns, 139
   Cornish Pasties, 92
   Curried Turnovers, 140
   Eccles Cakes, 124
   Golden Butterflies, 138
   Golden Egg Puffs, 138
   Golden Sesame Dumplings, 138
   Mincemeat, Cranberry and
      Pumpkin Tartlettes, 70
   Mushroom Tarts with Béarnaise
      Sauce, 58
   Pastry, 12, 58, 70, 93
   Pastry, Julia's Quick Puff, 132
   Savory Pumpkin, 36
   Spicy Chinese Doughnuts, 139
   Vegetarian Samosas, 112

Pineapple Beets, 76
Pinenut Sponge Cake,
   Steamed, 138
Pizza, Quick and Easy, 155
Plaice with Mustard Glaze, 137
Pollo Pipian, 188
Poppy Seed Cake, 124
Poppy Seed Noodles, 17
PORK
   Baked BBQ Pork Buns, 139
   BBQ Sausages, 155
   Pork and Banana Curry, 24
   Pork Medallions and Julienne of
      Sweet Pepper, 16
   Taco Pork with Lemon, 155

Terrine of Ham and Sweet
   Potatoes, 10

Posole Salad, 183
POULTRY
   CHICKEN
      Blanquette of Chicken, 132
      Breast of Chicken in Herbed
         Wine Sauce, 90
      Chicken Curry, 24
      Chicken with Preserved
         Lemons, 128
      Crisp Spicy Chicken Strips, 183
      Gai Hor Bai Toey (Chicken in
         Screwpine Leaves), 49
      Lemon Chicken, 178
      Makhani Murgh, 113
      Paper Wrapped Chicken, 145
      Pollo Pipian, 188
      Sichuan Chicken Salad, 195
      Tandoori Chicken, 114
   DUCK
      Roast Duck Calvados Stuffed
         with Barley Pilaf, 32
      Roasted Duck and Orange
         Salad, 158
   GOOSE, with Orange
      Stuffing, 67
   PHEASANT, with Rice and
      Fruit Stuffing, 81
   TURKEY, Escalopes with
      Cranberry Coulis and Sage
      Sauce, 12

Pralines, 41
Prawns (see SHELLFISH, SOUPS)
Pumpkin Bars with Cream Cheese
   Frosting, 37
Pumpkin Blossoms, Fried, 33
Pumpkin Conserve, 37
Pumpkin-Hazelnut Mousse with
   Autumn Leaves, 13
Pumpkin Ice Cream, 37
Pumpkin Seed Sauce, Spicy, 36
Pumpkin Seeds, Toasted, 33
Punjabi Garam Masala, 112
Punjabi Vegetarian Samosas, 112

Q

Quenelles of Pike Mousseline with
   Red Pepper Purée, 118
Quick Croissants, 101
Quick Glazed Onions, 73

R

Ravioli alla Piemontese, 51
Red Pepper and Tomato Timbale
   with Spinach Purée, 86
Red Pepper Purée, 119
RICE
   Arroz Fiesta, 188

Barley Pilaf, 32
Basmati, 25
Bhasmati, 114
Green Rice, 41
Paella a la Valenciana, 189
Pudding with Orange Sauce, 29
Rice Medley, 98
Risotto, 54, 119
Two-Rice Pilaf, 90
Wild Rice, 170

Risotto with Wild
    Mushrooms, 119
Rotolo with Tomato Sauce, 150

S

SALADS
    Carrot, in Lettuce Cups, 31
    Cranberry, Chestnut and
        Pear, 73
    Curly Endive, 151
    Dahi Raita, 113
    Double Melon, 100
    Ensalada di Nopale, 188
    Hearts of Romaine with
        Homemade Croutons, 119
    Insalata di Finocchi, 51
    Lobster, Caviar and Endive, 86
    Melon-Tomato, 174
    Mushroom and Endive Salad
        with Creamy Tarragon
        Dressing, 57
    Nouvelle Potato, 98
    Papaya and Pepper, 105
    Pasta, 98
    Posole, 183
    Rice Medley, 98
    Roasted Duck and Orange, 158
    Seafood with Tarragon and
        Mustard Dressing, 67
    Shrimp, Alison's, 195
    Sichuan Chicken, 195
    Sicilian, 98
    Spinach Chiffonade with
        Mustard Vinaigrette, 166
    Spinach with Balsamic
        Vinegar, 81
    Tomato and Egg, 29
    Warm Squab, 20
    Watercress, 170
    Which Came First Salad, 99

Salmon (see FISH)
Salsa, Daryl's Hot, 183
Samosas, Vegetarian Punjabi, 112
Sangria, 189
SAUCES/CONDIMENTS
    SAVORY:
        Avocado Salsa, 185
        Basic Salsa Ranchera, 188
        Béarnaise Sauce, 58
        Black Bean Sauce, 136, 143

Blackberry Butter Sauce, 137
Brown Butter, 136
Creole Meunière Sauce, 40
Cumberland Sauce, 67
Curry Sauce, Basic, 24
Daryl's Hot Salsa, 183
Fresh Carrot Pickle, 113
Fresh Cucumber Chutney, 25
Kefta Sauce, 128
Madeira Sauce, 63
Mint Chutney, 113
Mung Dhal, 114
Mushroom, 73
Nam Prik, 49
Onion Chutney, 25
Onion Relish, 70
Pickled Lemons, 113, 128
Pumpkin Cranberry Sauce, 36
Pumpkin Conserve
    (Chutney), 37
Red Pepper Purée, 119
Remoulade Sauce, 16
Sauce Espagnole (Brown
    Sauce), 81
Spicy Pumpkin Seed Sauce, 36
Tamarind Chutney, 113
Tartar Sauce, 137
SWEET:
    Apple Butter, 101
    Apricot Pineapple
        Conserve, 101
    Blueberry Lime Jam, 163
    Brandy Butter, 70
    Chocolate Sauce, 21
    Gooseberry Jam, 163
    Judy's Rhubarb Marmalade, 101
    Orange Sauce, 29
    Raspberry Sauce, 77
    Strawberry Rhubarb
        Conserve, 163

Scones, Cream, 121
Scones, Yeast, 121
Seafood (see FISH, SHELLFISH)
SHELLFISH
    Alison's Shrimp Salad, 195
    Mussel Curry, 49
    Mussels on the Half Shell in
        Vinaigrette, 159
    Periwinkles, 135
    Prawn Frittata, 162
    Prawns in Black Bean Sauce, 143
    Seafood Salad, 67
    Shrimp Curry, 24
    Shrimp Mousse, 80
    Shrimp Soufflé Role, 100
    Steamed Clams, 164

Sherried Carrot Consommé, 28
Shortbread, 124, 125
Sicilian Salad, 98
Sopa de Tortilla, 188
Sopaipillas, 185

SOUPS
    Avocado and Prawn
        Gaspacho, 158
    Avocado Soup, 194
    Broccoli Bisque, 62
    Consommé of Corn Topped
        with Fresh Herb Pastry, 11
    Country Pumpkin, 33
    Creamed Pea and Parsley with
        Clams, 194
    Cream of Oyster and
        Artichoke, 40
    Creamy Carrot, 92
    Curried Nut, 80
    Dom Yam Gung (Hot and Sour
        Prawn Soup), 48
    Double Mushroom, 55
    Duck Soup with Bannock
        Dumplings, 170
    Fresh Corn, 173
    Gazpacho, 189
    Gazpacho Sorbet, 194
    Il Minestrone di Roma, 108
    Melon, 145
    Sherried Carrot Consommé, 28
    Shrimp and Oyster Bisque, 72
    Sopa de Tortilla, 188
    Sorrel and Lettuce, 118
    Zuppa di Porri, 50

Spaghetti Squash with Tomatoes
    and Mushrooms, 106
Spinach and Beef, 145
Spinach Purée, 90
Spinach Salad, 81
Squab Salad, Warm, 20
Squash Stuffed with Seasonal
    Vegetables and Fresh Herbs, 21
Steamed Christmas Pudding, 70
Strawberry Meringues, 151
Strawberry Pinwheel with
    Raspberry Sauce, 76
Strawberry Rhubarb
    Conserve, 163
Strawberry Shortcake with Devon
    Style Cream, 120
SWEETS
    Cashew Butter Chocolates, 71
    Chocolate Truffles, 77
    Chocolate Walnut Fudge, 77
    Creamy Pralines, 41
    Grand Marnier Truffles, 71
    Homemade Chocolates, 71
    Pistachios in White
        Chocolate, 71
    Sugar Plums, 77

Swordfish (see FISH)

T

Taco Pork with Lemon, 155
Tagine of Brochettes or Kefta, 128

Tandoori Chicken, 114
Tartar Sauce, 137
Terrine, Classic Country, 150
Terrine of Ham and Sweet
    Potatoes, 10
Tomato and Egg Salad, 29
Tomato Gervaise, 72
Tomatoes with Bell Peppers, 129
Torta Terremoto (Earthquake
    Cake), 54
Tostada with Avocado Salsa and
    Crab, 184
Trout with Roasted Pecans and
    Creole Meunière Sauce, 40
Turkey (see POULTRY)

V

Veal, Classic Country Terrine, 150
VEGETABLES
    Baby Vegetables Marinated in
        Vinaigrette, 179
    Baked Eggplant and
        Provolone, 174
    Cauliflower and Broccoli
        Bhaji, 114
    Chinese Long Beans, 106
    Confetti Broccoli with Red
        Peppers, 69
    Fried Pumpkin Blossoms, 33
    Ginger Beets, 70
    Glazed Vegetables, 63
    Green Beans Amandine, 76
    Kohlrabi with Remoulade
        Sauce, 16
    Mung Dhal (Green Dhal
        Curry), 114
    Mushroom Pâté in Brioche
        Cases, 59
    Mushroom Sauce, 73
    Mushrooms in Parchment, 58
    Mushroom Tarts with Béarnaise
        Sauce, 58
    Pineapple Beets, 76
    Potato Latkes, 45
    Potatoes, Creamed, 67
    Potatoes in Tarragon Cream, 83
    Potatoes, Ranch-Cut, 21
    Potatoes, Roasted with Herbs
        and Garlic, 144
    Quick Glazed Onions, 73
    Red Pepper and Tomato
        Timbale with Spinach
        Purée, 86
    Spaghetti Squash with Sun-
        Dried Tomatoes and Wild
        Mushrooms, 106
    Squash Stuffed with Seasonal
        Vegetables and Fresh
        Herbs, 21
    Steamed Nettles, 170
    Stuffed Hairy Melon, 147
    Sun-Dried Tomatoes, 162
    Sweet Potato Croquettes, 73

Tomato Gervaise, 72
Tomatoes with Bell
    Peppers, 129
Vegetable Omelette, 154
Vegetable Pâté, 83
Vegetarian Samosas, 112
Vegetables Vinaigrette, 133
Warm Red Cabbage, 31
Wild Mushroom and Bacon
    Sauté, 59

VINEGARS and MAYONNAISE
    Balsamic Vinaigrette, 81, 99
    Basil, 99
    Boiled Dressing, 29
    Caper Mayonnaise, 62
    Creamy Tarragon Dressing, 57
    Curry Mayonnaise, 132, 166
    Egg Vinaigrette, 105
    French Vinaigrette, 99
    Ginger Mayonnaise, 195
    Green Mayonnaise, 166
    Hazelnut Oil Vinaigrette, 86
    Homemade Mayonnaise, 132,
        137, 166
    Horseradish Mayonnaise, 11
    Italian Vinaigrette, 99
    Lemon French Dressing, 99
    Mustard Mayonnaise, 166
    Mustard Vinaigrette, 99
    Oil and Vinegar, 194
    Red Wine Vinaigrette, 99
    Seafood Mayonnaise, 166
    Sweet and Sour Vinaigrette, 99
    Tarragon and Mustard
        Dressing, 67
    Tartar Sauce, 137
    Tomato Mayonnaise, 166
    Vinaigrette, 120, 133, 174, 179
    Walnut Oil Dressing, 99, 151

W

Walnut Bread, 76
Walnut Oil Dressing, 99, 151
Walnut Soufflé Torte, 17
Warm Red Cabbage, 32
Watercress Salad, 170
Welsh Cakes, 123
Which Came First Salad, 99
Wild Rice Bread, 20

Y

Yoghurt, Homemade, 109
Yorkshire Puddings, 76

Z

Zuppa di Porri, 50